HUMAN RIGHTS IN THE WORLD

BY THE SAME AUTHOR

Books

Characterization in the Conflict of Laws (Harvard, 1940)
The Council of Europe (London, 1956; second edition 1961; French
edition 1962)
European Institutions (London, 1959; second edition 1966; third edition
1973)
Human Rights in Europe (Manchester, 1963; second edition 1977)

Published Lectures

'Legal problems of European integration', *Recueil des Cours*, Académie de
Droit International, The Hague, 1957
The Law of International Institutions in Europe (Melland Schill lectures,
University of Manchester, 1961)
Constitutional Developments in the Council of Europe (Institut d'Etudes
Européennes, Brussels, 1964)
The International Protection of Human Rights (Montague Burton
lecture, University of Nottingham, 1970; Spanish translation, Mexico,
1970)
'Le Conseil de l'Europe' and 'La Convention européenne des Droits de
l'homme', in *Les Organisations Régionales Internationales*, Paris, 1970
'Human rights: a global assessment' and 'The Helsinki Agreement and
human rights', in *Human Rights and American Foreign Policy*, Notre
Dame, Indiana, 1979

Books edited by the Author

Human Rights in National and International Law, Manchester, 1967
Privacy and Human Rights, Manchester, 1973

HUMAN RIGHTS IN THE WORLD

AN INTRODUCTION TO THE STUDY OF THE INTERNATIONAL PROTECTION OF HUMAN RIGHTS

Second edition

by

A. H. ROBERTSON
B.C.L. (Oxon.), S.J.D. (Harvard)

former *Professeur Associé*, University of Paris I
former Simon Visiting Professor at the University of Manchester
former Director of Human Rights, Council of Europe

ST. MARTIN'S PRESS   NEW YORK

First edition 1972

All rights reserved
For information write:
St. Martin's Press Inc.,
175 Fifth Avenue,
New York, NY 10010

Printed in Great Britain

First published in the United States of America
in 1982

ISBN 0-312-39961-8

Library of Congress Cataloging in Publication

Robertson, A. H. (Arthur Henry), 1913—
   Human rights in the world.

   Includes bibliographical references and index
     1. Civil rights (International law)   I. Title.
K3240.4.R6   1982   341.4'81
ISBN 0-312-39961-8

HUMAN RIGHTS IN THE WORLD

AN INTRODUCTION TO THE STUDY OF THE INTERNATIONAL PROTECTION OF HUMAN RIGHTS

Second edition

by

A. H. ROBERTSON
B.C.L. (Oxon.), S.J.D. (Harvard)

former *Professeur Associé*, University of Paris I
former Simon Visiting Professor at the University of Manchester
former Director of Human Rights, Council of Europe

ST. MARTIN'S PRESS   NEW YORK

First edition 1972

Printed in Great Britain

First published in the United States of America
in 1982

ISBN 0-312-39961-8

Library of Congress Cataloging in Publication Data

Robertson, A. H. (Arthur Henry), 1913–
    Human rights in the world.

    Includes bibliographical references and index.
    1. Civil rights (International law)   I. Title.
K3240.4.R6   1982   341.4'81   82-10238
ISBN 0-312-39961-8

CONTENTS

PREFACE

The international protection of human rights is a subject which is receiving ever-increasing attention in our universities. Nor is this surprising. The number of Declarations, Conventions and Covenants adopted and the number of new organs – committees, commissions and courts – established in recent years is such as to provide extensive material for study and research for the lawyer and the political scientist.

Since the first edition of this book was written ten years ago, the importance of human rights in international affairs has increased immeasurably. This has become evident in many areas of the world, in the bi-lateral relations between States and in many international conferences, including those concerned with the application of the Helsinki Agreement on Security and Co-operation in Europe. In the international organisations, the two Covenants on Human Rights concluded by the United Nations in 1966 entered into force ten years later; they now apply to more than sixty States, and the new Human Rights Committee has been at work for several years; the American Convention on Human Rights came into force in 1978 and the Inter-American Court has been set up; the case law of the European Commission and Court of Human Rights has developed tremendously and is having an increasing influence on the law of European countries.

In this new edition I have attempted to describe and analyse these developments and also to give a brief account of the human rights work of the International Labour Organisation and UNESCO, the European Social Charter and the new Protocols to the Geneva Conventions on humanitarian law of 1977.

Since the Organisation of American States, the Arab League and the Organisation of African Unity are (at least in Europe) less well known than the United Nations and the Council of Europe, I have included in the relevant chapters short sections giving general information about those three organisations, which I hope will be found useful.

It would have been logical to call this book 'The International Protection of Human Rights'. But since at least five other books with that title have already been published in recent years, I have instead chosen for a title *Human Rights in the World*, which also indicates that this volume is, in a certain sense, complementary to my book *Human Rights in Europe* (first published in 1963, second edition 1977) which gives a fuller account of the European Convention and of the functions and work of the European Commission and Court of Human Rights.

As so often happens, certain parts of the book have previously been published as separate articles. The appropriate references are given in the end-notes.

In conclusion, I wish to thank Mme Catherine Abadie for her patient and efficient secretarial assistance.

Strasbourg   A. H. ROBERTSON
30 April 1981

To

R.C.A.R.

Chapter one

INTERNATIONAL CONCERN WITH HUMAN RIGHTS

I. WORLD PUBLIC OPINION AND HUMAN RIGHTS

One of the most striking developments in international law since the end of the Second World War is its concern with the protection of human rights. This development is the reflection of a wider phenomenon: the increased concern of large numbers of men and women all over the world with the treatment accorded to their fellow human beings in other countries, particularly when that treatment fails to come up to minimum standards of civilised behaviour. Legal rules are the reflection of social standards because, as the French Revolution reminded us, the law is the expression of the general will. This newly developed concern of international law with the protection of human rights is thus seen to be the result of a change in social attitudes towards a human problem. The first half of the nineteenth century saw a similar development when the abhorrence of slavery led to the acceptance of legal rules prohibiting, first, the slave trade and subsequently the institution of slavery itself. In the second half of the twentieth century we are witnessing the development of legal rules prohibiting internationally many other forms of uncivilised behaviour. Genocide is an obvious example. Others are arbitrary arrest, detention without trial, political executions and torture. The fact that such violations of human rights continue to occur does not mean that attempts to prevent them by international action are vain or useless — any more than the existence of crime at the national level refutes the value of criminal law. Widespread violations of human rights teach us that the attempts to prevent them at the international level are not as effective as we would wish and that much remains to be done to improve the existing international procedures. But in order to improve them we need to know what they are and how they function. That is what this book is about.

The revolutionary nature of the concept of the international protection of human rights is shown by the fact that the classic doctrine of international law had no place for it at all. We have quoted elsewhere the statement of Oppenheim, the leading authority on international law in the United Kingdom at the beginning of this century, that the 'so-called rights of man' not only do not but cannot enjoy any protection under international law, because that law is concerned solely with the relations between States and cannot confer rights on individuals.[1] Traditionally it was the accepted doctrine that relations between individuals and the States of which they were nationals were questions to be determined exclusively by the national law of those States; such matters were exclusively within their domestic jurisdiction. To change this traditional attitude into a new doctrine which recognises that international standards concerning the fundamental rights of the individual have been established by international law, and that international remedies are available if those standards are not respected, is a major operation requiring important modifications in the theory and practice of governments. It is not surprising if such a change takes time. We are at present in the middle of this process of transformation and, as we shall see in this book, much resistance is encountered and many governments seek to shelter behind the classic doctrine of international law and hide their actions behind the cloak of national sovereignty. This will appear with particular force when we come to discuss the work of the United Nations. But such obscurantist policies cannot alter the fact that the protection of human rights has found a place in international law which it never occupied in earlier times and that there is widespread recognition of the need to render the system of international protection more effective. These general observations are set out at the beginning of this book in order to rebut the common criticism which asserts that constant violations of human rights in many parts of the world prove that international law is powerless to prevent them. The answer is that it is not yet strong enough to prevent all violations, but it has succeeded in preventing some and in condemning many more; our task is to make it progressively more effective and thus limit or reduce further the number of violations that occur. The magnitude of the task is a challenge, but not a reason to desist or despair.

If we take a realistic view, we must recognise that there are probably more countries in the world today where fundamental rights and civil liberties are systematically violated than countries where they are effectively protected. Amnesty International estimated not long ago that there were sixty countries in which there was systematic use of torture and that the number of political prisoners in the world approached half a million.[2] We are told that the principles of liberal democracy, with its respect for fundamental rights, are observed in fewer than thirty countries today. However, something is changing in the world: international opinion, as expressed by the United Nations and many other international organisations; national opinion in many countries; and, for innumerable people throughout the world, individual opinion.

The non-governmental organisations (such as Amnesty International, the International Commission of Jurists, the International League for the Rights of Man and, in the educational field, the International Institute of Human Rights) are tireless in their work in this field and increasingly numerous and influential. Can we deny that there is a public conscience which is slowly but progressively making its influence felt? World public opinion on these matters has changed in the last fifty years in a way which would have seemed inconceivable when some of us were young; it is bound to go on changing in the years to come. It is our task in the pages which follow to see how this change in the public conscience is reflected in international law and in the action of the international organisations concerned with human rights.

II. DIFFERENT CULTURES AND THEIR APPROACH TO HUMAN RIGHTS[3]

1. The liberal tradition of the Western democracies

When we come to consider the philosophical foundations for our belief in human rights, it seems reasonably clear that the main stream (but not, as we shall see later, the only stream) has its origins in the liberal democratic tradition of Western Europe – that tradition which we have described elsewhere as the product of Greek philosophy, Roman law, the Judaeo-Christian tradition, the Humanism of the Reformation and the Age of Reason. It is the parliamentary democracies of Western Europe which are the direct heirs of this tradition; other countries which have inherited their political philosophy have carried the tradition to other parts of the world; yet others have absorbed some of it – but to varying degrees and incompletely.

When we seek a detailed formulation of that philosophy as applied to the specific problem of human rights, we find it in the *French Declaration of the Rights of Man and the Citizen of 1789* and particularly in its second article: 'The aim of all political association is the conservation of the natural and inalienable rights of man. These rights are: liberty, property, security and resistance to oppression.' The Declaration does not discuss why these rights are 'natural' and 'inalienable' (in French: 'imprescriptibles'). No doubt its authors would have considered that to be self-evident. Some would believe that they can be deduced from the nature of man as a sentient and intelligent being; others, remembering Aristotle, from his nature as a political animal; yet others, drawing inspiration from their Bible, from the nature of man created by the Almighty in his own image. The doctrine of natural law, holding that there are laws of nature or laws of God above and beyond positive law edicted by man, also contributed to this belief. We may note in passing that this belief in natural law as the basis of certain rights and duties finds expression in the twentieth century in the Constitution of Ireland of 1937, which recognises the family as 'a moral institution possessing inalienable and imprescriptible rights, antecedent and superior to all positive law'; it also acknowledges that man 'has the natural right, antecedent to positive law, to the private ownership of external goods'.

The French Declaration proclaimed a number of the rights which are now generally called civil and political: the basic principle that all men are born and remain free and equal in their rights; also particular rights, including equality before the law, freedom from arrest except in conformity with the law, the presumption of innocence, protection against retroactivity of the law, freedom of opinion, freedom of expression and the well known definition of liberty as freedom to do anything which is not harmful to others. The Declaration and the philosophy which it enshrined inspired liberals and romantics all over Europe and led the poet Wordsworth to write the famous lines:

> Bliss was it in that dawn to be alive,
> But to be young were very heaven.

Its political impact on the French nation and on other peoples struggling against authoritarian governments was such that Lord

Acton, the historian, described it as 'a single confused page . . . that outweighed libraries and was stronger than all the armies of Napoleon'. Its relevance to problems which are perennial is indicated by the fact that one of the French political parties in 1977 reprinted the Declaration of 1789 and distributed it all over France.

But if the French Declaration of 1789 constituted the proclamation of rights which is the most widely known and the most far-reaching in its consequences on the continent of Europe, other historic texts fulfilled a similar role in the English-speaking countries. Englishmen consider *Magna Carta of 1215* as the foundation of their liberties. It guaranteed to the citizen freedom from imprisonment or from dispossession of his property and freedom from prosecution or exile 'unless by the lawful judgment of his peers or by the law of the land'. It also included a primitive formulation of the right to a fair trial in the famous words 'To none will we sell, deny or delay right or justice'. These and other provisions of the charter were of such importance that it was confirmed and reissued no fewer than thirty-eight times by later sovereigns in succeeding centuries. The civil war and the peaceful revolution of the seventeenth century led to the *Habeas Corpus Acts* and the *Bill of Rights of 1689* (just a century before the French Declaration) which assured the supremacy of Parliament, the right to free elections, freedom of speech, the right to bail, freedom from cruel and unusual punishments and the right to trial by jury. The independence of the judiciary and freedom of the press were established shortly thereafter; and the philosopher John Locke clothed in political theory the constitutional arrangements which had been elaborated on a pragmatic basis. He held that sovereignty pertains not to the monarch but to the people as a whole, and that government is an instrument for securing the lives, the property and the well-being of the governed without enslaving them in any way. 'Government is not their master; it is created by the people voluntarily and maintained by them to secure their own good.' The individual conveys to society his own right to exercise certain functions; all other natural rights he retains. The theory of reserved natural rights is the basis of the maintenance of fundamental liberties; they belong to the individual by nature, have not been surrendered to the community and therefore cannot be limited or denied by the State.

This political philosophy was inherited by the colonists in North America. Their most eloquent spokesman was Thomas Jefferson, who had studied Locke and Montesquieu, and asserted that the Americans were a 'free people claiming their rights as derived from the laws of nature and not as the gift of their Chief Magistrate'. The first Continental Congress in its Declaration of Rights of 14 October 1774 considered 'the immutable laws of nature' as the principal source from which the colonies derived their rights. It was therefore not surprising that when Jefferson came to draft the Declaration of Independence in the summer of 1776 he referred to the necessity for a people 'to assume among the powers of the Earth the separate and equal station to which the Laws of Nature and of Nature's God entitled them'. This leads on directly to the belief in natural rights expressed in the second sentence:

We hold these truths to be self-evident, that all men are created equal, that they are endowed by their Creator with certain unalienable rights, that among these are life, liberty and the pursuit of happiness.

This has much in common with the second article of the French Declaration (quoted above), notably that the rights of man are 'natural and inalienable'; but it will be observed that Jefferson selects as the three cardinal rights life, liberty and pursuit of happiness, whereas the French Declaration chooses liberty, property, security . . . ('Resistance to oppression', which also comes in the second article of the French Declaration, follows in the next paragraph of the Declaration of Independence.) Immediately after the reference to the three cardinal rights we read: 'that to secure these rights Governments are instituted among men, deriving their just powers from the consent of the governed; that whenever any form of government becomes destructive of these ends, it is the right of the people to alter or abolish it . . .'. We hear the voice of Locke echoed in Philadelphia.

It is evident, then, that there is much in common between the two Declarations; and the demonstration could be carried further, because the American text refers to a number of other fundamental rights – not so much by proclaiming them as such as by complaining of their violation: independence of the judiciary, subordination of the military to the civil power, freedom of trade, freedom from taxation without consent, the right to trial by jury. When to these are added equality before the law, and the rights to life, liberty and the pursuit of happiness, we have an extensive catalogue. But the Declaration, important as it was, did not form part of the positive law of the infant republic. It was not made part of the federal constitution drafted in 1787, which was criticised by reason of the fact that it did not include a statement of fundamental rights. Two years later, therefore, twelve amendments to the Constitution were drafted by the first Congress in New York and approved on 25 September 1789 – just a month after the French Declaration. When ten were ratified by the states, they entered into force in 1791; they are generally known as the Bill of Rights and include the more important civil and political rights, as we call them today.

The fact that there is much in common – as regards the content, though not the drafting – between the American texts and the French Declaration need not surprise us. The main objective was the same on both sides of the Atlantic: to protect the citizen against arbitrary power and establish the rule of law; the French philosophers, including both Montesquieu and Rousseau, were studied in the Americas; fifty years earlier Voltaire in his *Lettres philosophiques* had studied and described the English constitutional arrangements resulting from the peaceful revolution and the Act of Settlement; Lafayette was a member of the drafting committee of the Constituent Assembly which produced the French Declaration and submitted to it his own draft based on the Declaration of Independence and the Virginia Bill of Rights; the *rapporteur* of the Constitutional Commission proposed 'transplanting to France the noble idea conceived in North America'; Jefferson himself was present in Paris in 1789, having succeeded Benjamin Franklin as American Minister to France.

We thus find in 1789 two parallel and broadly similar currents, the American and the French – the former largely inspired by English doctrines on the liberty of the subject – which together go to make up what we called above the 'main stream' of the philosophical and historical foundation for our belief in human rights. (This is not to deny that there were similar phenomena in other European countries, but they were less notable in their results.) And it is this same main stream which, after the horrors of the Second World War, found expression in the *Universal Declaration of Human Rights of 1948*. Is it a coincidence that the chairman of the Human Rights Commission which drafted it was Mrs Eleanor Roosevelt, while one of the principal authors was René Cassin and one of the most important documents considered by the Commission was the draft presented by the United Kingdom?[4] Be that as it may, the Universal Declaration – accepted, as it was, without a dissentient vote, and with few abstentions, by all States

members of the United Nations at that time – is a clear expression of
the concept of human rights evolved by the main stream of political
and philosophical thought which we have attempted to describe. It
is the human rights conception of one culture, namely the culture of
the parliamentary democracies.

2. The universal tradition

But there are other 'streams' of thought and other cultures.

At the *International Conference on Human Rights in Tehran*, on
the occasion of Human Rights Year, 1968, the late Shah of Iran in
his opening address told us that the ancestor of the documents
recognising the rights of man was promulgated in his country by
Cyrus the Great about two thousand years earlier.[5] Christian
Daubie has recently recounted the magnanimity and clemency of
Cyrus to subject peoples – in marked contrast to the practice of
earlier conquerors – and particularly his respect for their religion;
the author deduces from the '*Charter of Cyrus*' the recognition and
protection of what we now call the rights to liberty and security,
freedom of movement, the right of property and even certain
economic and social rights.[6]

Cyrus was not the only precursor in antiquity in the Middle East.
Ambassador Polys Modinos in 'La Charte de la Liberté de l'Europe'
quotes one of the Pharaohs of ancient Egypt giving instructions to
his Vizirs to the effect that 'When a petitioner arrives from Upper or
Lower Egypt . . . make sure that all is done according to the law,
that custom is observed and the right of each man respected'. He
goes on to cite the *Code of Hammourabi*, King of Babylon two
thousand years before Christ, in which the monarch records his
mission 'to make justice reign in the kingdom, to destroy the wicked
and the violent, to prevent the strong from oppressing the weak . . .
to enlighten the country and promote the good of the people'.[7]
Elsewhere the same author reminds us that the essential problem of
Sophocles' *Antigone* is the perennial conflict between the positive
law of the sovereign maintaining order in his country and the
unwritten law of the gods or of nature which commands respect for
the dead and love of a brother.

The number of cultures which have made their contribution to
the elaboration and dissemination of the rights of man is legion. As
a special contribution to International Human Rights Year in 1968
UNESCO published a collection of texts gleaned from different

cultural traditions and periods of history, which illustrate strikingly the universality in time and space of the concept of the rights of man – or, to quote the title of the book, *The Birthright of Man*. It is fascinating to select at random the *dicta* of sages, philosophers, prophets and poets from different countries and many faiths in all continents, including (to mention a few) India, China, Japan, Persia, Russia, Turkey, Egypt, Israel, several countries of black Africa and the pre-Columbian civilisations of South America. It is apparent therefore that human rights have been cherished through the centuries in many lands; as we have written elsewhere, the struggle for human rights is as old as history itself, because it is always apparent in the endeavour to protect the individual against the abuse of power by the monarch, the tyrant or the State. If we have referred above to a mainstream manifested in the political traditions of the parliamentary democracies of Western Europe, this is not because they have any monopoly of the subject, it is rather because they have produced its best-known formulations and instituted the most effective systems of implementation – both nationally and internationally.

This leads on naturally to a further question: are human rights more specially the concern of any particular culture? This question concerns not the formulation of texts, but the more fundamental problem whether the need and the desire to protect such rights are more characteristic of certain political systems than of others. The question is a topical one, because we are often told that the rights proclaimed in the historic texts we have mentioned, and the majority of the rights proclaimed in the Universal Declaration, are the product of a bourgeois or capitalist society with little – or, at least, less – relevance to the socialist States based on Marxist principles. Again, the argument is that rights which are considered important in industrially developed countries are relatively unimportant in developing countries or, if their value is admitted, that they are luxuries which the people of the Third World cannot afford.

3. The socialist concept

Some years ago Dr Imre Szabo and other members of the Hungarian Academy of Sciences explained the 'Socialist Concept of Human Rights'; other writers have done so more recently.[8] It is beyond the scope of this chapter to analyse this concept – or perhaps, rather, conception – in any detail, but we must note that we are faced with what is essentially a different culture with a fundamentally different approach to the philosophy of human rights. The point of departure is of course Marxist. Socialist theory 'rejects the natural-law origin of citizens' rights and is unwilling to deduce them from either the nature of man or from the human mind'. Equally, it rejects the idea that citizens' rights reflect the relationship between man and society or between an abstract 'man' and the State. The basis is rather society organised in a State; 'these rights should reflect the relationship between the state and its citizens'. This relationship in a socialist society is very different from that under bourgeois conditions and 'is tied up with the fact that the production and distribution process . . . are owned by the state, and the socialist state is in charge of organising the national economy'. 'As national economy in a socialist economy becomes state-run, this creates the conditions for uniformly securing citizens' rights as state rights.' The State 'has to give expression to the class-will, the will of the working class, which will is ultimately determined by the socialist production relations'.

This emphasis on the primordial role of the State – which itself is seen as the guardian or incarnation of the interests of the workers – places human rights in an entirely different light from that known in the Western democracies. It is claimed that since the State represents by definition the interests of the people, then the citizens can have no rights against the State. At the same time, this emphasis on the role of the State as the source of citizens' rights leads to a belief in the absolute sovereignty of the State and a refusal to admit any form of international control over its actions. No conflict, it is said, can exist between individuals and the State, since the latter assures the economic well-being and the cultural development of the former; the individual must therefore behave as required by the State, because such behaviour corresponds to the interests of society as a whole. The socialist State expresses the will of the mass of the workers, and the individual owes to it absolute obedience. At the international level, we are told that 'co-operation of states in the field of human rights must be combined with unfailing observance of the principles of sovereign equality of states and non-interference in the affairs which are essentially within their domestic jurisdiction'. The 'U.N. Charter, as well as the post-war agreements in the field of human rights, refer the direct provision and protection of human rights and freedoms exclusively to the domestic jurisdiction of the states'. Exceptions to this rule are admitted in certain clearly defined circumstances: under the trusteeship system (Chapter VI of the U.N. Charter) and in colonial territories; when violations of human rights are perpetrated on a mass scale, which endangers international peace and security, in which case Chapter VII of the Charter comes into play; when U.N. organs decide to set up special bodies of investigation, as in the case of the *ad hoc* working groups concerned with southern Africa and Chile and the Special Committee concerned with human rights in the territories occupied by Israel. Even when there are systems of 'international control', as in the two U.N. Covenants of 1966, the organs of control, we are told, may only make 'general recommendations'; the U.N. bodies

have no right to make concrete recommendations on specific measures to be taken to implement particular human rights and freedoms. The elaboration and implementation of such measures is the internal affair of states. International control over the activity of states in securing human rights and freedoms must be exercised with strict observance of their sovereignty and non-interference in their internal affairs.

It is not the aim of this book to engage in polemics for or against any particular theory, but rather to analyse the varying conceptions of different cultures towards human rights. We see therefore in the socialist States (if the texts quoted above are representative) a quite different approach to human rights from that of the liberal democracies, rejecting the view that they are 'natural' to human personality and 'inalienable', but asserting that they are the emanation of the State, which itself is the incarnation of the interests of the workers in a State-run national economy; the sovereignty of the State is pre-eminent and no limitation thereon may be accepted, either nationally or internationally.

Certain comments, however, may be formulated. This emphasis on the sovereignty and infallibility of the State reminds us of doctrines current in the West at an earlier period, and particularly those of Machiavelli and Hobbes. It has even much in common with the doctrine of English law to the effect that 'the King can do no wrong' – a doctrine which has been largely abandoned in practice in recent years. The real difficulty with the doctrine of infallibility of the State, however, is that it bears so little relation to practical realities. In modern industrialised societies, whether 'capitalist' or 'socialist', the State controls or directs or interferes with the daily lives of the citizens to a degree that would have been inconceivable a hundred years ago. The practical problem which results from this concerns the relationship of the individual not with an abstract conception of the State but with the army of officials (including on occasion policemen and gaolers) who represent it and who purport to apply laws and regulations promulgated in the name of the State by fallible human beings. Even if, in theory, the State can do no wrong, in practice an awful lot of wrongs can be committed in its name by such fallible human beings. Hence the need to protect the individual from these wrongs; that is what human rights is all about.

This applies both nationally and internationally. It leads to the question whether a system of international control violates the principle of non-interference in matters which are within the domestic jurisdiction of States; this we will discuss in more detail below. It must suffice for the present to say that matters with regard to which States have accepted international obligations by treaty thereby become subject to rules of international law and are no longer exclusively within their domestic jurisdiction. Moreover, any system of international control becomes meaningless if the matters to be controlled are exclusively subject to the sovereign will of the States concerned. Acceptance of the United Nations Charter, of the Universal Declaration and of the United Nations Covenants involves progress beyond nineteenth-century conceptions of national sovereignty and recognition of a common allegiance to what the late Wilfred Jenks called 'the Common Law of Mankind'.

4. Developing countries and human rights

We must now consider briefly the other main problem which arises in relation to different cultures and their approach to human rights; is it true that the rights which are considered important in industrially developed countries are relatively unimportant in developing countries or, if their value is admitted, that they are luxuries which the people of the Third World cannot afford? This is a vast subject which involves consideration of the relationship between, and the comparative importance of, the two main categories of human rights: civil and political, on the one hand; economic, social and cultural, on the other.

We may start with three simple propositions which, we believe, will be generally accepted. First, that the traditional approach of the Western democracies has been principally (some would say excessively) concerned with civil and political rights and that insufficient attention has been paid in the past to economic, social and cultural rights. Secondly, that there is general recognition now of the importance of the second category; as was said at the *Tehran Conference*: 'In our day, political rights without social rights, justice under law without social justice, and political democracy without economic democracy no longer have any true meaning'. As the conference stated in its Resolution XXI: 'the problems of economic, social and cultural rights should receive due and increasing attention . . . in view of the increasing importance of realising these rights in the modern world'.[9] Thirdly, that the socialist countries tend to attach more importance to the second category than to the first, and that this is perhaps their distinctive contribution to the realisation of human rights in the world.

What is the relevance of this dichotomy to the Third World?

In the first place, let us note that it was the General Assembly of the United Nations which decided in 1952 (reversing an earlier decision of 1950) that there should be two separate international covenants dealing with the two separate categories of rights. Secondly, that whereas two separate covenants were approved by the General Assembly in 1966, and entered into force in 1976 after receiving thirty-five ratifications, almost all states which have ratified one covenant have also ratified the other. (The exception is the Philippines, which ratified the Covenant on Economic, Social and Cultural Rights, but not that on Civil and Political Rights). In other words, the practice of States appears to be in favour of accepting both categories of rights *pari passu*.

What then of the argument that developing countries attach less importance to civil and political rights? As regards undertakings in international law, this argument cannot stand. By 1 January 1981 more than sixty States had ratified the two U.N. Covenants. Half of them were States from what is generally considered the Third World, and all but one had ratified both covenants. Nevertheless, from the point of view of political and social realities, it is evident that many developing countries are more concerned with economic and social rights than with their civil and political counterparts. This is not surprising, having regard to the immediate needs of their peoples: nor is it cause for regret, provided that one category of rights is not sacrificed to the other.

The great specialist on the attitude of African States to human rights is Kéba M'Baye, President of the Supreme Court of Senegal and a former President of the U.N. Commission on Human Rights. In his writings he has examined the problem with which we are now concerned. He recognises that in many African countries governments struggling to combat famine, illness and ignorance tend to overlook the classic liberties of the Western world; they consider that in the fight against underdevelopment they are in a state of war or emergency which permits derogations to be made – a new application of a principle generally recognised in national constitutions and international texts. At the same time he looks forward to a future when economic and social development will have been largely achieved and the general respect of the classic rights and liberties secured. He deduces a *'right to development'* as a necessary corollary of the other fundamental rights recognised in international texts; in particular, it is the logical result of the right of self-determination and the right of all peoples freely to dispose of their natural wealth and resources – rights which are proclaimed in both the U.N. Covenants.[10] It is generally recognised now that there is an essential correlation between the enjoyment of human rights and economic development. Neither is possible without the other; rather there is an essential connection between them. Thus the International Conference on Human Rights at Tehran in 1968 stated in its Resolution XVII:

The enjoyment of economic and social rights is inherently linked with a meaningful enjoyment of civil and political rights, and ... there is a profound interconnection between the realisation of human rights and economic development.

This affords an appropriate conclusion to our study of the varying approaches of different cultures to human rights. It is vain to argue that one category of rights is more important than the other; it is equally vain to hurl opprobrium at others who adopt a different system of priorities. Rather should we recognise that the different categories of rights – civil and political, economic, social and cultural – are interrelated and all desirable, even necessary, to the proper realisation of the human personality, whether we consider men and women individually or in the context of the State. Only in that way can we achieve a balanced well-being in society or, to use a classic concept that still remains valid, the greatest happiness of the greatest number.[11]

III. THE FIRST INTERNATIONAL MEASURES FOR THE PROTECTION OF HUMAN RIGHTS

1. The abolition of slavery

It is at the beginning of the nineteenth century that we see the first international texts relating to what we should now call a human rights problem. This problem was slavery. Shocking as it now seems, the institution of slavery was generally legal under national law at the end of the eighteenth century; it remained legal in the United States until 1863, in Brazil until 1880 and in some countries into the twentieth century. In England it was illegal at least since *Somersett's case* in 1772,[12] and at the turn of the century a humanitarian movement, largely inspired by Wilberforce, sought to prohibit it internationally. Since it was not possible to secure immediately the liberation of slaves legally held in servitude in other countries, the first step was to secure the abolition of the slave trade, and therefore prevent the increase in the number of slaves. It was prohibited in the British colonies in 1807. The institution of slavery was also abolished in France, and by the Treaty of Paris of 1814 the British and French governments agreed to co-operate in the suppression of the traffic in slaves. This undertaking was generalised and accompanied by a solemn condemnation of the practice by Austria, France, Great Britain, Portugal, Prussia, Spain, Sweden and Russia at the Congress of Vienna in 1815.[13]

A series of bilateral treaties on the subject (more than fifty in number) were concluded between 1815 and 1880, and the Conference of Berlin on Central Africa of 1885 was able to state in its General Act that 'trading in slaves is forbidden in conformity with the principles of international law as recognised by the signatory powers' (which numbered fifteen); it was agreed that the territories of the Congo basin should not serve as a market or means of transit for the trade in slaves and that the powers would employ all means at their disposal for putting an end to the trade and punishing those engaged in it.

Matters were taken a step further at the Brussels conference in 1890. An anti-slavery Act was signed, and later ratified by eighteen States, including the United States, Turkey and Zanzibar. It not only condemned slavery and the slave trade, but drew up a list of agreed measures for their suppression both in Africa and on the high seas, including the right of visit and search, the confiscation of ships engaged in the trade and the punishment of their masters and crew; it also provided for the establishment of a special office attached to the Belgian Foreign Ministry and for an International Maritime Office in Zanzibar to assist in implementing these provisions – one of the earliest examples of 'international measures of implementation'.

The General Act of the Brussels conference was the most comprehensive instrument on the subject until the outbreak of the First World War. Thereafter, the mandate system established by Article 22 of the League Covenant proclaimed the principles that the well-being and development of the peoples in the mandated territories should form a 'sacred trust of civilization' and that the mandatory powers should administer the territories under conditions 'which will guarantee freedom of conscience and religion . . . and the prohibition of abuses such as the slave trade'. Both the Convention of St Germain-en-Laye of 10 September 1919 and the International Convention on the Abolition of Slavery and the Slave Trade, concluded under the auspices of the League of Nations on 25 September 1926, proclaimed as their object 'the complete suppression of slavery in all its forms and of the slave trade by land and sea'. The story was taken a stage further after the Second World War; Article 4 of the Universal Declaration proclaimed: 'No one shall be held in slavery or servitude; slavery and the slave trade shall be prohibited in all their forms', while the Supplementary Convention on the Abolition of Slavery, the Slave Trade and Institutions and Practices Similar to Slavery was concluded in 1956 and entered into force on 30 April 1957.[14] Moreover, Article 13 of the Geneva Convention of 1958 on the Law of the High Seas provides in its Article 13 that the High Contracting Parties will prevent and punish the transport of slaves in their vessels and that any slave taking refuge thereon shall be free; while Resolution 1232 (XLII) of the Economic and Social Council of 6 June 1967, adopted on the proposal of the Commission on Human Rights, affirmed the need to review the Conventions of 1926 and 1956 and recommended that various measures should be taken by the Commission on the Status of Women, the ILO, UNESCO and the World Health Organisation.

This evolution over a period of 150 years shows that the right to freedom of the person, and the concomitant prohibition of slavery and the slave trade, have by now not only become matters of concern to international law but are subject to established rules of international law; one may indeed say that there is a customary rule of international law according to which slavery and the slave trade are prohibited. The problem today — for unfortunately a problem still exists — is not one of establishing the law but rather of its enforcement; in other words, it is no longer a question of agreeing on the rules but, by police action (in the widest sense), of seeing that they are observed.

2. Humanitarian law

The second development by which international law began to be concerned with human rights — or, as some would prefer to say, a kindred subject — was the evolution of humanitarian law. Though there have been notable exceptions through the ages, the vanquished in war was normally at the mercy of the victor, and frequently little mercy was shown. The atrocities which accompanied the Thirty Years' War were notorious. During the eighteenth century a more enlightened attitude appeared. Louis XV, after the battle of Fontenoy in 1745, ordered that the enemy wounded were to be treated in the same way as his own soldiers 'because once they are wounded they are no longer our enemies'. The English General Amherst applied the same rule at the siege of Montreal in 1762. Vattel advocated similar principles, while Rousseau wrote in his *Contrat Social* in 1762:[15]

The object of war being the destruction of the enemy State, one has the right to kill its defenders only when they have weapons in their hands; but immediately they put them down and surrender, thus ceasing to be enemies or agents of the enemy, they once more become ordinary men and one no longer has any right to their life. Sometimes one can extinguish a State without killing a single member of it; moreover, war confers no right other than that which is necessary for its purpose. These principles are not those of Grotius; they are not founded on the authority of poets, but they flow from the nature of things and are founded upon reason.

The transformation of these principles into positive law was due to the work of the Swiss philanthropist Henry Dunant. Having gone to Castiglione to see the emperor Napoleon III, he witnessed the battle of Solferino; appalled at the slaughter and the suffering of the wounded, he personally succoured more than a thousand of them and called on the local inhabitants to assist him in the work. Determined as a result of this experience to institute a permanent system for humanitarian relief whenever its services might be required, he founded with the Geneva lawyer Gustave Moynier and others in 1863 the *Comité International et Permanent de Secours aux Blessés Militaires*. Later that same year he organised a conference at which sixteen States were represented, and the delegates agreed to set up in their own countries private societies to supplement the work of the national army medical corps; they chose as their emblem the Swiss flag in reverse, i.e. a red cross on a white background. The official recognition of governments for these arrangements was accorded in the following year by the *Geneva Convention of 22 August 1864*, in which twelve States undertook to respect the immunity of military hospitals and their staff, to care for sick and wounded soldiers whatever their nationality and to respect the emblem of the Red Cross. This convention formed the basis of humanitarian activities during the Franco-Prussian War (1870), the Spanish-American War (1898) and the Russo-Japanese War (1904); it was revised and developed by a diplomatic conference in 1906, and further revised and improved in the light of the experience of the First World War, by the Geneva Convention of 1929.[16] The further development of humanitarian law during the last half century is summarised in Chapter VII.

It was, of course, necessary to extend a similar system of protection to the sick and wounded in naval warfare. This was achieved in a different framework, that of the Hague Peace Conferences of 1899 and 1907. The Hague Convention No. III of 1899 extended to maritime warfare the provisions of the Geneva Convention of 1864; when the latter had been revised in 1906, its principles were extended to war at sea by the Hague Convention No. X of 1907. This remained in force for more than forty years, during both the First and the Second World Wars, and was not replaced until 1949.

Another branch of humanitarian law relates to a field of activity for which the Red Cross is particularly well known – the care of prisoners of war. This concerns in the first place their identification and the communication of information on their whereabouts and their physical condition to their home countries; secondly, to arranging facilities for correspondence with their families and the despatch of parcels; thirdly, it covers visits to prisoner-of-war camps and the furnishing of medical supplies; fourthly, to the repatriation (usually on an exchange basis) of the seriously wounded.

The Hague Convention No. IV of 1907, dealing with the Laws and Customs of War on Land, was the legal basis for this work. In accordance with its provisions, the International Committee of the Red Cross set up during the First World War an International Agency for Prisoners of War in Geneva; this body established an index of over five million cards containing particulars of the identity and whereabouts of prisoners of war.

The humanitarian work of the Red Cross during the First World War was of such value for all the belligerents that the authors of the Covenant of the League of Nations inserted in the treaty as Article 25 the following provision:

The Members of the League agree to encourage and promote the establishment and co-operation of duly authorized voluntary national Red Cross organizations having as purposes the improvement of health, the prevention of disease and the mitigation of suffering throughout the world.

It had thus become clearly established by a number of treaties, and finally by the explicit recognition of the Red Cross in the League Covenant, that the condition of the sick and wounded and the care of prisoners of war had become matters of concern to international law; this contributed to the gradual evolution which led up to the result that human rights in general became the concern of international law and respect for human rights an obligation on all members of the United Nations.[17]

3. The protection of minorities

The third main development whereby international law came to be concerned with the rights of individuals (and not only of States) relates to the protection of minorities. This was principally the result of the redrawing of frontiers which formed part of the peace settlement in 1919, though in the Treaty of Berlin of 1878 Bulgaria, Montenegro, Serbia, Roumania and Turkey had all assumed obligations to grant religious freedom to their nationals. The political changes of 1919 and 1920, including the restoration of Poland and the creation of successor States after the dissolution of the Austro-Hungarian Empire, respected as far as possible the principle of nationality, but the populations in many areas were so mixed – perhaps as the result of a happier age when less importance was attached to nationality – that, wherever the frontiers were drawn, it was impossible to avoid the existence of minorities on the other side of the line.

The new arrangements took three main forms. First, there were five special treaties on minorities with the allied or newly created States: with Poland (Versailles, 28 June 1919), with Czechoslovakia and Yugoslavia (St Germain-en-Laye, 10 September 1919), with Roumania (Trianon, 4 June 1920) and with Greece (Sèvres, 10 August 1920). Secondly, chapters on the rights of the minorities within their borders were included in the peace treaties with the ex-enemy States: with Austria (St Germain-en-Laye, 10 September 1919), with Bulgaria (Neuilly, 27 November 1919), with Hungary (Trianon, 4 June 1920) and later with Turkey (Lausanne, 24 July 1923). Thirdly, certain States made declarations before the Council of the League of Nations as a condition of their admission to the League: Finland (27 June 1921, as regards the Åland Islands), Albania (21 October 1921), Lithuania (12 May 1922), Latvia (7 July 1923), Estonia (17 September 1923) and later Iraq (30 May 1932).[18]

Generally speaking, these various arrangements for the protection of the rights of minorities provided for equality before the law in regard to civil and political rights, freedom of religion, the right of members of the minorities to use their own language and the right to maintain their own religious and educational establishments. It was also usual to provide for teaching in the language of the minority in State schools in districts where the minority constituted a considerable proportion of the population. It was recognised that these various provisions protecting the rights of minorities constituted 'obligations of international concern' which were placed under the guarantee of the League of Nations and could not be modified without the consent of the Council of the League. Minority groups could bring their complaints before the League; the usual procedure was that, if the Secretary-General considered the case admissible, the Council would appoint an *ad hoc* Minorities Committee to investigate the matter and try to reach a friendly settlement; if this failed, the complaint was referred to the full Council. The Council could refer the matter to the Permanent Court of International Justice; one well known case in which this occurred was that of the *Minority schools in Albania*, in which the Court insisted on the need to maintain equality in fact as well as equality in law and held that the closing of the minority schools destroyed equality of treatment.[19]

Of particular importance – both for its practical effect at the time and for the precedent it created for the future – was the *German–Polish Convention of 15 May 1922 on Upper Silesia*, a region which was divided into two parts, one on each side of the frontier between Germany and Poland. This Convention not only contained guarantees for the protection of the minorities on both sides of the frontier but also set up an elaborate system of measures of implementation: a Minorities Office in each part of Upper Silesia, a Mixed Commission and an Arbitral Tribunal. The commission and the tribunal each had an independent president appointed by the League Council. The Mixed Commission dealt with more than 2,000 cases during the fifteen years of its existence (1922–37), and was essentially concerned with conciliation, while the Arbitral Tribunal was a judicial body, with competence to hear claims by individuals, and pronounced judgments which were binding on the courts and administrative authorities of the two countries.[20] Either government could refer any difference of opinion as to questions of law or of fact to the Permanent Court of International Justice; one case so referred in 1928, after the failure of settlement before the Mixed Commission and the League Council, was that of the *Rights of minorities in Upper Silesia*, in which the Court held that the question whether a person belonged to a racial, linguistic or religious minority (which was the criterion for admission to the German-speaking minority schools in Poland) 'is subject to no verification, dispute, pressure or hindrance whatever on the part of the authorities'.[21]

We thus see that by the end of the inter-war period there were a number of matters with regard to which it had been established that international law was concerned with the status or the treatment of the individual – and not merely with relations between States. However, this was true only in relation to a limited number of subjects – slavery, humanitarian questions, the rights of minorities – so that it remained necessary to generalise the field of application of this principle and extend it to all the basic rights of the individual. Moreover, it was only in very rare cases – under the minority treaties – that the individual possessed a remedy which would permit him to take action on the international scene to protect his rights, so that the question of international enforcement measures had barely been touched. International law was, however, ripe for development in both these respects. The cataclysm of the Second World War brought this home to the conscience of mankind and thus set the stage for the developments which have occurred since 1945 and which are the subject of this book.

NOTES

1   *Human Rights in Europe*, second edition, Manchester University Press, 1977, p. 149, quoting a paragraph from the first edition of Oppenheim's *Treatise on International Law*, 1905. When Sir Hersch Lauterpacht prepared the eighth edition of Oppenheim in 1955 he modified this passage considerably, as shown in Sohn and Buergenthal, *International Protection of Human Rights*, New York, 1973, p. 5. But see also *infra*, Chapter II, n. 61.

2   Report on Torture published by Amnesty International on the occasion of its conference in Paris, December 1973. Its report in 1980 recounted forty-five missions to thirty-three countries and work to assist over 4,000 individual prisoners of conscience.

3   This section is based on an article entitled 'The right to culture' in the UNESCO review *Cultures*, V, No. 1, 1978. See also H. Gros Espiell in reference given below in n. 11.

4   The Director of the Division of Human Rights in the U.N. Secretariat, to whom much credit should also be given, was Professor John Humphrey of Canada.

5   *The Final Act of the International Conference on Human Rights*, Tehran, 1968, is published in U.N. document A/Conf. 32/41.

6   Christian Daubie, 'Cyrus le Grand – un précurseur dans le domaine des Droits de l'Homme', *Human Rights Journal*, V, 1972, p. 293.

7   Polys Modinos, 'La Charte de la Liberté de l'Europe', *Human Rights Journal*, VIII, 1975, pp. 677–8; 'Introduction à l'étude des droits de l'homme', *ibid*., p. 650.

8   Imre Szabo, Isran Kovacs *et al*., *The Socialist Concept of Human Rights*, Hungarian Academy of Sciences, Budapest, 1966, particularly pp. 53–81. See also Imre Szabo, *Cultural Rights*, Budapest, 1974; Franciszek Przetacznik, 'L'attitude des Etats socialistes à l'égard de la protection internationale des droits de l'homme', *Human Rights Journal*, VIII, 1974, p. 175; V. Kartashkin, 'Human rights and peaceful coexistence', *Human Rights Journal*, IX, 1976, p. 5.

9   See *supra*, n. 5. See also U.N. General Assembly Resolution 32/130 (1977) and references given in Chapter II, n. 84.

10 Kéba M'Baye: 'Les réalités du monde noir et les droits de l'homme', *Human Rights Journal*, II, 1969, p. 382; 'Le droit au développement comme un droit de l'homme', *ibid*., V, 1972, p. 505; Th. C. Van Boven, 'Some remarks on special problems relating to human rights in developing countries', *ibid*., III, 1970, p. 383. See also below, Chapter VI, section 4.

11 For the text adopted by the Tehran conference see *supra*, n. 5. Cf. also U.N. General Assembly Resolution 32/130 of 16 December

1977: 'All human rights and fundamental freedoms are indivisible and interdependent; equal attention and urgent consideration should be given to the implementation, promotion and protection of both civil and political, and economic, social and cultural rights'. Further discussion of different approaches to the protection of human rights may be found in H. Gros Espiell, 'The evolving concept of human rights: Western, socialist and Third World approaches'; Theo C. van Boven, 'United Nations policies and strategies: global perspectives?'; B. G. Ramcharan, 'Standard-setting: future perspectives'; and M. Moskowitz, 'Implementing human rights: present status and future prospects', all in *Human Rights: Thirty Years after the Universal Declaration*, ed. Ramcharan, The Hague, 1979.

12   20 *State Trials*, p. 1.

13   For a summary of international action for the suppression of slavery see *Oppenheim's International Law*, eighth edition (ed. Lauterpacht), 1955, pp. 732–5; M. Ganji, *The International Protection of Human Rights*, Paris, 1962, pp. 87–110; J. R. P. Montgomery, 'Slavery', in *Human Rights*, published by the U.K. Committee for Human Rights Year, London, 1968.

14   *Human Rights – a Compilation of International Instruments*, U.N. doc. ST/HR/1 Rev. 1, 1978, p. 52. By 1 January 1980 it had been ratified by ninety-three States.

15   Quoted by Draper, *op. cit.* n. 16, p. 63.

16   For the history of the humanitarian Conventions see H. Coursier, 'L'Evolution du droit international humanitaire', ADI *Recueil des Cours*, 1960, I, p. 357, and G. I. A. D. Draper, 'The Geneva Conventions of 1949', *ibid.*, 1965, I, p. 63. See also Oppenheim, *op. cit.*, seventh edition (ed. Lauterpacht, 1952), pp. 353–97, and below, Chapter VII.

17   The relationship between humanitarian law and human rights law is discussed below in Chapter VII.

18   For an account of the system established under the protection of the League see *Oppenheim's International Law*, eighth edition, 1955, pp. 711–16; M. Ganji, *op. cit.* n. 13, pp. 45–85; L. C. Green, 'Protection of minorities in the League of Nations and the United Nations', in *Human Rights, Federalism and Minorities*, Toronto, 1970; Sohn and Buergenthal, *op. cit.*, n. 1, pp. 213–335.

19   Opinion of 6 April 1935, *Publications of the Permanent Court of International Justice*, series A–B, No. 64.

20   Ganji, *op. cit.*, pp. 57–69; G. Kaeckenbeck, *The International Experiment of Upper Silesia*, London, 1942.

21   *P.C.I.J.: Publications of the Court*, series A, No. 15, pp. 46–7.

Chapter two

THE UNITED NATIONS AND HUMAN RIGHTS: THE INTERNATIONAL COVENANT ON CIVIL AND POLITICAL RIGHTS

I. THE CHARTER

As is well known, the Charter of the United Nations contains a number of references to the promotion of human rights. The first is in the Preamble, written by Field-Marshal Smuts:

We the peoples of the United Nations, determined . . . to reaffirm faith in fundamental human rights, in the dignity and worth of the human person, in the equal rights of men and women and of nations large and small . . . have resolved to combine our efforts to accomplish these aims.

Then, among the purposes of the United Nations set out in Article 1, is 'to co-operate . . . in promoting respect for human rights and fundamental freedoms for all'. The most important provisions are probably those contained in Articles 55 and 56 of the Charter. Article 55 provides that the United Nations shall promote, *inter alia*, 'universal respect for, and observance of, human rights and fundamental freedoms for all without distinction as to race, sex, language or religion'; while in Article 56 'all members pledge themselves to take joint and separate action in co-operation with the Organisation for the achievement of the purposes set forth in Article 55'. Other references in the Charter are in Article 13, which authorises the General Assembly to make studies and recommendations about human rights; Article 62, which contains a somewhat similar provision about the Economic and Social Council; Article 68, which requires the Council to set up Commissions in the economic and social fields and for the promotion of human rights; and Article 76, which lists the promotion of human rights and fundamental freedoms for all without distinction among the basic objectives of the trusteeship system.

What is less well known is that the Charter very nearly gave to human rights 'only a passing reference'. Professor John P. Humphrey has recounted how the Dumbarton Oaks proposals for the United Nations, prepared in 1944 by the four great powers, contained only one general provision about human rights; but the delegations of several smaller countries and the representatives of a number of non-governmental organisations who attended the San Francisco conference as consultants to the United States delegation were able, by their energetic lobbying, to secure the inclusion in the Charter of the much more positive provisions summarised above.[1] The obligation now contained in Article 56 was at one stage intended to be stronger. The first draft would have required member States 'to take separate and joint action and to co-operate with the Organisation for the promotion of human rights', thus clearly implying an obligation for them to act individually, irrespective of the action, or failure to act, of other States. But this formulation was not approved, and the undertaking finally accepted was 'to take joint and separate action in co-operation with the Organisation'.[2] Professor Louis B. Sohn has also traced the history of these provisions and recounted how certain delegations at San Francisco considered that the phrase *promoting respect* for human rights' was too weak; various suggestions were made to substitute the words 'assure' or 'protect' for 'promote', and to require the 'observance' of human rights rather than merely 'respect' for them.[3] But these proposals were not accepted. However, in view of the fact that a number of delegations and influential non-governmental organisations considered that the human rights provisions of the Charter were too weak (even though markedly stronger than the original Dumbarton Oaks proposals), it was agreed that a Bill of Rights should be drawn up separately and as soon as possible thereafter.[4] There had, indeed, been suggestions, notably by Panama, for the incorporation of a Bill of Rights in the Charter itself; but this proved impossible, partly for lack of sufficient support and partly for reasons of time. President Truman, in his closing speech to the conference, stated that:

We have good reason to expect the framing of an international bill of rights, acceptable to all the nations involved. That bill of rights will be as much a part of international life as our own Bill of Rights is a part of our Constitution. The Charter is dedicated to the achievement and observance of human rights and fundamental freedoms. Unless we can attain those objectives for all men and women everywhere − without regard to race, language or religion − we cannot have permanent peace and security.[5]

II. THE UNIVERSAL DECLARATION

No time was lost in acting on this proposal. The Charter was signed in June 1945 and entered into force on 24 October of the same year. The Preparatory Commission in the autumn of 1945 recommended that the Economic and Social Council should immediately establish a Commission on Human Rights and direct it to prepare an international Bill of Rights; the General Assembly approved this recommendation on 12 February 1946; the Economic and Social Council acted on it four days later.[6] The Commission on Human Rights was constituted within a matter of months, first with a nucleus of nine members, who recommended by majority vote in May 1946 that, since the Council consisted of representatives of governments, the members of the Commission should be elected by the Council from a list of nominees submitted by governments but serve in an individual capacity. The U.S.S.R., however, opposed this proposal, and ECOSOC decided in June 1946 that the Commission should consist of eighteen members, appointed by the governments which were selected by the Council; later in the same year the Council decided to leave it to the governments concerned to decide whether to appoint government officials or independent persons. It is, therefore, governments which are members of the Commission, and its members in fact attend as representatives of governments.[7] In 1962 the membership was increased to twenty-one; in 1966 to thirty-two; in 1980 to forty-three.

The first regular session of the Commission opened in January 1947, and its first task was the drafting of the International Bill of Rights. It decided later in the year that this should have three parts: a Declaration, a Convention containing legal obligations, and 'measures of implementation' – that is to say, a system of international supervision or control. Work started immediately on the Declaration, for which purpose a drafting committee of eight members was appointed: the representatives of Australia, Chile, China, France, Lebanon, the United Kingdom, the United States and the U.S.S.R. The chairman of the Commission and of the drafting committee was Mrs Eleanor Roosevelt. The full commission examined and revised the draft Declaration thus prepared, and submitted it through the Economic and Social Council to the General Assembly in 1948; it also submitted at the same time a draft Covenant prepared by the drafting committee. The Assembly, at its third session, held in Paris in the autumn of

1948, decided to consider only the draft Declaration. The Third Committee devoted eighty-one meetings to examination of this text and to the 168 amendments which were tabled; in due course it submitted a revised version to the General Assembly. After a Soviet proposal to postpone further consideration of the matter until the following year had been defeated, the Declaration was adopted on 10 December 1948, with forty-eight votes in favour, none against and eight abstentions (the Soviet bloc, South Africa and Saudi Arabia).[8]

The Universal Declaration was adopted by *Resolution 217 (III) of the General Assembly*. It was not conceived as imposing legal obligations on States. The operative part of the Resolution read as follows:

Now, therefore, the General Assembly proclaims this Universal Declaration of Human Rights as a common standard of achievement for all peoples and all nations, to the end that every individual and every organ of society, keeping this Declaration constantly in mind, shall strive by teaching and education to promote respect for these rights and freedoms and by progressive measures, national and international, to secure their universal and effective recognition and observance, both among the peoples of Member States themselves and among the peoples of territories under their jurisdiction.

Mrs Roosevelt stated in the General Assembly that the Declaration was 'first and foremost a declaration of the basic principles to serve as a common standard for all nations. It might well become the Magna Carta of all mankind'. She considered that its proclamation by the General Assembly 'would be of importance comparable to the 1789 proclamation of the Declaration of the Rights of Man, the proclamation of the rights of man in the Declaration of Independence of the United States of America, and similar declarations made in other countries'.[9] Professor Sohn draws the following conclusion:[10]

There seems to be an agreement that the Declaration is a statement of general principles spelling out in considerable detail the meaning of the phrase 'human rights and fundamental freedoms' in the Charter of the United Nations. As the Declaration was adopted unanimously, without a dissenting vote, it can be considered as an authoritative interpretation of the Charter of the highest order. While the Declaration is not directly binding on United Nations Members, it strengthens their obligations under the Charter by making them more precise.

But if this was the position in 1948, the Universal Declaration has since acquired a greatly reinforced status not only as 'a common standard of achievement for all peoples and all nations' but also as an agreed statement of the law which all States should observe. It has been reaffirmed by the General Assembly on a number of occasions, of which the most striking were perhaps the adoption of the Declaration on Colonialism in 1960, by ninety votes in favour, none against and nine abstentions (reaffirmed in 1962 by 101 votes in favour, none against and four abstentions), which stated, *inter alia*:[11] '*All States shall observe faithfully and strictly* the provisions of the Charter of the United Nations, the Universal Declaration of Human Rights and the present Declaration . . .'; and the unanimous adoption in 1963 (without abstentions) of the *Declaration on the Elimination of Racial Discrimination*, which contained a similar provision.[12]

At the International Conference on Human Rights in Tehran in 1968, the Secretary-General of the United Nations, U Thant, was able to say that there are no fewer than forty-three constitutions adopted in recent years which are clearly inspired by the Universal Declaration, and that examples of legislation expressly quoting or reproducing provisions of the Declaration can be found in all continents.[13]

We may therefore safely conclude, with Professor Humphrey, that the impact of the Universal Declaration has probably exceeded the most sanguine hopes of its authors; and with Professor Sir Humphrey Waldock that the constant and widespread recognition of its principles clothes it with the character of customary international law.[14]

III. THE INTERNATIONAL COVENANT ON CIVIL AND POLITICAL RIGHTS

Resolution 217 (III) of 10 December 1948 not only approved the text of the Universal Declaration, it also decided that work should go ahead on the other two parts of the Bill of Rights: a Covenant containing legal obligations to be assumed by States, and measures of implementation. The Commission had indeed already prepared and submitted a preliminary draft for the Covenant, but it was not yet ready for adoption and was referred back by the General Assembly.

1. The history of the Covenant

There then began a period of discussion, drafting and negotiation which lasted for eighteen years. The story is fascinating for those interested in the international protection of human rights, and we are indebted to Professor Louis B. Sohn for an enthralling summary of it.[15] No more than the bare outline can be given here.

The initial work of the Commission resulted in a text devoted to the classic civil and political rights, but when the General Assembly was consulted in 1950 for certain basic policy decisions, it decided that economic, social and cultural rights should also be included.[16] The Commission proceeded to draft accordingly in 1951, but when the Council considered the results, and particularly the differences in the two categories of rights, it recommended that the General Assembly should reconsider its decision. As a result, the Assembly, after a long debate, and on the proposal of India and the Lebanon, supported by Belgium and the U.S.A., decided in 1952 that there should be two separate Covenants, with as many similar provisions as possible, and that both should include an article on 'the right of all peoples and nations to self-determination'.[17]

The articles on measures of implementation gave the Commission much more trouble than the normative provisions, principally because the views of its members were sharply divided on the basic question how far governments could be expected to accept a system of international control. A number of far-reaching proposals were considered, including an Australian suggestion for an International Court of Human Rights, a proposal by Uruguay for the establishment of an Office of a United Nations High Commissioner (or Attorney-General) for Human Rights and a French proposal for an International Investigation Commission, coupled with the appointment of an Attorney-General of the Commission; India proposed that the Security Council should be seized of alleged violations, investigate them and enforce redress, while Israel suggested the creation of a new Specialised Agency for the implementation of the Covenants.[18] The attitude of the United Kingdom and the United States was more cautious; they proposed that Human Rights Committees should be set up on an *ad hoc* basis, but only for inter-State disputes.[19] The Soviet Union was consistently opposed to all arrangements of this sort on the ground that they would interfere in the internal affairs of States, contrary to Article 2(7) of the Charter, undermining their sovereignty and independence.[20] The Commission finally decided by seven votes to six, with one abstention, in favour of the establishment of a permanent Human Rights Committee to consider complaints of violations of human rights on an inter-State basis; but it rejected (seven–four–three) the possibility of considering complaints by non-governmental organisations and (eight–three–three) petitions by individuals.[21]

Since there will be many references in this book to the problem of the meaning and effect of Article 2 (7) of the Charter, it will be appropriate to examine the question in a little more detail and to summarise the issues involved. Different governments have taken different positions at different times, depending on the political context; perhaps not the least remarkable feat of U.N. diplomacy is the facility with which some delegates argue that it is outside the competence of the U.N. to discuss human rights situations on their own territory or on that of their allies, but quite proper to discuss alleged violations by their political opponents. Among the attitudes and statements which it is instructive to recall are those of Mr Vyshinsky (U.S.S.R.) in 1946 that Article 2 (7) did not prevent the U.N. from discussing the situation of Indians in South Africa; of Mr Santa Cruz (Chile) in 1949 that 'abuse of Article 2 (7) of the Charter might paralyse the action of the United Nations' and in 1952 that 'the international law created by conventions and agreements among countries removes a number of questions from the exclusive competence of States . . . since the adoption of the Charter, all fundamental human rights have formed part of international law since they are included in that multilateral treaty, the Charter'. Among the texts of major importance is the Report of the U.N. Commission on the Racial Situation in South Africa of 3 October 1953, which discusses at length the meaning of Article 2 (7) of the Charter, citing the views of such eminent jurists as Professors Lauterpacht, Cassin and Kelsen, and contains the following statement:

. . . The United Nations is unquestionably justified in deciding that a matter is outside the essentially domestic jurisdiction of a State when it involves systematic violation of the Charter's principles concerning human rights, and more especially that of non-discrimination, above all when such actions affect millions of human beings, and have provoked grave international alarm, and when the State concerned clearly displays an intention to aggravate the position.

When this report was discussed in the General Assembly in 1953,

South Africa introduced a draft resolution rejecting its conclusions and maintaining that the matters dealt with therein (principally racial policies in the Union) were 'matters essentially within the domestic jurisdiction of a Member State' and therefore outside the competence of the United Nations; this draft was rejected by an overwhelming majority of forty-two votes to seven, with seven abstentions – a fact which deserves to be remembered. The same position has, of course, been repeated on many subsequent occasions, as is illustrated by the Second Report on the Racial Situation in South Africa, and discussions in the Security Council in 1960 on the request of twenty-nine States that the Council should consider the Sharpeville massacre, and the discussions in the Security Council in 1963–64 on the report of the Special Committee on the Policies of Apartheid and in 1970 on the question of the arms embargo against South Africa. One may also retain from these discussions the statement of the American position by Mr Cabot Lodge on 30 March 1960:

We all recognise that every nation has a right to regulate its own internal affairs. This is a right acknowledged by Article 2, paragraph 7, of the Charter. At the same time, we must recognise the right – and the obligation – of the United Nations to be concerned with national policies in so far as they affect the world community. This is particularly so in cases where international obligations embodied in the Charter are concerned.

One might perhaps summarise the situation by saying that until 1945 international law considered that the manner in which a State treated its own nationals was (apart from the limited circumstances in which humanitarian intervention was permissible) a question within its own jurisdiction and competence, with which other States had no right to intervene. But since then the legal position has changed. Matters with regard to which States have accepted obligations in international law cease to be questions solely within their domestic jurisdiction. The unfettered rule of national sovereignty no longer applies to them. Other States which have accepted similar obligations have a legitimate interest in seeing that the common undertakings are respected. The fact that those undertakings relate to the maintenance by a State of the human rights of its own citizens does not justify a derogation from the fundamental rule of international law: *Pacta sunt servanda*.

The Commission on Human Rights completed its work on the draft Covenants by 1954, and submitted its texts to ECOSOC and the General Assembly.[22] In the following year the Secretary-

General prepared an analysis of the texts and of the issues which had been discussed during their preparation, which is a valuable additional source for understanding the provisions of the Covenants.[23]

When the draft Covenants prepared by the Commission on Human Rights were being considered by the Third Committee of the General Assembly, it devoted its attention principally, over a period of nearly ten years, to the substantive rights. There was much discussion of the right of all peoples to self-determination, which resulted in Article 1, common to both Covenants. During the years 1956–58 the articles relating to economic and social rights were approved with a good deal of detailed revision but with little major amendment. From 1958 to 1961 the same was done for the civil and political rights. In 1962 and 1963 discussion centred mainly on the introductory articles, i.e. the obligations of States to respect the rights enounced, with particular reference to the question whether the obligation is of immediate or progressive effect – a question to which we will return later. In 1964 and 1965 comparatively little attention was devoted to the Covenants, as the Third Committee was principally concerned with the Convention on the Elimination of All Forms of Racial Discrimination. In 1966 a determined and successful attempt was made to finish the work on the Covenants; it concentrated on the measures of implementation.

In this respect the Third Committee considerably revised the proposals of the Commission. It agreed to the establishment of a Human Rights Committee, but increased the number of its members from nine to eighteen; it also decided that the members should be elected by the States parties, instead of by the International Court of Justice, as had been proposed by the Commission. As regards the Covenant on Economic, Social and Cultural Rights, the committee retained the system of reports by contracting parties to the Economic and Social Council, on the basis of which the Council may adopt recommendations 'of a general nature', i.e. not referring to particular situations or even to particular States.[24] We will return to this subject in Chapter VI.

As regards the Covenant on Civil and Political Rights, the committee decided in favour of a double system of implementation, that is to say, a compulsory system of reporting to the new Human Rights Committee to be established under the terms of the Covenant; and an optional system of fact-finding and conciliation, which would apply only in relation to States which had expressly agreed to this procedure. This was supplemented by a provision for *ad hoc* Conciliation Commissions, if the parties to a dispute agreed. The Netherlands proposed a further optional clause providing for the possibility of individual petitions, which appeared to have more chance of success in 1966 than in previous years, since a comparable provision had been inserted in the Racial Discrimination Convention the year before. The attempt, however, was unsuccessful and the Third Committee decided by the narrowest majority (41–39–16) that a text permitting individual petitions or communications to the Human Rights Committee should be incorporated in a separate 'Optional Protocol' to the Covenant, and thus apply only to States which, by a separate act, ratify the Protocol.[25]

The Covenants, as revised by the Third Committee, were finally approved unanimously by the General Assembly on 16 December 1966[26] with more than 100 votes in favour; they required thirty-five ratifications and entered into force in 1976. The Optional Protocol was approved by majority vote (sixty-six to two, with thirty-eight abstentions) and required ten ratifications; it entered into force at the same time as the Covenant on Civil and Political Rights. By 1 January 1981, sixty-five countries had ratified the two Covenants, and twenty-five had ratified the Optional Protocol to the Covenant on Civil and Political Rights.[27]

This culmination of eighteen years' work in the unanimous approval of the Covenants by over a hundred States was in itself a remarkable achievement. Even the long period of time taken over the negotiations had one important advantage: whereas about fifty States participated in the initial discussions, this number had more than doubled by the time the texts were completed, with the result that the new members of the United Nations are also likely to feel some of the responsibilities – and, we may hope, the pride – of parenthood; they may thus be more likely to ratify instruments in whose preparation they participated, and for whose approval they cast their votes.

The contents of the two Covenants have already been the subject of much learned comment.[28] The Covenant on Economic, Social and Cultural Rights will be discussed in Chapter VI, and the Covenant on Civil and Political Rights in this chapter.

2. The general provisions of the Covenant

In accordance with the decision of the General Assembly taken in 1952, both Covenants start off in identical terms, with an article on the right of self-determination. This right is stated as one which exists and is of immediate application ('All peoples *have* the right of self-determination') and which results in their right to determine freely their political status. In subsequent paragraphs it entails the right of peoples to dispose freely of their natural resources, and the obligation of States to 'promote the realisation of the right of self-determination'.

This article of both Covenants is, of course, in accordance with the political philosophy of the General Assembly – which no one would question at this date, so long as it is expressed as a political philosophy. Our problem, however, is of a different nature. The Universal Declaration was an instrument for proclaiming rights in general terms; the Covenants are supposed to contain legal obligations of States to respect human rights – which is normally taken to mean the rights of individuals as human beings. The difficulty with the right of self-determination is twofold: first, it is a collective right and not an individual right, so that many people would question whether it is in its place in the present context – all the more so since it was proclaimed elsewhere in the 'Declaration on the Granting of Independence to Colonial Countries and Peoples' of 1960;[29] secondly, the right is stated as belonging to 'all peoples'. But what constitutes a 'people'? Merely to take a few cases in Western Europe, does the right of self-determination belong to the Scots and the Welsh, the Bretons, the Corsicans and the Alsatians, the Basques and the Catalans? The same question can be put in relation to many other parts of the world. The issue can, of course, be argued as one of policy or of expediency; the difficulty results from the attempt to transform a political principle into an enforceable right. It would appear that the inclusion of the articles on the right of self-determination in the two Covenants may well harbinger trouble in the years to come.

Articles 2–5 of both Covenants constitute Part II thereof; they contain in each case an undertaking to respect, or to take steps to secure progressively, the substantive rights which follow in Part III, and also certain other provisions of a general nature.

In the Covenant on Civil and Political Rights, Article 2 provides that each State party 'undertakes to respect and to ensure to all individuals within its territory and subject to its jurisdiction the rights recognised in the present Covenant . . .'. Does this impose on States an obligation of immediate application or only an obligation to do something in the future? From the words quoted above from the first paragraph of Article 2, one would conclude that the obligation is immediate. Schwelb states that, subject to certain exceptions, the Covenant 'imposes on States parties *the obligation to maintain a defined standard*'.[30] This would, indeed, appear to have been the intention as regards civil and political rights. At the same time it seems clear that some members of the United Nations cannot accept immediately all the obligations resulting from the Covenant, because the list of rights secured is (as we shall see shortly) very extensive; and it was thought desirable to obtain the largest possible number of ratifications. Paragraph 2 of Article 2 therefore provides for an obligation to take 'the necessary steps . . . to adopt such legislative or other measures as may be necessary to give effect to the rights recognised in the present Covenant' in cases where they are not already provided for in the national law. It thus appears that while the first principle is one of immediate obligation, the possibility of progressive application is also recognised; and a proposal to set a time limit for taking 'the necessary steps' which was made during the negotiations was not accepted. The immediate nature of the obligation is thereby somewhat weakened.

Article 2 of the Covenant on Civil and Political Rights also contains (in paragraph 1) a 'non-discrimination clause' in what may now be considered the standard form; and (in paragraph 3) the undertaking to make available an effective remedy to anyone whose rights set out in the Covenant are violated. The non-discrimination clause is amplified by Article 3, which contains an undertaking to respect the principle of equality of men and women in the enjoyment of the rights secured. Article 4 provides for the possibility of derogation 'in times of public emergency which threatens the life of the nation and the existence of which is officially proclaimed'; while Article 5 contains two separate provisions: the first is designed to prevent abuse of the rights and freedoms set out (based on Article 30 of the Universal Declaration); while the second is a general saving clause to the effect that nothing in the Covenant may be interpreted as limiting the rights and freedoms already existing or recognised under national law or under other conventions.

3. The rights protected

Part III of the Covenant on Civil and Political Rights sets out the rights which the Covenant is designed to protect. They are the following:

Article 6. The right to life.
   7. Freedom from torture and inhuman treatment.
   8. Freedom from slavery and forced labour.
   9. Right to liberty and security.
   10. Right of detained persons to be treated with humanity.
   11. Freedom from imprisonment for debt.
   12. Freedom of movement and of choice of residence.
   13. Freedom of aliens from arbitrary expulsion.
   14. Right to a fair trial.
   15. Protection against retroactivity of the criminal law.
   16. Right to recognition as a person before the law.
   17. Right to privacy.
   18. Freedom of thought, conscience and religion.
   19. Freedom of opinion and of expression.
   20. Prohibition of propaganda for war and of incitement to national, racial or religious hatred.
   21. Right of assembly.
   22. Freedom of association.
   23. Right to marry and found a family.
   24. Rights of the child.
   25. Political rights.
   26. Equality before the law.
   27. Rights of minorities.

It will be observed that this is an extensive list. The number of rights included is greater than in the Universal Declaration or the European Convention. A comparison with the latter instrument is contained in Chapter III; as compared with the Universal Declaration, it may be observed that the rights set out in the Covenant are generally defined in greater detail and include the following, which were not contained in the Declaration:

   10. The right of detained persons to be treated with humanity.
   11. Freedom from imprisonment for debt.
   20. Prohibition of propaganda for war and of incitement to hatred.

24. The rights of the child.
27. The rights of minorities.

On the other hand, the right of property, which was included in Article 17 of the Universal Declaration, is not included in either Covenant. It proved impossible in the United Nations to reach agreement between countries of widely different political philosophies on a definition of this right.

It is not proposed to examine in detail the definitions of the civil and political rights set out in the Covenant. Two general observations, however, may be made at this stage.

First, that not only is the number of rights protected in the Covenant greater than in other comparable instruments, but also that the definitions given are frequently more liberal or progressive. For example, Article 6 on the right to life does not actually prohibit the death penalty, but is clearly drafted with the intention of indicating that it should be abolished. It refers to countries which have not abolished the death penalty as if this is a temporary state of affairs which should be remedied, and states specifically that nothing in the article shall be invoked to prevent or delay the abolishment of capital punishment. Again, Article 10 provides positively that all detained persons shall be treated humanely and with respect for the inherent dignity of the human person; this is something more than the mere prohibition of inhuman treatment found in earlier texts. Moreover, Article 10 continues by laying down separate standards for accused persons and juveniles, who shall be separated from convicted persons; while paragraph 3 of this article provides that the aim of the penitentiary system shall be the reformation and social rehabilitation of prisoners.

Another example is afforded by Article 25, which sets out certain political rights; this appears to apply not only to the right to vote in national elections but also to the same right in local elections and to the right to take part in the government of one's country and in the public service. Another example is Article 27, which protects certain rights of minorities, i.e. 'to enjoy their own culture, to profess and practise their own religion, and to use their own language'.

Article 14 on the right to a fair trial is undoubtedly a provision of particular importance and is wide in scope. In addition to the usual guarantees of an independent and impartial tribunal, public hearings, the presumption of innocence and the rights of the defence, it also provides for: protection against self-incrimination; the right of appeal; compensation for miscarriage of justice; and the principle of *ne bis in idem*.

A second general comment is that if the list of rights enumerated in the Covenant is extensive, and if the definitions given are often more liberal or more advanced than in earlier texts, some of them are so general or imprecise that the texts appear to be more statements of political principle or policy than of legally enforceable rights. This point has already been made in relation to 'the right of self-determination of all peoples'. It could also be made as regards several other provisions, notably those relating to the aim of the penitentiary system (Article 10 (3)), the right to recognition as a person before the law (Article 16), the prohibition of propaganda for war (Article 20) and the right to take part in the conduct of public affairs (Article 25 (a)). Some of these points will be examined in greater detail in Chapter III, section I (5).

It is proposed to examine in greater detail the 'measures of implementation' of the Covenant on Civil and Political Rights, for the simple reason that the effectiveness of the system instituted by the Covenant depends not so much on the definitions of the rights to be protected, which are reasonably satisfactory, as on the measures instituted to control whether governments in fact respect the obligations they have assumed.

4. The Human Rights Committee

Article 28 of the Covenant provides for the establishment of the Human Rights Committee, which thus becomes the principal organ of implementation of the Covenant on Civil and Political Rights. This contrasts with the Covenant on Economic, Social and Cultural Rights, where no new body is created and that role will be played by the existing Economic and Social Council.

As already noted, the Third Committee doubled the number of members of the Human Rights Committee from the figure of nine, which had been proposed in the 1954 draft, to eighteen. This was eminently reasonable, having regard to the fact that the number of members of the United Nations had doubled by 1966.[31] As regards the qualifications of members of the Committee, they must in the first place be nationals of States which are parties to the Covenant; secondly, they must be 'persons of high moral character and recognised competence in the field of human rights'; thirdly, consideration shall be given 'to the usefulness of the participation of some persons having legal experience'. The Commission in 1954 had proposed 'some persons having a judicial or legal experience', but the Third Committee decided to delete the reference to judicial qualifications. The change in fact makes little difference, since the consideration of persons with legal experience clearly does not exclude judges, and, in any event, the clause is not of mandatory effect.

Under Articles 29 and 30 of the Covenant, the members of the Committee are elected by secret ballot by the States parties at a special meeting convened by the Secretary-General of the United Nations for the purpose. Each State party may nominate not more than two candidates, who must be nationals of that State. The detailed procedure for the election is set out in Article 30. The following article provides that the Committee may not include more than one national of any one State and that consideration shall be given to the principle of equitable geographical distribution and to the representation of the different forms of civilisation and of the principal legal systems.[32] The term of office is for four years, though that of nine members elected at the first election is for only two years, in order to avoid a complete change of membership at any one time (Article 32). Members of the Committee are eligible for re-election (Article 29). Articles 33 and 34 deal with the possibilities of incapacity and casual vacancies, while the following article provides that the members of the Committee shall receive emoluments from United Nations resources, thus emphasising the principle already stated in Article 28 that they 'shall serve in their personal capacity', that is to say, not as representatives of their governments. This principle is further emphasised in Article 38, which requires each member of the Committee to make a solemn declaration that he will perform his functions impartially and conscientiously.[33] Article 36 then provides that the Secretary-General of the United Nations shall provide the necessary staff and facilities for the functioning of the Committee.

The Covenant on Civil and Political Rights and the Optional Protocol entered into force on 23 March 1976, and the meeting of the States parties to elect the members of the Committee took place on 20 September 1976. By that time there were forty-four parties to the Covenant and sixteen to the Protocol. The principles of equitable geographical distribution and representation of the principal legal systems were in fact respected, as may be seen from the following indications of the nationality of the members of the Committee: there were five from Western Europe,[34] four from Eastern Europe,[35] two from Asia,[36] three from Africa,[37] one from North America[38] and three from Latin America.[39] The five Western Europeans were all from States which are parties to the European Convention, one of them being also a member of the European Commission of Human Rights;[40] the three Latin Americans were nationals of States parties to the American Convention on Human Rights. Only seven members of the Human Rights Committee were nationals of States which had ratified the Optional Protocol providing for the right of individual petition.[41]

The election of officers at the first session of the Committee in March 1977 equally respected the principle of geographical distribution: the Cypriot member was elected chairman; the three vice-chairmen were from Bulgaria, Mauritius and Norway; the *rapporteur* from Columbia.

The first two meetings of the Human Rights Committee were held in March and August 1977. The Committee was then principally concerned with organisational matters and, in accordance with Article 39 of the Covenant, with settling its rules of procedure (with the assistance of a working group of five members) – though at the second session it also considered the first periodic reports and individual petitions, to which we will revert below.

As regards the rules of procedure, the two most interesting points concerned the publication of the proceedings and the method of voting. It was agreed that reports, formal decisions and all other official documents of the Committee and its subsidiary bodies should be documents of general distribution, i.e. public, unless the Committee should decide otherwise in any particular case; also periodic reports by States parties and additional information submitted by them, should be public documents. On the other hand, documents and decisions relating to inter-State complaints under Articles 41 and 42 of the Covenant and to individual communications under the Optional Protocol should have only restricted distribution, that is to say that they should remain confidential.[42]

As regards the method of voting, there are certain rules established by the Covenant itself. Article 39 provides that the Committee shall establish its own rules of procedure, but paragraph 2 thereof stipulates that these rules shall provide *inter alia* (a) that twelve members shall constitute a quorum; and (b) that decisions shall be made by a majority vote of the members present. During the drafting of the rules of procedure, some members of the Committee argued that there has been a tendency in recent years in various legal bodies (both inside and outside the United Nations) towards the adoption of decisions on the basis of consensus. They urged that the Human Rights Committee should follow this method and thus 'underscore the resolve of members to work harmoniously and in a spirit of co-operation'.

Other members argued that, while consensus was desirable if possible, to establish a rule to this effect 'might considerably restrict the Committee's power of decision-making' and would be inconsistent with Article 39, paragraph 2 (b) of the Covenant (quoted above). Finally, it was agreed to incorporate in Rule 51 the method of decision by a simple majority, but to add a footnote indicating that there was general agreement that the 'method of work normally should allow for attempts to reach decisions by consensus before voting . . .'.[43] At the same time, in the procedures for the consideration of communications under the Optional Protocol, provision was made in Rule 94 that a summary of an individual opinion may be appended to the collective view of the Committee.

In 1979, after the tenth State had made a declaration under Article 41, bringing the inter-State complaints procedure into force, the Committee put into effect Rules 72–7 of its rules of procedure to govern such inter-State complaints. In general, these merely follow the provisions of Article 41, notably that the Committee will consider communications only if both States have made declarations under Article 41 and all domestic remedies have been exhausted (or have been unreasonably prolonged). Rule 75 provides that the Committee shall examine communications under Article 41 at closed meetings, but the Committee may, after consultation with the States parties concerned, issue communiqués, through the Secretary-General, for the use of the information media and the public. The Committee may, through the Secretary-General, request from either of the parties concerned additional information or observations in oral or written form and set a time limit for their submission. Under Rule 77 the parties have a right to be represented when the matter is considered by the Committee and to make submissions orally and/or in writing. The Committee shall adopt a report, in accordance with Article 41 (1) (h), within twelve months of the notice bringing the matter to the Committee's attention, but the parties do not have a right to be present during the Committee's deliberations concerning the adoption of the report. If the matter is not resolved to the satisfaction of the parties, the Committee may, with their prior consent, proceed to the conciliation procedure prescribed in Article 42.

These rules are sound, reasonable and promising, and their promulgation did not meet with efforts to limit the Committee's powers. Doubtless they were helped by the fact that most of the members of the Committee were nationals of countries that had not submitted to this regime, and their governments were not threatened by it. The few members of the Committee from countries that had accepted the system were eager to see it work, and their governments, having submitted to it voluntarily, were not disposed to try to weaken or frustrate it.

5. Reporting procedures

The 1954 draft Covenant prepared by the Commission on Human Rights envisaged as the principal measure of implementation the procedure of inter-State complaints before the Human Rights Committee; a reporting procedure was added only at the end of the relevant chapter, and it is clear from the context that it was considered as a less important or subordinate measure. In the final text of the Covenant the position was reversed: the reporting procedure becomes the principal measure of implementation and the inter-State procedure is optional.

The system of submission of reports by States parties and their examination by the Human Rights Committee is therefore likely to be of cardinal importance in the implementation of the Covenant on Civil and Political Rights, at least during the first years after its entry into force, and merits careful study.

Considerable doubt is felt in some quarters about the value of reports sent in by States on the way in which they have complied with their international obligations. Such reports will, of course, be compiled by national officials who have a natural tendency to give the best account they can of the situation in their own country; it is unlikely that they will draw the attention of an international body to any shortcomings or failures in their national record, that is to say (in the matter which concerns us) to violations by their government or other organs of the State of human rights. Is there, then, it is asked, any value in a reporting system?

There is, of course, much substance in this criticism. National reports *per se* do not constitute an effective measure of control. What matters is how they are dealt with after they have been received, that is to say whether there is an opportunity of critical examination, of drawing attention to gaps or inaccuracies in the information provided, of comparing official statements with other sources of information on the same subject – in short whether the system is such that a critical appraisal of the reports is possible.

Several elements are necessary to make a reporting system effective: (1) the co-operation of governments in providing full information; (2) the possibility of obtaining further (and perhaps critical) information from other responsible sources; (3) the examination of the information thus obtained by independent persons who are not government officials; and (4) the right of some organ or body taking part in the procedure to make suitable recommendations about any necessary improvements in the law or practice of the country concerned.

This emphasis on the need for independent scrutiny and on the power of recommending improvements is not dictated by prejudice or hostility towards particular governments. It arises from the complex nature of modern society, the vast range of subjects with regard to which government action effects the lives of the citizens – often beneficially, but not always so – and the huge apparatus of public administration engaged in implementing that action. Even with the best intentions, officials may make mistakes; occasionally their intentions may leave something to be desired. And the greater the centralisation of power in the hands of governments, the greater is the need for effective safeguards to protect the rights of the individual citizens. In how many countries are there laws and even constitutional provisions which are beyond reproach, but administrative action which fails to correspond? It is against this background of more general considerations that we need to look at the reporting system established by the Covenant on Civil and Political Rights.

Even the reporting system of limited efficacity enshrined in the Covenant was not accepted with general enthusiasm. In the early days, when such procedures were first discussed in the Commission of Human Rights, the objection was made that 'any such procedure was contrary to the United Nations Charter, in particular to Article 2 paragraph 7, and constituted a violation of national sovereignty.[44] This extreme and illogical view, however, was fortunately not repeated in the Third Committee; indeed, in 1963 the Eastern European representatives indicated that they were prepared to accept a reporting system, thus reversing their earlier position. A point of more substance that was made both in the Commission and in the Third Committee was that the requirement that States should report 'on the measures they have adopted which give effect to the rights recognised herein *and on the progress made in the enjoyment of those rights*' (emphasis added) would seem to imply that the rights and freedoms set out in this Covenant are to be the object of progressive implementation by the contracting parties. Now it is agreed that the economic, social and cultural rights set out in the other Covenant are to be ensured progressively; indeed, it would be physically impossible for a number of them (e.g. the right to work) to be implemented immediately and completely in many (if not all) countries. Civil and political rights, on the other hand, are as a general rule capable of immediate application, and a State should put its laws and administrative practice in compliance with the Covenant before ratifying it. Consequently, an article which speaks of 'the progress made in the enjoyment of those rights' seems to derogate from or diminish the immediate obligation to secure respect for civil and political rights.[45]

While there is much logic in this argument, it is not altogether realistic. Certainly the civil and political rights are intended to be of immediate application and should, so far as possible, be ensured at the time of ratification. But there may be certain legislative or administrative measures which require adjustment or amendment, and Article 2, paragraph 2, of the Covenant expressly recognises this possibility. Moreover, it would be foolish to pretend that no further progress can be made in the enjoyment of human rights after a State has ratified the Covenant. It is therefore reasonable and sensible (if not logical) to ask States to report on the progress which they have been able to make subsequent to the deposit of their instrument of ratification.

The obligation on States to report, then, relates to 'the measures they have adopted' to give effect to the rights set out in the Covenant, to 'the progress made in the enjoyment of those rights' and also, under paragraph 2 of Article 40, to 'the factors and difficulties, if any, affecting the implementation of the present Covenant'. The United States proposed an amendment to the effect that the reports should relate to 'the legislative, judicial or other action taken . . .', but certain speakers opposed this on the ground that it was more restrictive than 'measures' without qualification, and the amendment was not adopted.[46] The reports are to be presented within one year of the entry into force of the Covenant for the States parties concerned, and thereafter when the Committee so requests (Article 40, paragraph 1). This means that for the thirty-five States which first ratified the Covenant, as the result of which it entered into force on 23 March 1976, their first reports were due to be deposited by 23 March 1977, that is to say by the time when the Human Rights Committee held its first session (21 March to 1 April 1977).

Of the four conditions enumerated above for an effective reporting system, we can see that the first is provided for in the Covenant, that is to say the co-operation of governments in providing full information. It remains to be seen how far this will be achieved in practice, though the first signs are reasonably encouraging; also, how far the other three conditions have been met – as regards both the legal texts and the practice adopted.

The Human Rights Committee quickly established its intention of following in certain respects the practice of the Committee on the Elimination of Racial Discrimination, that is to say in requesting additional information from governments when required and in inviting governments to send representatives to discuss their reports with the Committee and answer questions. Of course, common sense requires such action and it may be thought surprising that we think it necessary to draw attention to the development of this procedure. The reason is that some governments are so extraordinarily sensitive about anything in the nature of international examination of their human rights record – invoking the arguments about national sovereignty and Article 2 (7) of the Charter to which we alluded at the beginning of this chapter – that it is a distinct achievement to get them to accept even the modest measures to which reference is made. One member of the Human Rights Committee argued that States had agreed to accept 'a reporting procedure, not an investigatory procedure' and that once they have submitted a report they have no further obligation to co-operate with the Committee.[47] The argument has even been put forward that Article 40 of the Covenant does not contain an express provision like that in Article 9 of the Racial Discrimination Convention authorising the Committee to 'request further information from the States Parties', and that the Committee should therefore not make such requests. It is hence a cause for satisfaction that this negative attitude has not prevailed.

As a result of these, and other, discussions, Rule 66 of the rules of procedure contains the general provisions about the submission of reports, including one to the effect that the Committee may inform States of its wishes as regards the form and contents of their reports; while Rule 68 provides that representatives of the States parties may be present when their reports are examined and that such a representative 'should be able to answer questions which may be put to him by the Committee and make statements on reports already submitted by his State, and may also submit additional information from his State'. It is clear, then, that both the rules of procedure and the initial practice of the Human Rights Committee are conceived in that spirit of 'constructive dialogue' which is so obviously necessary.

At its second session in August 1977 the Committee formulated general guidelines about the form and contents of reports, asking that they should be in two parts. The first should describe briefly the general legal framework within which civil and political rights are protected, including information as to whether they are protected in the constitution or by a separate 'Bill of Rights', whether the provisions of the Covenant are directly enforceable in internal law, and what remedies are available to an individual who thinks that his rights have been violated. The second part should deal with the legislative, administrative or other measures in force in regard to each right and include information about restrictions or limitations on their exercise. The Committee also requested information on any significant new developments at any time.[48]

The main defect in the procedure revealed at the Committee's session in August 1977 was that of the thirty-five initial reports which should have been received by 22 March 1977 only sixteen had in fact arrived in time and nineteen were overdue. Reminders were sent to governments and the fact reported to the General Assembly.

In 1978 the Committee found it necessary to hold three sessions and found that it was able to examine only a comparatively small number of reports at each session; in fact it examined the reports of six States[49] at its third session (January–February 1978), six States[50] at its fourth session (July–August 1978) and four States[51] at its fifth session (October–November 1978). In October 1978 there were still twelve reports overdue which should have been submitted in 1977.

It is evident, then, that there are two major problems already revealed in the reporting system: the delay in their receipt and the necessity for the Committee to have adequate time for the detailed scrutiny which is required. The importance of the first point should not be exaggerated; as a new system begins to operate, it is not surprising if a number of States (especially those with limited resources in their national administrations) fall behind the timetable. But the second point is more serious. If the Committee was behind with its work when it had hardly begun to consider individual communications submitted under the Optional Protocol and when the inter-State procedure set out in Articles 41 and 42 had not yet entered into force, what will the position be in the future? There is a strong case for treating membership of the Committee as a full-time occupation.

The second element in an effective reporting system, as indicated above, is the possibility of obtaining further, and perhaps dissenting, information from responsible sources other than the governments. This is provided for in the systems established by the I.L.O. for its international labour Conventions and by the Council of Europe for the European Social Charter. The Covenant on Civil and Political Rights does not institute any similar arrangements.

The nearest it comes to doing so is the provision in paragraph 3 of Article 40, which was introduced as an amendment by the United Kingdom in the Third Committee,[52] and authorises the Secretary-General of the United Nations, after consultation with the Committee, to 'transmit to the Specialised Agencies concerned, copies of such parts of the reports as fall within their field of competence'. Both the I.L.O. and UNESCO have expressed their willingness to co-operate with the Human Rights Committee in this respect,[53] and appropriate provision has been included in the rules of procedure.[54] It is too early to say what will be the practical result of these arrangements for consultation of the Specialised Agencies, but it would be wise not to expect too much from them, because comparatively few of the rights protected by the Covenant on Civil and Political Rights relate to matters within the competence of the I.L.O. and UNESCO;[55] moreover, the Specialised Agencies do not possess a *right* to comment on States' reports and may do so only if specifically requested by the Committee.[56] The I.L.O., UNESCO, F.A.O. and W.H.O. have been invited to send representatives to attend the public sessions of the Committee.

From what other responsible sources could the Committee obtain information to supplement, or possibly criticise, the information furnished by governments? The answer which springs readily to mind is: the non-governmental organisations having consultative status with the Economic and Social Council. Unfortunately, they have not been accorded any rights to lay information before the Human Rights Committee when it is considering the reports of governments. This is a real defect in the system. However, it does not prevent the N.G.O.'s supplying information to members of the Committee in their individual capacity, but this is not the same thing as presenting information officially to the Committee itself.

As regards the possibility of obtaining independent information one must therefore conclude that the situation is far from satisfactory. One cannot but hope that the members of the Committee will succeed in time in overcoming this difficulty, perhaps by an intelligent use of the right of any independent expert to do his own research work and use such sources of information as are available to him.

The third requirement which we have postulated as necessary in an effective reporting system is the independence of the persons who examine the reports. As we have seen in the previous section of this chapter, the text of the Covenant is satisfactory in this respect; Article 28, paragraph 3, states that the members of the Committee 'shall be elected and shall serve in their personal capacity'. What is perhaps more important is the provision of Article 38 of the Covenant requiring each member to make 'a solemn declaration in open committee that he will perform his functions impartially and conscientiously'; and that of Article 35 to the effect that the members of the Committee 'shall . . . receive emoluments from United Nations resources . . .'. Furthermore, Rule 16 of the rules of procedure reiterates the requirement of a solemn declaration of impartiality; while Rule 13 requires that in case of the resignation of a member of the Committee, this must be notified by him to the Chairman or the Secretary-General, thus eliminating the possibility that a government may decide to remove a member of the Committee and notify the Chairman or the Secretary-General to that effect.

The fourth requirement of an effective reporting system is the existence of a power to make suitable recommendations about any necessary improvements in the law or practice of the country concerned. In this respect the Covenant on Civil and Political Rights is sadly deficient. To understand why, we must look more closely at the *powers and procedure of the Committee when it has received the reports of States parties*. The principal relevant text is paragraph 4 of Article 40. This involves the following steps:

1. The Committee shall study the reports submitted by the States parties. (It may, as we have already seen, obtain the views of the Specialised Agencies on matters within their competence.)
2. The Committee must then draw up its own reports 'and such general comments as it may consider appropriate'. These must be transmitted to the States parties.
3. The Committee *may also* transmit these comments to the Economic and Social Council (but is not obliged to do so) together with the reports of the States parties.
4. The States parties *may submit* to the Committee their observations on the latter's comments on their reports. But nothing is said about submitting these observations to the Economic and Social Council if the Committee's comments have already been sent to that body.
5. Under Article 45 of the Covenant, the Committee is required to submit an annual report on its activities through ECOSOC to the General Assembly.

The reasons why these procedures are deficient are that:

1. The Committee is authorised only to make 'general comments'.
2. The States concerned are not required to take any action on the comments made by the Committee on their reports. They 'may submit . . . their observations on any comments that may be made . . .', but they may ignore them completely.
3. More generally, it is usual in reporting systems (for example, in the procedures of the I.L.O. and the Council of Europe) that the independent experts submit their conclusions to some political organ and that the latter is then empowered to make formal and specific recommendations to the government concerned. This stage of the procedure is lacking in the Covenant.

To summarise as regards the provisions of the Covenant on reporting procedures, one may say that the obligation on States parties to report is as it should be, which is also the case for the practice of establishing a constructive dialogue with governmental representatives and obtaining additional information from them. The fact that some governments are late in sending in their reports is regrettable but not too serious. Secondly, the opportunities for obtaining independent information are clearly inadequate, which will impose an additional problem for N.G.O.'s and an additional burden on members of the Committee. Thirdly, the provisions of the Covenant and rules of procedure about the independence of members of the Committee are adequate, though vigilance may be necessary to ensure that governments respect them scrupulously. Fourthly, the Covenant is clearly defective when one examines the possibility of recommending remedial action if it appears that the national measures are insufficient to give effect to the rights which the Covenant is designed to secure.

It is not surprising that there are weaknesses and deficiencies in the reporting system instituted by the Covenant on Civil and Political Rights when it is the product of the heterogeneous community enshrined in the United Nations, some of whose members were in complete disagreement on the fundamental question of instituting any system of international control at all. Seen in this perspective, the reporting system is a reasonable compromise. It will be a demanding challenge for the Human Rights Committee to make it as effective as possible.

6. Proceedings between States parties

As explained above, a great variety of proposals for implementation of the Covenants was put forward in the Commission on Human Rights when it was engaged on preparing its drafts between 1947 and 1954. These included suggestions for the establishment of an International Court of Human Rights, an International Investigation Commission, a High Commissioner or Attorney-General for Human Rights, a new Specialised Agency for the implementation of the Covenants, and the establishment of a panel of independent experts from which an *ad hoc* Human Rights Committee could be selected when occasion required. These proposals were launched during the period of enthusiasm for a new world order which succeeded the horrors of the Second World War. But before long the traditional methods of diplomacy and notions of sovereignty reasserted themselves and these ambitious new ideas did not receive the necessary measures of support. By 1950 the Commission decided that there should be a permanent body of independent persons to examine alleged violations of human rights but that it should be accessible only to States and not to individuals or to non-governmental organisations. This position remained unchanged when the Commission finished its work on the draft Covenants in 1954.

The Third Committee of the General Assembly, instead of strengthening the powers of the Human Rights Committee in dealing with inter-State disputes, did just the opposite. The most important change which it made was to render the competence of the Committee to examine inter-State complaints an optional procedure, instead of one applying automatically to all States parties, as in the 1954 draft. Thus Article 41 of the Covenant, which sets out in detail the procedure for considering inter-State 'communications', starts off with the words: 'A State Party . . . may at any time declare . . . that it recognises the competence of the Committee to receive and consider communications to the effect that a State Party claims that another State Party is not fulfilling its obligations under the present Covenant'. A separate declaration recognising this competence, in addition to the act of ratification, is therefore required. Moreover, it is not sufficient that the State alleged to be responsible for a violation has made such a declaration. Communications can be considered by the Committee only if the complaining State has also done so. There must be (in a new sense) 'equality of arms'. It is only States which have agreed to expose themselves to this procedure which have the right to use it against another State party. Furthermore, under paragraph 2 of Article 41, the procedure would come into force only when ten States had made the necessary declarations. This number was in fact achieved in 1979.[57] But it was clear that this procedure was far from constituting the principal measure of implementation provided for in the Covenant.

It is curious, and perhaps instructive, to compare different human rights treaties from the point of view of the obligatory or optional nature of the systems of international control. To take them in chronological order, the European Convention on Human Rights (drafted in 1950, entered into force in 1953) makes the procedure for inter-State complaints obligatory for all contracting parties (Article 24) and the procedure of individual petition optional (Article 25). The U.N. Covenant, as we have seen, makes both procedures optional, while the American Convention on Human Rights (drafted in 1969, entered into force in 1978) makes the procedure of individual petition obligatory for all contracting parties (Article 44) and the procedure of inter-State complaints optional (Article 45).

The second way in which the Third Committee watered down the Commission's 1954 proposals is that the Human Rights Committee no longer has the right to express an opinion on the question of violation. The procedure set out in Article 41 of the Covenant envisages, in the first place, bi-lateral negotiations between the two States concerned; secondly, if the matter is not thus settled, either State may refer it to the Human Rights Committee, which must examine the question in closed meetings and only after domestic remedies have been exhausted; the Committee may call for all relevant information and the States parties may be represented and make oral and written submissions; thirdly, the Committee is to make available its good offices with a view to a friendly settlement of the matter based on respect for human rights; fourthly, if this is not achieved, the Committee is required to submit a report *which is to be confined to a brief statement of the facts*, the written and oral submissions of the States parties being attached. It is apparent, therefore, that the functions of the Committee in relation to inter-State disputes are practically limited to establishing the facts, proposing its good offices and exercising them if the offer is accepted. As certain representatives stated in the Third Committee, the Human Rights Committee is 'no longer the same as the quasi-judicial body originally proposed by the Commission on Human Rights' but 'more in the nature of a functional organ'.[58]

There is, however, another procedural possibility opened by Article 42 of the Covenant. This provides that if a matter referred to the Committee under Article 41 is not resolved to the satisfaction of the States parties concerned, then the Committee may, if those States consent, appoint an *ad hoc* Conciliation Commission, which will in turn make available its good offices 'with a view to an amicable solution of the matter on the basis of respect for the present Covenant'. The commission is to consist of five members who are nationals of States which have accepted the Article 41 procedure but not nationals of the States parties to the dispute. Article 42 deals in some detail with the composition, method of election and procedure of the Conciliation Commission; in particular, it provides that the information obtained by the Human

Rights Committee shall be made available to the commission, which may also call on the States concerned for further relevant information.

When it has completed its work, or in any event within a year of being seized of the matter, the Conciliation Commission is to draw up its report. If an amicable solution has been reached, the report will contain a brief statement of the facts and of the solution reached. If an amicable solution has not been reached, the report will contain a full statement of the facts and the commission's views on 'the possibilities of an amicable solution of the matter'. Within three months of the receipt of the report, the States parties will indicate 'whether or not they accept the contents of the report of the Commission'.[59]

One may summarise the provisions of Articles 41 and 42 of the Covenant by saying that in inter-State disputes the function of the Human Rights Committee is one of good offices, while that of the Conciliation Commission is of good offices and perhaps conciliation; but that neither function can be exercised except in relation to States both of which have made an express declaration accepting the competence of the Committee to exercise this function and, as regards the Conciliation Commission, consented to its appointment. Having regard to the limited number of States which have made such a declaration, it would appear that a number of years must elapse before the Human Rights Committee will have any significant role to play in inter-State disputes. This conclusion is strengthened by the fact that of the first thirteen States to accept the competence of the Commission to consider inter-State disputes nine were parties to the European Convention on Human Rights[60] and (as we shall see in section I (5) of Chapter III) will not normally refer to the U.N. Committee matters which could be considered by the European Commission of Human Rights. Furthermore, the Communist States have made it clear that they will not accept this optional procedure, as they are opposed to the basic principle on which it rests. Indeed, it is hard to believe that any government other than that of a democratic country (in the traditional sense) with real guarantees of freedom of expression and association, free elections, protection against arbitrary arrest and due process of law will be willing to expose itself to the possibility of complaints by other States that it is violating civil and political rights. As we have noted, it is generally estimated that there are not more than about thirty democratic States in the modern world. Twenty of them are

members of the Council of Europe and parties to the European
Convention and will therefore use the Strasbourg procedures in
preference to those of Articles 41 and 42 of the U.N. Covenant. The
prospects of extensive use of the latter, therefore, are not
considerable.

IV. INDIVIDUAL COMMUNICATIONS: THE OPTIONAL PROTOCOL

The real test of the effectiveness of a system of international control
for the protection of human rights is to be found in the answer to the
question whether or not it permits the individual whose rights are
violated to seek a remedy from the international control organ.
One's reaction to this question is conditioned by one's whole
approach to the nature of international law and to the status of the
individual in international law.

There is no doubt that the classic conception of international
law, as it has evolved over the last hundred years, postulates that it
is the law which governs relations between States and that the
individual has no place therein.[61] His interests are supposed to be
protected by the State of which he is a national, and he has no *locus
standi* before international tribunals or international organisations.
Equally, there is no doubt that in the second half of the twentieth
century certain inroads upon, or exceptions to, this classic doctrine
have been established. The question which the modern
international lawyer has to face is whether these inroads and
exceptions are to be encouraged and further developed, or resisted
and restricted. Opinion among international lawyers has been
divided on this issue for thirty years, and the debate will no doubt
continue for at least another generation. There is an immense
literature on the subject;[62] and there have been and will continue to
be innumerable speeches about it in the United Nations organs and
elsewhere.[63]

To move from the general to the particular, there are two
practical arguments which are determinant in the view of the
present author.[64] The first is that the classic doctrine of
international law simply does not work in the context of the
protection of human rights. If an individual's rights are violated, it
will in the great majority of cases be the result of acts by organs or
agencies of the State of which he is a national. It is therefore

nonsense to say that his rights will be championed by the State of which he is a national when that State is *ex hypothesi* the offender. The second argument is that, as is well known, the United Nations receives thousands of communications each year complaining of violations of human rights throughout the world. Article 1 of the Charter states that one of the purposes of the United Nations is 'to achieve international co-operation ... in promoting and encouraging respect for human rights and fundamental freedoms for all ...' and there are seven other references in the Charter to the functions of the United Nations and its organs in relation to human rights. If – as was at one time the case – the organisation takes no action with regard to the communications it receives, this inevitably brings it into disrepute and shows that it is failing to fulfil one of its principal functions. Considerations both of common sense and of preserving the reputation of the United Nations therefore make it necessary to adopt a constructive and positive attitude to the question of access of the individual to international remedies.

These considerations have led to discussions which went on for many years in different U.N. organs about whether the Commission on Human Rights could take any action about communications from individuals and non-governmental organisations complaining about violations. These discussions finally led to the adoption by the Economic and Social Council in 1970 of its *Resolution 1503*, which authorised the Commission to examine 'communications, together with replies of governments, if any, which appear to reveal a consistent pattern of gross violations of human rights'.[65] The procedure is complicated, involving a triple screening, and the results so far have been disappointing. The Resolution 1503 procedure will be discussed in the following section of this chapter; its existence has been mentioned at this stage as the first timid recognition of the fact that the United Nations cannot totally ignore individual complaints of violation of human rights.

There is also a third important argument for allowing individuals who believe that their rights have been violated to appeal to an international organ of control. Once it is admitted that the international organ can be seized of inter-State complaints, then if no right of individual petition exists the only remedy available is an inter-State procedure. This means that aggrieved individuals will be tempted to look for another government that will champion their cause by bringing a case against the government of which they are nationals. Thus Greek citizens whose rights were violated by the military regime in their country in 1967 were led to appeal to the Scandinavian governments for help. It is obviously better in the interests of peaceful relations between States that what is essentially an individual or national problem should be dealt with as such and should not be transformed into an international dispute between States, with all the consequences which that may imply.

When the Covenant on Civil and Political Rights was being drafted, it became necessary to face squarely the question whether the measures of implementation to be included in the Covenant should include the right of individual petition to the Human Rights Committee. The Third Committee discussed the matter at length.[66] After it had approved the two articles on inter-State procedures (which became Articles 41 and 42) it considered an amendment by the Netherlands proposing the addition of a new article providing for the competence of the Human Rights Committee, on an optional basis, to receive and consider individual petitions – a text which was largely inspired by the corresponding provisions of the European Convention. Jamaica and France tabled further amendments, the French proposal being aimed at limiting the functions of the Committee to the simple receipt and transmission of communications. There followed a ten-power revised amendment, which followed the general lines of the earlier proposal of the Netherlands, but set out the procedure in greater detail and would have authorised the Committee, when examining individual communications, to 'forward its suggestions, if any, to the State Party concerned and to the individual'.

During the discussion in the Third Committee all the old arguments for and against the right of individual petition (some of which have been quoted above) were invoked. Finally the debate turned on the question whether such a procedure should be included in the Covenant itself, on an optional basis, or in a separate protocol thereto, which would also be optional. The representative of Lebanon made a formal proposal in the latter sense, which was adopted in a roll call vote by forty-one votes to thirty-nine, with sixteen abstentions.[67] It was thus decided by a very narrow majority to incorporate the right of individual petition in a separate legal text.

In a certain sense it seems regrettable that such an important measure of implementation should be altogether absent from the Covenant itself. On the other hand, this was probably a wise decision, because its inclusion in the Covenant would no doubt have rendered more difficult the procedure of ratification in a number of countries. There is also perhaps a certain psychological advantage in the fact that the measure is included in a separate Optional Protocol, because this fact draws more attention to the existence of the procedure of individual petition than would be the case if it were set out in a new Article 43 of the Covenant. The Protocol is now included separately in the list of United Nations treaties; ratifications are published and to some extent publicised; it is thus an object of greater attention than the optional procedure in Article 41 of the Covenant. One should not exaggerate the weight of this argument, but – on balance – nothing seems to be lost and probably something is gained by the fact that the Optional Protocol exists as a separate legal text.

When we come to consider the actual provisions of the Optional Protocol,[68] we see that any State party to the Covenant which ratifies the Protocol thereby 'recognises the competence of the Committee to receive and consider communications from individuals subject to its jurisdiction who claim to be victims of a violation by that State Party of any of the rights set forth in the Covenant'. Articles 2 and 3 of the Protocol introduce the rule of exhaustion of domestic remedies and provide that communications shall be considered inadmissible if they are anonymous, abusive or incompatible with the provision of the Covenant. Article 5, paragraph 2, introduces a further condition of admissibility, excluding communications which relate to a matter which is being examined under another procedure of international investigation or settlement. This rule is eminently reasonable in itself. What is curious about this paragraph is that it places on the Committee the positive obligation of ascertaining that the matter is not being examined under another international procedure – an obligation which may be difficult to fulfil – whereas it would seem more logical to provide that the Committee will not examine a communication if it is shown (by the respondent government or otherwise) that the matter is in fact being examined under another international procedure. The relationship between the procedures of the U.N. Committee and those of the European Commission on Human Rights will be examined in Chapter III, section I (5).

Paragraph 2 of Article 5 also repeats the rule of exhaustion of domestic remedies, adding that the rule shall not apply if the domestic remedies are unreasonably prolonged.

Article 4 and the remaining paragraphs of Article 5 deal with the procedure of the Committee when dealing with individual communications. They shall be communicated to the State party concerned, which shall within six months 'submit to the Committee written explanations or statements clarifying the matter and the remedy, if any, that may have been taken by that State'. Nothing is said about oral hearings of the case, and Article 5, paragraph 1, makes it clear that the proceedings shall be based on 'all written information made available . . . by the individual and the State Party concerned', which would seem to exclude oral hearings and information from other sources. Communications are to be examined at closed meetings and, under Article 5, paragraph 4, 'The Committee shall forward its views to the State Party concerned and to the individual'.

Finally, under Article 6 of the Protocol, the Committee will include a summary of its activities thereunder in its annual report to the General Assembly provided for in Article 45 of the Covenant.

From this brief summary of the provisions of the Protocol it will appear that the procedure instituted is not a contentious procedure, in the sense of permitting argument by counsel, examination of witnesses and so on, nor is it a judicial procedure in the sense of leading to a decision on the question of violation by the Human Rights Committee. Nevertheless, even with these limitations, it marks a big advance on any measures of implementation previously established by the United Nations.[69] Much will depend on how the Human Rights Committee interprets its powers under the Protocol, particularly in forwarding 'its views' to States parties under Article 5 (4) and in reporting to the General Assembly under Article 6.

As of 31 December 1980, twenty-five States had ratified the Optional Protocol.[70] The Committee's first reports to the General Assembly on its activities recorded the appointment of various working groups to consider the admissibility of individual communications, but since the proceedings are confidential, information was not published about the identity of the applicants, about the nature of the alleged violations or about the States against which the complaints were lodged. The Committee's first reports tell only the results of the procedural steps taken: decisions of inadmissibility; decisions to transmit communications to governments for their observations on admissibility; requests to applicants for further information, including steps to exhaust domestic remedies; and so on. The reports also give indications of the Committee's thinking on four topics: the standing of the author, the examination of complaints *ratione temporis*, the exhaustion of domestic remedies and the problem of determining whether a matter is being examined under another international procedure of investigation or settlement.

In 1979 the Committee for the first time 'forwarded its views to the State Party concerned and to the individual' (Article 5 (4)) and made public what was, in effect, its first 'decision' on a private communication under the Protocol. The Committee had received a 'communication' from a Uruguayan citizen alleging mistreatment of herself and three members of her family. Each had been charged with 'subversive association' or 'assistance to subversive association', and was allegedly detained without trial, held incommunicado and tortured. The Committee brought the communication to the attention of the government of Uruguay (Article 4 (1)). The government of Uruguay objected to the admissibility of the claim on the grounds that domestic remedies had not been exhausted, and that the alleged violations against the principal complainant had occurred before the Covenant entered into force for Uruguay. The Committee agreed that acts occurring before the Covenant's entry into force were outside its jurisdiction. As regards violations alleged to have occurred after that date, however, the Committee found that no further domestic remedy was available. It decided also that the 'close family connection' permitted the author of the communication to act on behalf of herself and the other victims. When, after six months (Article 4 (2)), the government of Uruguay failed to give a satisfactory explanation of its actions, the Committee formulated its views on the basis of the facts as alleged. It expressed the view that the facts disclosed several violations of the Covenant, including: torture and detainment in unhealthy conditions, contrary to Articles 7 and 10 (1)); imprisonment after a release order, contrary to Article 9 (1); failure to inform the prisoners of the charges against them contrary to Article 9 (2); denial of a prompt and fair trial contrary to Articles 9 (3) and 14; inadequate possibilities of appeal contrary to Article 9 (4); imprisonment incommunicado contrary to Article 10 (1); and denial of political rights contrary to Article 25. The Committee expressed the view that the government of Uruguay was obliged to 'take immediate steps to ensure strict observance of the provisions of the Covenant and to provide effective remedies to the victims.[71]

Further time must evidently elapse before we can form a balanced judgment on the effectiveness of the system instituted by the Optional Protocol. The evidence to date would seem to show that the Human Rights Committee has made a good beginning in the discharge of its important responsibilities thereunder.

V. CERTAIN OTHER UNITED NATIONS PROCEDURES

There are, of course, many other United Nations texts and procedures which concern human rights in addition to the Universal Declaration and the two Covenants, but space does not permit consideration of them in detail. We must, however, mention the more important Conventions, whose character is evident from their titles; they may be found in a useful compilation originally produced by the U.N. Secretariat for International Human Rights Year, 1968, and subsequently reissued.[72] They include the Convention on the Prevention and Punishment of the Crime of Genocide of 1948, the Supplementary Convention on the Abolition of Slavery and the Slave Trade of 1956, three Conventions on Nationality and Statelessness, i.e. on the nationality of married women (1957), on the Reduction of Statelessness (1961) and on the Status of Stateless Persons (1954), the Convention on the Status of Refugees (1951) and its Protocol (1966), the Convention on the Political Rights of Women (1952), and the Convention on the Non-applicability of Statutory Limitations to War Crimes and Crimes against Humanity (1968).

As is well known, the United Nations has been particularly concerned with the prevention of racial discrimination. This concern is reflected in the International Convention on the Elimination of All Forms of Racial Discrimination of 1965 (to which we shall revert shortly) and the International Convention on the Suppression and Punishment of the Crime of Apartheid of 1973. The Specialised Agencies, for their part, have produced conventions for the elimination of discrimination in employment (I.L.O.) and in education (UNESCO) which we will discuss in Chapter VI.

This considerable volume of international legislation is the product of what is called the *'promotional'* or *'standard-setting'* *function* of the United Nations, that is to say the establishment of rules of international law which lay down the norms or standards of human rights and related matters which all member States should observe. This was the principal activity of the organisation in the human rights field until 1966, when the Covenants were adopted, and it is not finished, because the Commission on Human Rights is still engaged in drafting texts on the prevention of torture and other forms of inhuman treatment, on the rights of the child and on the elimination of religious intolerance. A declaration on the last subject was finally adopted, after twenty years' work, in March 1981. Nevertheless, there has been a change of emphasis, and more attention has been given in recent years to the *protection* of human rights, that is to say to the prevention or remedying of violations which occur. Certain procedures designed to afford a remedy for violations were included in the Covenants and have already been described. We will now turn to other procedures of this nature.

One of the most important is that provided for in the *Convention on the Elimination of All Forms of Racial Discrimination*, adopted by the General Assembly on 21 December 1965.[73] This restates in precise legal and more developed form the principles set out in the Declaration on the Elimination of All Forms of Racial Discrimination approved by the General Assembly on 20 November 1963. In particular, it provides that the contracting parties will declare an offence punishable by law all dissemination of ideas based on racial superiority or hatred and all incitement to racial discrimination; also that they will declare illegal and prohibit organisations which engage in such activities. Moreover, the Convention contains elaborate measures of implementation which many people have thought could constitute a model for other U.N. instruments on human rights.

The Convention entered into force on 4 January 1969 and by 1 January 1980 had been ratified by 106 States, being the most widely ratified of all U.N. Conventions. Article 8 of the Convention provides for the establishment of a Committee on the Elimination of Racial Discrimination (C.E.R.D.) of eighteen independent experts, while Article 9 of the Convention contains an undertaking of the States parties to submit reports 'on the legislative, judicial, administrative or other measures which they have adopted and which give effect to the provisions of the Convention . . .'. The reports are to be submitted within one year of the entry into force of the Convention and thereafter every two years or on request. Article 9 also provides: 'The Committee may request further information from the States Parties'. It is clear that there is a rather close – but not complete – parallel between Article 9 of the Racial Discrimination Convention and Article 40 of the Covenant on Civil and Political Rights, and the experience gained in the implementation of the former has, as mentioned above, influenced the practice and procedure of the Human Rights Committee.

The Committee on the Elimination of Racial Discrimination has taken its task seriously and has succeeded in imposing its authority. It has indicated to States parties the form and character which their reports should take; it has refused to accept very brief reports merely stating that there is no racial discrimination in the country in question; it has required the production of demographic information about the existence of minorities and has had to explain unmistakably that racial discrimination is not practised only by whites against blacks; it requires specific information on the way in which States have complied with their obligation under Article 4 of the Convention to prohibit by law propaganda for racial discrimination and similar activities and organisations engaged therein; it requests supplementary information when necessary and, if the State concerned fails to supply it, reports this fact to the General Assembly. More important, since 1972 the Committee has, with the approval of the General Assembly, adopted the practice of inviting States parties which have submitted reports to send a representative to take part in the Committee's proceedings when the report is under examination. Almost all States parties have accepted such invitations and in this way a constructive dialogue has developed between the Committee and the governmental representatives, who answer questions, afford explanations, provide additional information, and so on. This procedure has the additional advantage that it permits the Committee to indicate informally, if necessary, that a government is not fully complying with its obligations, without the necessity for a formal decision to that effect. The Committee appears to have established a basis of mutual confidence with governments (or the majority of them) which augurs well for its future work.[74]

Apart from the reporting procedure, there is provision in Article 11 to the effect that any State party may bring an alleged violation of the Convention by another party to the attention of the Committee; it will be communicated to the State concerned, which then has three months to submit to the Committee written explanations or statements clarifying the matter. If the matter is not adjusted to the satisfaction of both parties, either State has the right to refer the matter again to the Committee, whose chairman must then appoint an *ad hoc* Conciliation Commission.

There is also in Article 14 an optional provision for individual complaints. A State party may at any time declare that it recognises the competence of the Committee on Racial Discrimination to consider communications from an individual or a group of individuals within its jurisdiction claiming to be the victim of a violation by that State of any of the provisions of the Convention. A somewhat complicated procedure is set out by which the Committee is to deal with such petitions: it involves investigation by the Committee, subject to certain safeguards (including the exhaustion of domestic remedies) and permits the Committee to formulate its suggestions and recommendations. This procedure appears to be inspired, in part, by the provisions of the European Convention on Human Rights relating to the right of individual petition. But it will enter into force only when ten States have made declarations accepting to be bound by this procedure. By 1 January 1980 only seven States had made declarations to that effect, so that this procedure was not yet in force.

A system of periodic reports is also provided for in the *Convention on the Suppression of Apartheid* of 30 November 1973.[75]

A less happy development in the United Nations relates to the procedure for dealing with individual communications relating to violation of human rights which cannot be dealt with under the terms of the Optional Protocol to the Covenant on Civil and Political Rights. Indeed, this problem arose many years before the Optional Protocol was drafted or entered into force.

The Secretary-General receives thousands of such communications each year. The Commission on Human Rights considered for many years that it had 'no power to take any action in regard to any complaints concerning human rights'. This attitude was approved by the Economic and Social Council in 1947 (Resolution 75 (V)) and reaffirmed by the Council in 1959 (Resolution 728 (F)). Various attempts to reverse this negative approach were made in subsequent years, but were regularly countered by the argument (advanced particularly by the Soviet Union and its allies) that the consideration of individual complaints by the Commission would constitute 'intervention in matters which are essentially within the domestic jurisdiction of States', in violation of Article 2 (7) of the Charter.

However, the situation changed after 1965. The principal reason was the large increase of Afro-Asian members in the United Nations and the increase in the membership of the Commission on Human Rights to permit the participation of the new members, who were particularly concerned with such problems as racial discrimination and apartheid, colonialism and underdevelopment.[76]

This new orientation both of the Commission and of the organisation as a whole produced a new attitude towards the role of the United Nations in considering human rights problems. At first this was limited to matters raised by governments. In 1966 the General Assembly, in its *Resolution 2144 (XXI)*, invited the Economic and Social Council and the Commission 'to give urgent consideration to ways and means of improving the capacity of the United Nations to put a stop to violations of human rights wherever they might occur'. After the Commission had considered the matter early in 1967, the Council in June 1967 adopted its *Resolution 1235*, approving the Commission's decision to give annual consideration to an item entitled 'Question of the violation of human rights and fundamental freedoms, including policies of racial discrimination and segregation and of apartheid, in all countries, with particular reference to colonial and other dependent countries and territories'. The Council also approved the Commission's intention to make a thorough study of situations which reveal *a consistent pattern of gross violations of human rights*.

This 'Resolution 1235 procedure' can be initiated by a member State or group of member States, or by the Sub-commission on the Prevention of Discrimination and the Protection of Minorities. The Commission itself decides whether or not to act on a proposal that is made to it, and its decision is not uninfluenced by political considerations. The procedure is public. If the Commission decides to make a thorough study of a particular situation, it may appoint a working group or a special *rapporteur* to study and report thereon, or ask the Secretary-General to do so; it may adopt a text condemning a particular situation or send a telegram to the government concerned; in all cases it will report, through the Council, to the General Assembly. The appointment of special working groups will be considered further below.

While the above procedure is public and undertaken on the proposal of governments or of an official organ of the United Nations, the problem remained whether action could be taken on individual complaints of violations of human rights. This has also been the subject of new developments in recent years.

At its twenty-sixth session in 1970 the Commission on Human Rights approved a procedure whereby it would be authorised to examine 'communications, together with replies of governments, if any, which appear to reveal a consistent pattern of gross violations of human rights'; but it was significant that this was by fourteen votes in favour, with seven against and five abstentions. Later in the same year the Economic and Social Council, in its Resolution 1503, approved the proposal and authorised the Commission on Human Rights to act accordingly. This system is therefore known as the *Resolution 1503 procedure.*[77]

It seemed at the time that this represented an important breakthrough and that it would change an attitude which had been described by the Secretary-General as long ago as 1949 as one which 'is bound to lower the prestige and authority not only of the Commission on Human Rights but of the United Nations in the opinion of the general public'.[78] These hopes, however, were short-lived. The procedure was to operate at three levels, which would involve a triple screening: first, in a working group of the Sub-commission on Prevention of Discrimination and Protection of Minorities, then in the sub-commission itself; they are required to examine the 'communications' addressed to the Secretary-General. The sub-commission then refers to the Commission on Human Rights any 'situation' which it thinks merits further attention. The Commission, however, is not obliged to consider the complaints thus filtered but decides whether they require a thorough study and whether they should be the object of an investigation by an *ad hoc* committee 'to be appointed by the Commission after obtaining the consent of the State concerned'.

In fact the Commission on Human Rights has inserted a fourth stage in the procedure: it considered that it would not have sufficient time to examine in detail and in plenary session the matters submitted to it by the sub-commission and therefore appointed its own working group of five members to undertake this task. The results of this cumbersome system have been – at least over the first few years – disappointing, consisting for the most part of references from one group to another for further study. As the whole procedure is confidential, little is known about what actually happens, though a slight lifting of the veil has occurred by reason of the fact that since 1978 the chairman of the Commission has announced in public sessions that the Commission has taken certain decisions in private sessions and has mentioned by name the countries concerned. In 1980, for example, the following countries were mentioned as being the subject of investigation under the Resolution 1503 procedure: Bolivia, Ethiopia, Indonesia, Paraguay, the republic of Korea, Uganda, Uruguay, Argentina and the Central African Republic. In one case, concerning Equatorial Guinea, the Commission decided to change to the Resolution 1235 procedure, so that the proceedings became public.

Another aspect of the matter is that, under the terms of the decision of the Economic and Social Council in 1970, the whole procedure was to be reviewed after the entry into force of the Covenant on Civil and Political Rights and the establishment of the new Human Rights Committee, so that it is hard to be optimistic about the future effectiveness of this procedure for examining individual complaints about violations of human rights.

The last type of procedure established by the United Nations which we must mention in this chapter is the appointment of special working groups or individual *rapporteurs* to examine the situation of human rights in a particular country or group of countries and report back to the organ by which they were appointed. This may be done under the Resolution 1235 procedure or independently of it. Decisions to this effect have been taken both by the Commission on Human Rights and by the General Assembly. It would seem at first sight that this would be an effective method of establishing the facts in serious cases of violation of human rights and drawing public attention to such situations with a view to remedial measures being taken. Indeed, some useful work has been done in this way. But it has not constituted a generally effective procedure, principally for two reasons: first, that such a working group or *rapporteur* has no right to undertake investigations in a particular country without the agreement of the government concerned, which may be difficult or impossible to obtain; secondly, that the decision to investigate – or not to investigate – a particular situation is usually motivated to a considerable extent by political considerations which have little concern with respect for human rights. Thus it is only when a majority in the General Assembly or the Commission on Human Rights are prepared to offend the State incriminated (such as South Africa or Chile) that action will be taken; proposals to examine the situation of human rights in Uganda (of Amin Dada) or in the Soviet Union have been rejected for reasons which have little to do with the human rights record of the country concerned but, as often as not, result from the voting strength of the different regional groupings in the United Nations organs.

The first group to be appointed with a mission of investigation and enquiry was the *Ad Hoc Working Group of Experts on the situation of human rights in Southern Africa*. It was established by the Commission in March 1967 (Resolution 2 (XXIII)), originally with a mandate to investigate and report on the torture and ill-treatment of prisoners and persons arrested by the police in South Africa. Its mandate has been renewed annually and enlarged so as to extend to other countries in Africa: Namibia and, until they obtained their independence, the Portuguese colonies of Angola, Mozambique and Guinea Bissau, and also Southern Rhodesia (now Zimbabwe). This Ad Hoc Group of Experts was unable to visit the countries concerned, because permission to do so was not granted, but did visit neighbouring countries, where they heard witnesses and considered communications from interested parties. For example, in 1974 they heard over a hundred witnesses on the situation in the territories concerned, on the basis of which they drew up reports for the Commission and the Economic and Social Council. The resolutions and recommendations of these bodies are then communicated to all organs of the United Nations concerned with the situation in southern Africa and given wide publicity.

A second example is afforded by the *Special Committee to investigate Israeli practices in the Occupied Territories*, that is to say the territories occupied by Israel as a result of the war in June 1967. This special committee was created directly by the General Assembly in December 1968, after earlier discussions in the Security Council and at the International Conference on Human Rights in Tehran in the spring of that year. The government of Israel proposed that the terms of reference of the special committee should be extended to cover the treatment of Jewish minorities in Arab countries, and when this request was refused and after various difficulties had arisen about the appointment of the members of the special committee (*inter alia* as a result of the death of the President of the General Assembly, who was supposed to appoint them) Israel refused to co-operate with it or to admit its members to the territories in question.

The special committee nevertheless obtained such information as it could from various sources, including investigations in neighbouring countries, and has produced reports which have been considered by the General Assembly and by the Commission on Human Rights, which has kept this question regularly on its

Agenda.

A third example is afforded by the *Ad Hoc Working Group on the situation of human rights in Chile*. After the *coup d'état* in that country in September 1973, the situation there was discussed at the session of the Commission on Human Rights in February 1974 and a telegram was sent to the Chilean government expressing concern at the numerous reports of flagrant and massive violations of human rights. In the summer of that year the sub-commission requested the Commission at its next session to study the situation in detail and invited both governmental and non-governmental organisations with information about torture and inhuman treatment in Chile to submit it to the Commission. The General Assembly in the autumn of 1974 supported this request and asked the Commission to undertake an investigation. The Commission at its next session (February 1975) decided to do so, and appointed an Ad Hoc Working Group of five members for the purpose, asking the Chilean government to grant to it all necessary facilities (Resolution 8 (XXXI)).

The government at first promised to do so, and arrangements were made for the group to visit Chile in July that year. But when its members met in Lima on 7 July *en route* for Santiago, they learned that the authorisation for their visit had been cancelled. They therefore had recourse to other, and less satisfactory, methods, such as collecting information from other sources and hearing witnesses outside the country. On this basis the Ad Hoc Working Group, whose mandate was renewed annually, submitted several reports to the General Assembly and the Commission to the effect that flagrant violations of human rights continued to take place in Chile. The Assembly and the Commission renewed their appeals to the Chilean government to remedy the situation.

Of course, one wants to know whether all these exercises have any practical effect. They are certainly less effective than one would wish. But few governments are entirely insensitive to international public opinion, and qualified observers have reported that the situation in Chile did improve somewhat in the years 1976–78. In 1978 the Chilean government did finally agree to a two-week visit by the Ad Hoc Working Group, during the course of which it had meetings with government officials and judges, representatives of the Churches and of private organisations; it also visited detention centres and interviewed prisoners. In its reports to the General Assembly and the Commission[79] it stated that the situation of human rights had improved to a certain extent, but that there were still frequent and serious violations.

In March 1979 the Commission once more demanded that the Chilean government should take a series of measures to restore human rights in Chile, decided to continue to follow the situation in that country and appointed a special *rapporteur* for the purpose.[80] This put an end to the mission of the Ad Hoc Working Group itself, but not to the interest of the United Nations in the Chilean situation. Though the proceedings had been slow and fraught with difficulties, they constituted the first case of a United Nations mission of enquiry carried out on the territory of a member State which was likely to become an important precedent for the future.[81]

The procedure of appointing a special *rapporteur* to examine the situation of human rights in a particular country was used with happier results in the case of Equatorial Guinea. Originally the examination of complaints against the Macias dictatorship in that country was undertaken as a confidential procedure under Resolution 1503. But in 1979 the Commission decided to make a public enquiry under Resolution 1235 and appointed a special *rapporteur* for the purpose. In August 1979 Macias was overthrown by a *coup d'état*, following which the special *rapporteur* was able to visit the country and investigate the situation. The Commission considered his report in 1980; it indicated a considerable improvement as regards respect for human rights; and appealed to the Commission to provide Equatorial Guinea with assistance which the new government wished to receive for restoring human rights on its territory.[82] The Commission responded by asking the Secretary-General to provide the assistance required.

VI. APPRAISAL

This summary account of the principal developments in the United Nations over a period of thirty-five years aimed at securing a more effective respect for human rights throughout the world leads one to make several comments.

First of all, it is necessary to bear in mind that the Charter itself does not (as is sometimes supposed) impose observance of human rights on all the members of the organisation. It requires them 'to co-operate . . . in promoting respect for human rights' (Article 1) and 'to take joint and separate action . . . for the achievement of the purpose' of promoting 'universal respect for, and observance of, human rights and fundamental freedoms for all . . .' (Articles 55 and 56). In other words, respect for human rights is an aim for which the member States are pledged to work; it is not set out in the Charter as a condition of membership. Indeed, this could not be otherwise in an organisation of a universal character with more than 150 members comprising nearly all the countries in the world, less than half of which observe the rule of law and the fundamental principles of democracy.

Secondly, the Universal Declaration of 1948, by reason of its constant reaffirmation by the General Assembly and in numerous other texts both international and national (including national constitutions) can now, after more than thirty years, be taken as a statement of customary international law establishing standards which all States should respect. But the Declaration lacks 'measures of implementation'. In other words, it sets standards but does not establish machinery for their enforcement.

Thirdly, it is the two Covenants of 1966 which reaffirm, and further elaborate, those standards, adding measures of implementation which, in the case of civil and political rights, mean the procedures of the Human Rights Committee which we have examined earlier in this chapter. However, those procedures are applicable only to the States which have ratified the Covenants (nearly half the members of the United Nations by the end of 1980), but even the measures which apply to all contracting States by virtue of their ratification – that is, the reporting system – are of only limited effect, and the more effective optional provisions, including the Optional Protocol, have been accepted only by a small number of States.

As regards the Charter, the Declaration and the Covenants, therefore, it appears that the United Nations has done much in the realm of promotion or 'standard-setting' but much less as regards protection or 'measures of implementation'. This conclusion is borne out when we consider the other activities of the organisation in the human rights field. Much has been done in standard-setting by the conclusion of other Conventions relating to genocide, war crimes and crimes against humanity, racial discrimination, apartheid and so on, but these instruments contain but weak provisions, if any, for their implementation and other attempts at establishing procedures for the protection of human rights, notably those instituted by ECOSOC Resolutions 1235 and 1503, have had, on the whole, disappointing results.

This is not to belittle the very great efforts made by a number of governments, by many delegates at U.N. meetings, by Secretariat officials and by non-governmental organisations working for the protection of human rights. It is, however, a recognition of a political reality, that is to say that an international organisation cannot do more than its member governments are prepared to accept and that the majority of members of the United Nations are not willing to accept an effective system of international control over their actions which affect the human rights of their citizens. Though the progress made over the last thirty-five years has been considerable as regards standard-setting, it has been modest as regards measures of implementation, and the unwillingness of governments to accept more effective measures is the explanation.

Many people, and some governments, are aware of these shortcomings, and many attempts have been made in recent years to improve the effectiveness of the U.N. procedures. One difficulty which has arisen in so doing centres around the dispute resulting from different political ideologies about the comparative importance of different categories of human rights, some governments attaching more importance to the classic civil and political rights, others to economic, social and cultural rights.[83] In 1977 the General Assembly tried to put an end to this dispute by affirming that all human rights and fundamental freedoms are indivisible and interdependent and that equal attention should be given to the implementation, promotion and protection of both civil and political, and economic, social and cultural rights (*Resolution 32/130* of 16 December 1977).

One of the proposals which has been made from time to time in order to reinforce the effectiveness of the United Nations in this field is for the appointment of a United Nations High Commissioner for Human Rights who, as an independent and high-level personality (comparable in some respects to the U.N. High Commissioner for Refugees), would have functions to be defined in relation to the investigation of alleged violations of human rights. Proposals on these lines have been made on various occasions over many years, starting with Uruguay and Costa Rica in earlier years and more recently by President Carter in 1977. At one stage the Commission, by a very narrow majority, decided to recommend the establishment of such a post, but the Economic and Social Council has not yet agreed to do so. In 1977 the General Assembly requested the Commission to undertake an overall analysis of the alternative approaches and ways and means within the United Nations system for improving the effective enjoyment of human rights and fundamental freedoms (*Resolution 32/130*), and in the following year asked it to include in its study a re-examination of the proposal for a High Commissioner, in the light of the views expressed by governments (*Resolution 33/105*). But, at its session in 1979, the Commission had to admit that it could not reach agreement. This was evidently on account of the unwillingness of many governments, which we have already mentioned, to submit their human rights record to international scrutiny.

Other ideas, however, were in the air. The undertaking of the 'overall analysis' was in itself a good sign.[84] This was to extend to the programme and methods of work of the Commission; also to consultation with the Specialised Agencies and with regional organisations concerned with human rights (Resolution 33/54). The enlargement of the Commission to forty-three members in 1980 (as the result of ECOSOC Resolution 1979/136) brought new blood and new vigour to its work, and its thirty-sixth session in that year was generally considered to have been particularly positive. One of its proposals was that the Division of Human Rights in the U.N. Secretariat should be enlarged and redesignated as a 'Centre for Human Rights', in order to recognise its increased responsibilities.

We may therefore conclude by saying that the United Nations over a period of thirty-five years has achieved a great deal in developing the international law of human rights, in particular as regards establishing international standards which the world community has now accepted as conventional or customary rules of law. If it has had less success in securing the 'universal and effective recognition and observance' of those standards (in the words of the Universal Declaration) that is because the organisation cannot exercise greater powers than its member States are prepared to give it, and to change the traditions and practice of governments and governmental agencies all over the world is an immense task requiring prolonged and persistent endeavour. We can still observe many governments voting for idealistic texts in New York or Geneva but ignoring these ideals in their daily conduct of affairs. But, as we said in Chapter I, if international law is not yet strong enough to prevent such violations, our task is to make it progressively more effective, and we may take hope from the fact that many people both inside and outside the United Nations are labouring with that end in view.

NOTES

1   John P. Humphrey, 'The U.N. Charter and the Universal Declaration of Human Rights', in *The International Protection of Human Rights*, ed. Evan Luard, London, 1967, pp. 39–58, at p. 40; *idem*, 'The Universal Declaration: its history, impact and juridical character', in *Human Rights: Thirty Years after the Universal Declaration*, ed. Ramcharan, The Hague, 1979. The classic work on the provisions of the Charter relating to human rights remains Sir H. Lauterpacht, *International Law and Human Rights*, London, 1950, Part III of which contains the author's own proposals for an International Bill of Human Rights.

2   Humphrey, *op. cit.* n. 1, pp. 43–4.

3   Louis B. Sohn, 'A short history of United Nations documents on human rights', in *The United Nations and Human Rights*, eighteenth report of the Commission to Study the Organisation of Peace, New York, 1968, pp. 39–186, at pp. 51–2.

4   Humphrey, *op. cit.* n. 1, pp. 40, 46–7; Sohn, *op. cit.*, n. 3, pp. 50–2.

5   Quoted by Sohn, *op. cit.*, n. 3, p. 55.

6   *Ibid.*, pp. 59–60.

7   Sir H. Hoare, 'The U.N. Commission on Human Rights', in *The International Protection of Human Rights*, *op. cit.* n. 1, pp. 60–1.

8   For the history of the Universal Declaration see the two chapters by Humphrey, cited in n. 1; Sohn, *op. cit.* n. 3; Egon Schwelb, *Human Rights and the International Community*, Chicago, 1964; H. Lauterpacht, *op. cit.* n. 1; R. Cassin, 'La Déclaration Universelle et la mise en oeuvre des droits de l'homme', in *Recueil des Cours de l'Académie de Droit International*, 1951, pp. 241–367; Albert Verdoodt, *La Naissance et Signification de la Déclaration Universelle des Droits de l'Homme*, Louvain, 1964. The members of the drafting committee referred to included Mrs Roosevelt (chairman), Dr P. C. Chang of China (vice-chairman), Dr Charles Malik of the Lebanon (*rapporteur*) and M. René Cassin of France. The Director of Human Rights in the U.N. Secretariat, who presented a preliminary draft to the drafting committee in June 1947, was Professor John P. Humphrey; the Deputy Director was Mr Egon Schwelb.

9   Quoted in Sohn, *op. cit.* n. 3, p. 70.

10 *Ibid.*, p. 71.

11 Resolution 1514 (XV), cited by Schwelb, *op. cit.* n. 8, p. 70.

12 Resolution 1904 (XVIII).

13 Final Act of the Tehran conference (A/Conf. 32/41, p. 37).

14 Sir H. Waldock, 'Human rights in contemporary international law and the significance of the European Convention', *I.C.L.Q.*

Supplement No. 11, 1965, p. 15. Similarly, the Montreal Assembly of Human Rights in March 1968 stated that 'the Universal Declaration of Human Rights constitutes an authoritative interpretation of the Charter of the highest order, and has over the years become a part of customary international law' (doc. A/Conf. 32/28, p. 2). The point is further developed by Schwelb, *op. cit.* n. 8, pp. 66–74; Sohn, *op. cit.* n. 3, pp. 72–4; and Humphrey, second work cited in n. 1, pp. 28–37.

15   Sohn. *op. cit.* n. 3, pp. 101–69. There is much literature about the U.N. Covenants. The following works and articles may be particularly mentioned: E. Schwelb, 'Some aspects of the international Covenants on human rights', and F. Capotorti, 'The international measures of implementation included in the Covenants on human rights', in *Nobel Symposium 7: International Protection of Human Rights*, New York and Stockholm, 1968; *idem*, 'The early legislative history of the measures of implementation of the Covenants', in *Mélanges offerts à Polys Modinos*, Paris, 1968, pp. 270–89; *idem*, 'The Nature of the obligations of the States parties to the International Covenant on Civil and Political Rights', in *Liber Amicorum Discipulorumque René Cassin*, Paris, 1969, pp. 301–24; *idem*, 'Measures of Implementation in the U.N. Covenants on Human Rights', *Texas Interantional Law Journal*, XII, Nos. 2–3, 1977, pp. 141–86; K. Das, 'Institutions et Procédures issues des conventions relatives aux droits de l'homme . . .', in *Les Dimensions Internationales des Droits de l'Homme*, ed. K. Vasak, UNESCO, 1978 (cited below as 'UNESCO Manual'), pp, 409–31. An English edition of this important work is in preparation under the title *International Dimensions of Human Rights* (1982). Also A. Glenn Mower Jr, 'The implementation of the U.N. Covenant on Civil and Political Rights', in *Human Rights Journal*, X, 1977, pp. 271–95; and 'Organising to implement the Covenant: first steps by the Committee', in *Human Rights Review*, III, 1978, pp. 122–31; B. G. Ramcharan, 'Implementing the international Covenants on Human Rights', in *Human Rights: Thirty Years after the Universal Declaration*, The Hague, 1979, pp. 159–95; Max E. Tardu, *Human Rights: the International Petition System*, Dobbs Ferry, 1979–80, Vol. II, Part I, Section 1, pp. 1–132. The most detailed study is *The International Bill of Rights: the Covenant on Civil and Political Rights*, ed. L. Henkin, New York, 1981. Some of this chapter is taken from the author's contribution to the last-named collective work.

16   Resolution 421 (V) of 4 December 1950.

17   Resolutions 543 (VI) and 545 (VI) of 5 February 1952.

18   Sohn, *op. cit.* n. 3, pp. 103, 105, 125, 132, 137.

19   *Ibid.*, p. 139.

20   *Ibid.*, pp. 127, 132, 154, 163.

21   *Ibid.*, pp. 143–4, 161.

22   *Report of the tenth session of the Commission*, doc. E/2573, pp. 62–72.

23   Document A/2929 of 1 July 1955.

24   Sohn, *op. cit.* n. 3, pp. 163–4.

25 *Ibid.*, pp. 164–9. See further section IV of this chapter.
26 Resolution 2200 of 16 December 1966. The chairman of the Third Committee in 1966 was Mme Warzazi (Morocco); the Director of Human Rights was M. Marc Schreiber.
27 In addition, the Philippines had ratified the Covenant on Economic, Social and Cultural Rights, but not the Covenant on Civil and Political Rights. The list of ratifications is given in U.N. doc. ST/HR/4/Rev. 3.
28 See *supra*, n. 15.
29 Resolution 1514 (XV) of 14 December 1960. On self-determination as a right, cf. J. E. S. Fawcett, 'The role of the United Nations – is it misconceived?' in *Nobel Symposium 7* (see n. 15), pp. 95–101.
30 Schwelb has examined in detail 'The nature of the obligations of the States parties to the International Covenant on Civil and Political Rights' in the *Liber Amicorum Discipulorumque René Cassin* (hereafter cited as *Mélanges Cassin*), Paris, 1969, at pp. 301–24, and reaches the firm conclusion that this Covenant creates an immediate obligation to respect and guarantee the rights recognised.
31 It is however interesting to compare the different systems adopted by the regional organisations. The European Commission of Human Rights established under the European Convention on Human Rights of 4 November 1950 consists of a number of members equal to that of the High Contracting Parties (twenty in December 1980). By contrast the Inter-American Commission of Human Rights, established by resolution of the Ministers for Foreign Affairs of the Organisation of American States in 1959 (and subsequently made a statutory organ of the Organisation by the Protocol of Buenos Aires of 1967) consists of only seven members. This is repeated in Article 34 of the American Convention on Human Rights of 1969.
32 Cf. Article 9 of the Statute of the International Court of Justice, which requires that 'the representation of the main forms of civilisation and of the principal legal systems of the world should be assured'.
33 The same principle is established in Article 23 of the European Convention and in Article 36 of the American Convention.
34 Cyprus, Denmark, Federal Republic of Germany, Norway, United Kingdom.
35 Bulgaria, German Democratic Republic, Roumania, U.S.S.R.
36 Iran, Syrian Arab Republic.
37 Mauritius, Rwanda, Tunisia.
38 Canada.
39 Colombia, Costa Rica, Ecuador.
40 Mr Torkel Opsahl of Norway. In 1980 the British member of the U.N. Committee (Sir Vincent Evans) was elected a judge on the European Court of Human Rights, while the Austrian member of the European Commission was elected to the U.N. Committee.
41 The members from Canada, Colombia, Costa Rica, Denmark, Ecuador, Mauritius, Norway.
42 First Annual Report of the Human Rights Committee to the General

Assembly, doc. A/32/44 (1977), paras. 46–47.

43   *Ibid.*, paras 28–32.

44   U.N. doc. A/2929, Chapter VII, para. 161.

45   *Ibid.*, paras. 162–6; U.N. doc A/6546, para. 382. But see *supra*, n. 30.

46   U.N. doc. A/6546, para. 384.

47   *I.C.J. Review*, No. 20, 1978, p. 25.

48   First Report of the Human Rights Committee, doc. A/32/44 (1977), Annex IV, pp. 69–70.

49   Czechoslovakia, Denmark, German Democratic Republic, Libyan Arab Republic, Sweden and the United Kingdom.

50   Federal Republic of Germany, Iran, Jordan, Madagascar, Norway and Yugoslavia.

51   Byelorussian S.S.R., Mauritius, the U.S.S.R. and a supplementary report of Ecuador. Examination of the report of Chile was postponed, pending receipt of the report of the U.N. Ad Hoc Working Group which had recently visited Chile.

52   U.N. doc. A/6546, 1966, paras, 378 and 385.

53   Human Rights Bulletin No. 17 (January–June 1977), p. 63.

54   Rule 67, para. 1 provides for the transmission to the Specialised Agencies of copies of such parts of the reports as fall within their competence.

55   At its fourth session (July–August 1978) the Committee agreed that extracts of reports concerning Articles 22 and 24 of the Covenant should be sent to UNESCO, but no agreement was reached as to how Specialised Agencies should comment on States' reports. Co-operation with Specialised Agencies is discussed in some detail in the Committee's Annual Report, 1978, doc. A/33/40, at pp. 103–105.

56   Rule 67, para. 2, states that the Committee 'may invite the Specialised Agencies . . . to submit comments on those parts . . .'. In other words, they may do so only on request.

57   By 1 January 1981 such declarations had been made by Austria, Canada, Denmark, the Federal Republic of Germany, Finland, Iceland, Italy, Netherlands, New Zealand, Norway, Sri Lanka, Sweden and the United Kingdom.

58   U.N. doc. A/6546 (1966), para. 308.

59   Article 42, para. 7, sub-paras. (c) and (d).

60   Austria, Denmark, the Federal Republic of Germany, Iceland, Italy, Netherlands, Norway, Sweden and the United Kingdom.

61   This was not, however, the view of Grotius, generally considered 'the father of international law' – see W. J. M. van Eysinga, 'Grotius resurgens', *Grotiana*, Assen (Netherlands), I, 1980, p. 5. See also *supra* Chapter I, section I.

62   See the many works cited in Sohn and Buergenthal, *International Protection of Human Rights*, New York and Indianapolis, 1973, at pp. 19–21; and in Council of Europe, *Bibliography on the European Convention on Human Rights*, third edition, 1978, pp. 42–6; also F. Ermacora, 'Human rights and domestic jurisdiction', *A.D.I. Recueil des Cours*, 1968, II.

63   See references given in n. 65 below.

64 His views are set out more fully in his treatment of the right of individual petition to the European Commission of Human Rights – *Human Rights in Europe*, Manchester, second edition 1977, pp. 42–6.

65 The discussions which finally led to the adoption of ECOSOC Resolution 1503 are reproduced at length in Sohn and Buergenthal, *op. cit.* n. 62, in Chapter VI, section C, pp. 739–856, and summarised in *Human Rights Journal*, VIII, No. 1, 1975, pp. 293–5. The procedures are described by Marc Schreiber in 'La pratique récente des Nations Unies dans le domaine de la protection des droits de l'homme', Hague Academy *Recueil des Cours*, 1975, II, pp. 351–8; in the UNESCO manual *Dimensions Internationales des Droits de l'Homme*, 1978, pp. 322–7; and in Max Tardu, *Human Rights: the International Petition System*, Dobbs Ferry, 1979–80, Vol. I, Part I, Section 1A, and Vol. II, Part I, Section 2, pp. 1–133. For the earlier history, T. C. van Boven, 'The United Nations Commission on Human Rights and violations of human rights', *Nederlands Tidschrift*, XV, 1968, p. 393.

66 Report of the Third Committee, doc. A/6546 (1966), paras. 474–85.

67 *Ibid.*, para. 485. Most of the Soviet bloc, Asian and African States voted in favour. Most of the Western group and Latin American States voted against. Among the abstentions were: Brazil, China, Cyprus, Greece, Israel and Turkey. When it came to the vote in the General Assembly on 16 December 1966, the Optional Protocol was approved by sixty-six votes to two, with thirty-eight abstentions.

68 The Protocol was in part inspired by Article 14 of the Convention on the Elimination of All Forms of Racial Discrimination of 21 December 1965. For an analysis of its provisions see Tardu, *op. cit.* n. 65, Vol. I, Part I, Section 1A, pp. 1–24, and Vol. II, Part I, Section 1, pp. 1–132.

69 The Committee on the Elimination of Racial Discrimination will have slightly greater powers, when considering individual communications under Article 14 of the Racial Discrimination Convention, because it 'shall forward its *suggestions and recommendations*, if any, to the State Party concerned and to the petitioner'. But this is also an optional procedure which will enter into force when ten States have accepted it, which was not the case by 31 December 1980.

70 Barbados, Canada, Colombia, Costa Rica, Denmark, Dominican Republic, Ecuador, Finland, Iceland, Italy, Jamaica, Madagascar, Mauritius, Netherlands, Nicaragua, Norway, Panama, Peru, Senegal, Surinam, Sweden, Trinidad and Tobago, Uruguay, Venezuela, Zaire.

71 Report of the Human Rights Committee, 1979 (doc. A/34/40), Annex VII. In 1980 the Committee found five further cases of violation by the government of Uruguay and one case in which that government had taken appropriate remedial measures (doc. A/35/40, Annexes V–X).

72 *Human Rights: a Compilation of International Instruments*, United

Nations, New York, 1978, ST/HR/1/Rev. 1.
73 *Ibid.*, pp. 24–30.
74 Further information on the Convention and its application may be found in Natan Lerner, *The U.N. Convention on the Elimination of All Forms of Racial Discrimination – a Commentary*, Leyden, 1970; Thomas Buergenthal, 'Operating the U.N. Racial Convention', *12 Texas International Law Journal*, 1977, pp. 187–221; Marc Schreiber, *op. cit.* n. 65, pp. 333–8; the UNESCO Manual (*supra*, n. 15), chapter 11; K. J. Partsch, 'Elimination of racial discrimination in the enjoyment of civil and political rights', *14 Texas International Law Journal*, 1979, pp. 193–250.
75 *Op. cit.* n. 72, pp. 30–3. The Convention entered into force on 18 July 1976. By 1 January 1980 it had been ratified by fifty-four States. Under the terms of Article 9, the periodic reports are considered by a group of three members of the Commission on Human Rights who are also 'representatives of States Parties to the . . . Convention'.
76 On the Commission on Human Rights in general see: Sir S. Hoare, 'The U.N. Commission on Human Rights', in *The International Protection of Human Rights* (*op. cit.* n. 1), pp. 60 ff.: John Carey, *U.N. Protection of Civil and Political Rights*, New York, 1970; M. Schreiber, *op. cit.* n. 65; UNESCO Manual, *op. cit.* n. 65; J. B. Marie, *La Commission des Droits de l'Homme de l'ONU*, Paris, 1975; *idem*, 'La Pratique de la Commission des Droits de l'Homme de l'ONU', in *Revue Belge de Droit International*, 1980.
77 For references see above, n. 65.
78 *Report on Communications concerning Human Rights*, doc. E/CN.4/165 of 2 May 1949.
79 Documents A/33/331 (1978) and E/CN.4/1310 (1979).
80 Report of the thirty-fifth session of the Commission, doc. E/1979/36, p. 124.
81 See General Assembly Resolution 33/176 of 20 December 1978 on the importance of the experience of the Special Working Group.
82 Document E/CN.4/1371 of 12 February 1980.
83 Cf. *supra*, Chapter I, section II and the references given in Chapter I, n. 11.
84 Though one highly qualified observer considers that *Resolution 32/130*, by seeking to grant priority to such notions as threats against national sovereignty, self-determination and the realisation of a new international economic order, 'challenges the very validity of the Universal Declaration of Human Rights', that it abounds in 'cant and compulsory clichés' and 'is only symptomatic of the intellectual chaos which pervades the international human rights field'. See Moses Moskowitz, 'Implementing human rights: present status and future prospects', in *Human Rights: Thirty Years after the Universal Declaration*, ed. Ramcharan, The Hague, 1979, pp. 109–30. On the other hand, Theo van Boven, Director of the Division of Human Rights in the U.N. Secretariat, takes a more favourable view of *Resolution 32/130* and concludes that 'the Universal Declaration is not superseded but supplemented by new concepts, new approaches

and new instruments'. Theo van Boven, 'United Nations policies and strategies: global perspectives', *ibid.*, p. 83, at pp. 88–92.

Chapter three

THE PROTECTION OF HUMAN RIGHTS IN EUROPE

I. THE EUROPEAN CONVENTION ON HUMAN RIGHTS

1. The origin and history of the Convention

The same factors which led the United Nations to concern itself with the protection of human rights produced a similar result, but to a more marked degree, in Europe.

The first of these factors was a natural reaction against the Nazi and Fascist systems which had provoked the Second World War and wrought such havoc on the rights of millions during the course of that conflict. The denial of human rights was not merely an incidental result of these systems; it was a deliberate instrument of policy and even a precondition of their establishment. If the dictators had built their empires by suppressing individual freedoms, then an effective system for the protection of human rights would constitute a bulwark against any recrudescence of dictatorship.

Secondly, during the immediate post-war years it soon became evident that the democratic systems of Western Europe needed protection not only against a possible revival of the pre-war dictatorships but also against another kind of regime which had established its hold on half the continent. The principles championed by the French Revolution, some of which had already been enshrined in the Bill of Rights and even in Magna Carta, were menaced by a new political philosophy in which the dictatorship of the proletariat gave all power to the State and reduced the individual to a cypher. The preservation of democracy and the maintenance of the rule of law necessitated foundations (in the words of Robert Schuman) 'on which to base the defence of human personality against all tyrannies and against all forms of totalitarianism'. Those foundations were the effective protection of the rights of man and of fundamental freedoms.

As early as August 1941 the Atlantic Charter proclaimed the famous Four Freedoms and also (which is often forgotten) the right of self-determination. These principles were reaffirmed in the Declaration of the twenty-six United Nations on 1 January 1942, and three years later came the well known provisions of the United Nations Charter. These texts, however, were but proclamations or undertakings of a very general nature. It was left to the Congress of Europe at The Hague in May 1948 to announce:

We desire a united Europe, throughout whose area the free movement of persons, ideas and goods is restored;

We desire a Charter of Human Rights guaranteeing liberty of thought, assembly and expression as well as the right to form a political opposition;

We desire a Court of Justice with adequate sanctions for the implementation of this Charter;

We desire a European Assembly where the live forces of all our nations shall be represented.

The essence of this message lay in the words 'guarantee' and 'sanctions'. Something more was required than declarations of intention: an organised system was necessary to ensure the collective guarantee of human rights in the proposed European Union.

It was to the task of designing such a system that the Consultative Assembly of the Council of Europe directed some of its energies during its first session in August and September 1949. The Statute creating the Council of Europe was signed in London on 5 May 1949; it laid down that the maintenance and further realisation of human rights and fundamental freedoms were one of the means to be employed for the achievement of the aim of the Council, which is a greater unity between its members; while Article 3 of the Statute actually made respect for human rights a condition of membership. On 12 August 1949 three separate proposals were made as regards measures for the protection and development of human rights. The Assembly's Committee on Legal and Administrative Questions met under the chairmanship of Sir David Maxwell Fyfe (later Lord Chancellor Kilmuir) with M. Pierre-Henri Teitgen as *rapporteur*; the Legal Committee studied a revised proposal for the establishment of 'an organisation within the Council of Europe to ensure the collective guarantee of human rights' and before the end of the session presented its conclusions in the famous Teitgen Report of 8 September 1949. The committee proposed that a list of ten rights from the Universal Declaration should be the object of a collective guarantee; that the member States should bind themselves to respect the fundamental principles of democracy and to hold free elections; and that a European Commission for Human Rights and a European Court of Justice should be established, the former to hear complaints of alleged violation and attempt conciliation, the latter to take decisions, if necessary, as to whether a violation had occurred.

This is not the place to describe in detail the negotiation of the Convention on Human Rights.[1] It will suffice to recount that the Committee of Ministers of the Council of Europe appointed two separate governmental committees which met successively during the first half of 1950. After further consultation of the Assembly in the summer of that year the Convention was signed in Rome by the Foreign Ministers on 4 November 1950.[2] The rights guaranteed are substantially the same as those proposed by the Assembly in the previous year, and the organs of control are a Commission and a Court of Human Rights, but the right of individuals to lodge complaints with the Commission (as the Assembly had proposed) was made conditional on the express acceptance of this procedure by the State concerned; the possibility of bringing a case before the Court was also made conditional on the agreement of the State concerned to accept the Court's jurisdiction, and the Committee of Ministers of the Council of Europe was brought in as the final arbiter in cases which are not referred to the Court of Human Rights.

The Convention entered into force on 3 September 1953, when ten ratifications had been deposited; by the end of 1980 there were twenty contracting parties (Austria, Belgium, Cyprus, Denmark, France, the Federal Republic of Germany, Greece, Iceland, Ireland, Italy, Luxembourg, Malta, the Netherlands, Norway, Portugal, Spain, Sweden, Switzerland, Turkey and the United Kingdom), that is to say, all the members of the Council of Europe except Liechtenstein.

The Convention recorded in its Preamble that it had been concluded in order 'to take the first steps for the collective enforcement of certain of the rights stated in the Universal Declaration'. Further steps were envisaged and were not long in coming. Already in the summer of 1950, before the Convention was signed, the Assembly had proposed the inclusion of three additional rights; they were subsequently included in the First Protocol, signed on 20 March 1952, which entered into force two years later.

Four further Protocols were concluded during the years 1963 to 1966. The Second Protocol, of 6 May 1963, confers on the Court the competence in certain circumstances to give advisory opinions, while the Third Protocol (of the same date) modifies in certain respects the procedure of the Commission, notably by abolishing the system of sub-commissions. The Fourth Protocol securing four additional rights required only five ratifications to enter into force, and this was achieved on 2 May 1968. The Fifth Protocol concerning the procedure for the election of members of the Commission and the Court required ratification by all contracting parties and entered into force in 1974. The Agreement relating to Persons participating in the Proceedings of the Commission and the Court entered into force in 1971.

2. The rights guaranteed

The first article of the Convention provides: 'The High Contracting Parties shall secure to everyone within their jurisdiction the rights and freedoms defined in Section I of this Convention'. It will be observed that the obligation assumed by each State is not limited to protecting the rights of its own nationals, nor even to protecting those of the nationals of the other contracting parties; the obligation extends to all persons within the jurisdiction, whatever their nationality or legal status and however short the length of their sojourn.[3] Secondly, the obligation – though extensive as regards the category of the beneficiaries – is strictly limited to the rights and freedoms defined in the first part of the Convention.

The rights there defined include, as we shall see shortly, the principal civil and political rights necessary in a democratic society. But they do not include all the rights which one might wish to see guaranteed in an ideal commonwealth. Should the list have been made more extensive when the Convention was drafted? This point was considered by M. Teitgen when he presented his proposals in September 1949. He said on that occasion:[4]

The Committee on Legal and Administrative Questions had first to draw up a list of freedoms which are to be guaranteed. It considered that, for the moment, it is preferable to limit the collective guarantee to those rights and essential freedoms which are practised, after long usage and experience, in all the democratic countries. While they are the first triumph of democratic regimes, they are also the necessary condition under which they operate.

Certainly, professional freedoms and social rights, which have themselves an intrinsic value, must also in the future be defined and protected. Everyone will, however, understand that it is necessary to begin at the beginning and to guarantee political democracy in the European Union and then to co-ordinate our economies, before undertaking the generalisation of social democracy.

The Convention thus 'began at the beginning' with the basic civil and political rights, though others were to be added later. But, as a result, a very large number of individual applications to the Commission of Human Rights have had to be thrown out because the applicant alleged the violation of a right which – however necessary or desirable – was not specifically included in the Convention or its Protocols. This has been the case with applications based on the denial of the right to a pension, the right to a nationality, the right to practise as a lawyer, the right to reside in one's own country, the right to a career in the public service, the right to political asylum, the right to be compensated for Nazi persecution, the right to a passport, the right to social security benefits, and many other others.

Part I of the Convention sets out twelve rights and freedoms which are specifically guaranteed. These are:

1. The right to life (Article 2).
2. Freedom from torture and from inhuman or degrading treatment or punishment (Article 3).
3. Freedom from slavery and servitude (Article 4).
4. The right to liberty and security of the person (Article 5).
5. The right to a fair trial (Article 6).
6. Protection against retroactivity of the criminal law (Article 7).
7. The right to respect for one's private and family life, one's home and one's correspondence (Article 8).
8. Freedom of thought, conscience and religion (Article 9).
9. Freedom of expression (Article 10).
10. Freedom of assembly and association (Article 11).
11. The right to marry and found a family (Article 12).
12. The right to an effective remedy if one's rights are violated (Article 13).

The First Protocol of 20 March 1952 added three further rights:

13. The right to property (Article 1).
14. The right of parents to ensure the education of their children in conformity with their own religious and philosophical convictions (Article 2).
15. The right to free elections (Article 3).

The Fourth Protocol adds four more rights:

16. Freedom from imprisonment for debt (Article 1).
17. Liberty of movement and freedom to choose one's residence (Article 2).
18. Freedom from exile and the right to enter the country of which one is a national (Article 3).
19. Prohibition of the collective expulsion of aliens (Article 4).

These nineteen rights and freedoms are, of course, defined in a considerable measure of detail. In many cases, the first sentence or paragraph of the article contains a general affirmation of the right, often based on the text of the Universal Declaration, and the following paragraphs set out the limitations to which that right may be subjected. For example, the right to liberty can be restricted after conviction by a competent court or in the event of lawful arrest or detention; while several other rights, such as freedom of expression, of assembly and of association, may be limited in the interests of national security, public safety, protection of the rights and freedoms of others, and so on. But the limitations are carefully formulated and, in general, permitted only when they are prescribed by law and necessary in a democratic society in the public interest.

Articles 14–18 of the Convention relate to the exercise of the rights guaranteed. Article 14 contains a widely drawn prohibition of discrimination. Article 15 permits the suspension of some (but not of all) rights 'in time of war or other emergency threatening the life of the nation', but only 'to the extent strictly required by the exigencies of the situation' and after a notice of derogation has been filed with the Secretary-General of the Council of Europe.

Article 17 of the Convention provides that 'nothing in this Convention shall be interpreted as implying . . . any right to engage in any activity or perform any act aimed at the destruction of any of the rights and freedoms set forth herein'.

Finally, Article 18 stipulates that the restrictions which are permitted under the Convention may not be applied for any purpose other than those for which they have been prescribed.

The rights and freedoms discussed above are those which are generally described as 'civil and political rights'. But, as we have indicated in Chapter I, there are other rights which the State should secure to its citizens and which some consider of equal, or even greater importance: economic, social and cultural rights. The Council of Europe began at the beginning, as M. Teitgen had proposed in 1949, but, once the Convention and First Protocol had been concluded, turned its attention to 'the generalisation of social democracy'. The result was the conclusion in 1961 of the *European Social Charter*, which we will discuss in Chapter VI.

3. The system of international control

The rights discussed above are the subject of an undertaking by the contracting parties that they will be ensured to 'everyone within their jurisdiction'. But the authors of the Convention did not consider that such a conventional obligation was sufficient; they sought the institution of something more, an international guarantee. For this purpose they decided to create a Commission of Human Rights and a Court of Human Rights, and also to make use of the existing governmental organ of the Council of Europe: the Committee of Ministers.

(a) The European Commission of Human Rights The Commission consists of as many members as the High Contracting Parties. In fact (though not necessarily) there is one national of each State; they act in an individual capacity and – by contrast with the members of the U.N. Commission on Human Rights – not as governmental delegates. The Commission elects its President.[5] Under Article 24 of the Convention, any party may refer to the Commission an alleged breach of the Convention by any other party.

This system of international control is valuable, but is still not sufficient. The reason is that the object of the Convention is to protect not States but individuals. As we pointed out above in discussing the Optional Protocol to the U.N. Covenant on Civil and Political Rights, the real party in interest, if a violation occurs, is the individual whose rights have been denied; and the violation will in the great majority of cases be the result of acts by organs or agencies of his own government. Under the classic concept of international law, the individual has no *locus standi*, on the theory that his rights will be championed by his government. But how can his government be his champion when it is *ex hypothesi* the offender? What is necessary, therefore, is to give the individual a right of appeal to an international organ which is competent to afford him a remedy even against the government of the State of which he is a national.

It is the great merit of the European Convention on Human Rights that it institutes a procedure which permits an individual to complain to the European Commission even against his own government. This was a remarkable innovation in international law; so much so, indeed, that some governments hesitated to accept it. The right of individual petition was therefore made optional, and thus applies only in relation to States which have expressly declared that they accept it, in accordance with the provisions of Article 25 of the Convention. It is to their credit that sixteen European governments have agreed to this procedure (Austria, Belgium, Denmark, France, the Federal Republic of Germany, Iceland, Ireland, Italy, Luxembourg, the Netherlands, Norway, Portugal, Spain, Sweden, Switzerland and the United Kingdom) and thus made this remedy available to about 300 million persons; it is hoped that the other contracting parties will follow their example and thus render the Convention fully applicable in their territories.

From its creation in 1954 the Commission was competent to examine cases brought by one State against another. In fact, only ten inter-State applications have been lodged in twenty-five years. They constituted five groups: two cases brought by Greece against the United Kingdom in 1956 and 1957, relating to the situation in Cyprus at a time when the island was still a British colony; a case brought by Austria against Italy in 1960 concerning the trial for murder of six young men who were members of the German-speaking minority in the South Tyrol; two cases brought by Denmark, Norway and Sweden against Greece in 1969 and 1970 (the Netherlands being a joint applicant in the first case) relating to the situation in Greece after the *coup d'état* of April 1967; two cases brought by Ireland against the United Kingdom in 1971 and 1972, relating to the situation in Northern Ireland; three cases brought by Cyprus against Turkey in 1974, 1975 and 1977 concerning the situation in Cyprus resulting from the Turkish intervention in 1974.[6]

The competence of the Commission to consider individual applications entered into force on 5 July 1955, when six States had recognised the 'right of individual petition', that is to say, the right of redress accorded by Article 25 to 'any person, non-governmental organisation or group of individuals claiming to be the victim of a violation by one of the High Contracting Parties of the rights set forth in this Convention'. By 31 December 1980 the Commission had been seized of 9,231 individual applications.

The first task of the Commission when it considers an application is to decide whether it is admissible. In this matter strict rules apply. Article 26 of the Convention lays down two conditions which apply both to inter-State cases and to individual applications. The Commission may deal with a case only after all domestic remedies have been exhausted (unless no domestic remedies are available or they are unreasonably delayed) and within a period of six months from the date of the final decision at the national level. Moreover, under Article 27, which applies only to individual cases, the Commission must reject as inadmissible any application which is anonymous, substantially the same as a matter already examined by the Commission or under another international procedure, incompatible with the provisions of the Convention, manifestly ill-founded or which constitutes an abuse of the right of petition.

It thus appears that there are seven separate grounds on which an application may be declared inadmissible; in these circumstances, it is hardly surprising that the great majority of individual applications have been thrown out at this stage. By 31 December 1980, 234 had been held to be admissible. The ground of inadmissibility which is most difficult to apply is that of 'manifestly ill-founded'. The Commission is not competent to decide that an application is ill-founded on the merits – that is a decision for the Committee of Ministers or the Court – but it must throw out the application as inadmissible if the fact that it is ill-founded is 'manifest'. Where is the line to be drawn between these two concepts? This is clearly a matter of difficulty and of delicacy. An English lawyer would be tempted to say that a case is manifestly ill-founded if there is no *prima facie* appearance of a violation. The Commission itself has said:

In a long series of previous decisions the Commission has consistently acted on the principle that an application should be declared inadmissible as being manifestly ill-founded only when a preliminary examination of the case docs not disclose any appearance of a violation of the Convention.

If the Commission declares a case to be admissible, it has the task, under Article 28 of the Convention, of undertaking an examination of the application 'with a view to ascertaining the facts'; this examination is effected 'together with the representatives of the parties'. This means in practice a hearing of a judicial nature at which the individual applicant and the respondent government are represented by counsel on a footing of complete equality. The difference between the procedure of the European Commission of Human Rights and that of the U.N. Human Rights Committee established by the Covenant on Civil and Political Rights (described in the previous chapter) thus becomes strikingly apparent.[7]

Article 28 of the Convention also authorises the Commission to undertake, if necessary, an investigation, for the effective conduct of which the State or States concerned are obliged to 'furnish all necessary facilities, after an exchange of views with the Commission'. It will be observed that the consultation concerns the modalities of the investigation – the date, the place, the detailed arrangements – but not the major question whether or not the investigation shall take place. On that point there is no discussion; the States concerned, by ratifying the Convention, have accepted the obligation to agree to an investigation if the Commission so desires. Once more the difference between the European procedures and those of the United Nations is striking.

The most impressive example of an investigation carried out *in situ* was in the Greek case in 1969. A sub-commission met in Athens in March that year and heard thirty-four witnesses as regards the allegations of torture in Greece, visiting and photographing the premises of the Security Police; it also heard twenty witnesses about the existence of a state of emergency, including three former Prime Ministers, the chief of the armed forces and the Director-General of Security.[8]

Once the Commission has completed its investigation, Article 28(b) of the Convention requires it to try to secure a friendly settlement of the matter 'on the basis of respect for human rights as defined in this Convention'. A number of friendly settlements have thus been effected in practice.[9] In that event the Commission draws up a report, which is published, containing a brief statement of the facts and of the solution reached (Article 30). If a friendly settlement is not achieved, the Commission draws up a detailed report, setting out the facts and stating its opinion as to whether the facts found disclose a violation of the Convention. The report is transmitted to the Committee of Ministers of the Council of Europe; the Commission may make in its report such proposals as it thinks fit (Article 31).[10]

(b) The Committee of Ministers The Committee of Ministers consists of the Ministers for Foreign Affairs (or their deputies) of the member States of the Council of Europe;[11] it is essentially a political organ, but judicial or quasi-judicial functions were conferred on it by the Convention on Human Rights. Article 32 provides that if the case is not referred to the Court of Human Rights, the Committee of Ministers shall decide whether or not a violation has occurred. It takes this decision by a two-thirds majority, even though its more important decisions in other spheres require unanimity.

The Committee does not have the power to order a government to take remedial measures, but paragraph 2 of Article 32 requires it to prescribe a period of time during which the State concerned must take the measures required by the Committee's decision. In other words, if the Committee decides that a violation has occurred, it is for the respondent government to draw its own conclusions and take the remedial action that may be necessary within the time fixed by the Committee. The contracting parties agree to be bound by the Committee's decision (Article 32, paragraph 4).

A certain sanction is contained in paragraph 3 of Article 32. If the government concerned has not taken satisfactory measures within the prescribed period, the Committee is required to decide what further action is necessary and to publish the report of the Commission. This sanction is more powerful than might at first appear, because no government of a democratic State can accept without grave concern the publication of a report by a competent and impartial international organ declaring that it is violating its international obligations to respect human rights. Moreover, in the last resort, a much more powerful sanction is in the hands of the Committee of Ministers. Article 8 of the Statute of the Council of Europe empowers the Committee to expel from the organisation any member which violates Article 3 of the Statute requiring respect for the rule of law and the enjoyment by all persons within its jurisdiction of human rights and fundamental freedoms. It is apparent therefore that the Committee of Ministers disposes of strong means of pressure, should this be necessary, to ensure compliance with its decisions.[12]

(c) The European Court of Human Rights The Court contains as many judges (twenty-one) as the number of members of the Council of Europe (Article 38). The judges act, of course, in complete independence, and must possess the same qualifications as the members of the International Court of Justice at The Hague (Article 39 (3)). The Court elects its own President.[13]

The jurisdiction of the Court is contingent, however. A case may be referred to the Court only by the Commission or a State party concerned and not by an individual applicant (Article 44); and only if the defendant State has accepted its jurisdiction. This may be done *ad hoc* for a particular case (Article 48) or by a general declaration accepting the jurisdiction of the Court as compulsory, in accordance with Article 46 of the Convention. Eighteen States have made such declarations to date (Austria, Belgium, Cyprus, Denmark, France, the Federal Republic of Germany, Greece, Iceland, Ireland, Italy, Luxembourg, the Netherlands, Norway, Portugal, Spain, Sweden, Switzerland and the United Kingdom).

Article 43 of the Convention provides that for each case brought before it the Court shall consist of a chamber composed of seven judges, which shall include *ex officio* the judge who is a national of any State party concerned, the remaining judges being chosen by lot. This indeed remains the normal procedure. But Rule 48 of the rules of procedure has added a further provision to the effect that a chamber may relinquish jurisdiction in favour of the plenary Court if the case pending before it 'raises a serious question affecting the interpretation of the Convention'. Such relinquishment is obligatory if there is a possibility of conflict with a previous judgment of a chamber or of the plenary Court. In practice this arises not infrequently, with the result that consideration of cases by the plenary Court is not uncommon.

The jurisdiction of the Court extends to all cases concerning the interpretation and application of the Convention submitted to it (Article 45), but the case must be submitted within a period of three months after the report of the Commission has been transmitted to the Committee of Ministers (Article 47). It is then for the Court to decide whether or not the facts found constitute a violation of the Convention.

If a violation has occurred, the Convention is silent on the question whether the Court has the power to order remedial measures. This contrasts with the American Convention on Human Rights, which, as we shall see in the following chapter, specifically confers such powers on the Inter-American Court. The European Court has not, to date, undertaken to order such measures, and it may be thought that, in the absence of an express provision in the Convention, it does not have this power. Article 50 of the Convention, on the other hand, specifically empowers the Court to award 'just satisfaction' or damages to an injured party if the internal law of the country concerned does not afford an adequate remedy. In recent years the Court has taken advantage of this provision on a number of occasions.

The contracting parties undertake to abide by the decision of the Court in any case to which they are parties (Article 53). Moreover, the judgment of the Court is transmitted to the Committee of Ministers of the Council of Europe, which has the responsibility of supervising its execution (Article 54). This means in practice that the representative of the government concerned will explain to the Committee what action his government has taken in order to give effect to the judgment of the Court – for example, by amending its legislation or affording damages to an injured party – and the Committee will decide whether such action satisfies the requirements of the situation. In this respect the powers of the European Court of Human Rights are less extensive than those of the Inter-American Court or the Court of Justice of the European Communities, both of which can make an order for damages which is directly enforceable in the country concerned; but the European system works adequately in practice and the requirement that a government should explain to the Committee of Ministers what action it has taken to comply with the judgment of the Court is undoubtedly of value.

4. The application of the Convention

More than twenty volumes (many of them containing nearly a thousand pages each) have been published reproducing decisions and reports of the European Commission of Human Rights, decisions of the Committee of Ministers and judgments of the Court.[14] It is obviously impossible to summarise this voluminous case law in the framework of the present chapter.[15] Consequently, we propose to limit ourselves to summaries of the two most important inter-State cases and to a bare statement of the issues raised in the various cases referred to the Court.

(a) The Greek case On 3 May 1967 (that is to say, shortly after the *coup d'état* of 21 April 1967) the permanent representative of Greece addressed a letter to the Secretary-General of the Council of Europe in which, invoking Article 15 of the Convention on Human Rights, he stated that, by royal decree No. 280 of 21 April 1967, the application of various articles of the Greek constitution had been suspended in view of internal dangers threatening public order and the security of the State. In subsequent letters of 25 May and 19 September 1967 the Greek government gave further information in regard to Article 15.

In identical applications of 20 September 1967 to the European Commission of Human Rights the governments of Denmark, Norway and Sweden, after referring to the suspension of the above provisions of the Greek constitution, submitted that, by royal decree No. 280 and other legislative measures, and by certain administrative practices, the Greek government had violated Articles 5, 6, 8, 9, 10, 11, 13 and 14 of the Convention. In relation to all these allegations they contended that the government had failed to show that the conditions of Article 15 of the Convention permitting measures of derogation were satisfied. The government of the Netherlands, in an application of 27 September 1967, made submissions which corresponded in substance to those of the first three applicant governments. The four applications were joined by the Commission on 2 October 1967.

The respondent government, in its written observations in reply of 16 December 1967, submitted primarily that the Commission was not competent to examine the applications because they concerned the actions of a revolutionary government. It also stated with regard to Article 15 of the Convention that, in accordance with the Commission's jurisprudence, a government enjoyed a 'margin of appreciation' in deciding whether there existed a public emergency threatening the life of the nation and, if so, what exceptional measures were required.

On 24 January 1968 the Commission declared the four applications admissible.[16]

In a further joint memorial of 25 March 1968 the three Scandinavian governments extended their original allegations to Articles 3 and 7 of the Convention and Articles 1 and 3 of the First Protocol. On 31 May 1968 these further allegations were also declared admissible.

Protracted hearings took place over the next eighteen months.

More than eighty witnesses were heard in Strasbourg and in Athens. As mentioned above, an inspection was made – and photographs were taken – of the Security Police building in Athens. More than 300 pages of the Commission's report were devoted to the question of torture. Many victims were heard as witnesses. At the same time, it is impossible to read the report without being impressed by the objective manner in which the Commission required corroboration of the allegations made, offered the government every opportunity to rebut the evidence produced and even examined the possibility that (as alleged) many of the accounts of torture were deliberately fabricated as part of a plot to discredit the government.

After carefully reviewing all the evidence at its disposal the Commission concluded that torture had been inflicted in eleven cases; that there were indications, *prima facie* cases or strong indications in seventeen other cases, with regard to which the sub-commission had been prevented from completing its investigation; that there was a practice of torture and ill-treatment by the Athens Security Police of persons arrested for political reasons; and that the Greek authorities, confronted with numerous and substantial complaints and allegations of torture and ill-treatment, had failed to take any effective steps to investigate them or remedy the situation.

The Commission, of course, also examined the other allegations made by the applicant governments. It concluded that there was not in Geece on 21 April 1967 a public emergency threatening the life of the nation, as a consequence of which the Greek derogations were invalid; also that there were violations of nine other articles of the Convention and the First Protocol, including the right to liberty, the right to a fair trial, freedom of association, and the right to free elections. Its conclusions were contained in a report transmitted to the Committee of Ministers of the Council of Europe on 18 November 1969.[17]

Consideration of the *Greek case* was complicated by the fact that two parallel procedures were pursued in the Council of Europe at the same time. On the one hand, there was the case brought before the Commission of Human Rights under Article 24 of the Convention; on the other, the Consultative Assembly of the Council of Europe, basing itself on certain articles of the Statute, had recommended that the Committee of Ministers should expel the Greek government from the organisation. The relevant provisions were Article 3, which requires that every member must respect the rule of law and ensure the observance of human rights and fundamental freedoms, and Article 8, the sense of which is that a State which has seriously violated Article 3 may be suspended from membership. While the proceedings under Article 24 of the Convention were continuing before the Commission – and quite understandably they took some time, slightly more than two years – the Assembly considered that, irrespective of the result of those proceedings, there was a strong case for holding that the Greek government had violated Article 3 of the Statute and that the Committee of Ministers should therefore act under Article 8 without waiting for the result of the proceedings before the Commission of Human Rights. A recommendation was addressed to the Committee of Ministers in this sense in January 1969.[18] When the Ministers met in London for their forty-fourth session in May 1969 strong pressure was put upon them both by parliamentarians and by several governments to the effect that they should act accordingly. Knowing that the report of the Commission was nearly ready, they promised a decision at their next session.

This was held in Paris on 12 December 1969. The Commission's report had been sent to governments on 18 November; its contents were therefore known to the Ministers, even though it was not formally on the agenda of the meeting, because Article 32 of the Convention provides that a period of three months shall elapse, during which the case may be referred to the Court, before the Ministers can take a decision.

The Ministers in December 1969 discussed the situation in Greece and the question whether that country could remain a member of the organisation. At a dramatic meeting, during which a draft resolution for the suspension of Greece circulated among the delegations and received a wide measure of support, the Greek Foreign Minister announced the decision of his government to withdraw from the Council of Europe and to denounce the Convention on Human Rights. However, the denunciation of the Convention would take effect only after the expiry of a period of six months and the denunciation of the Statute at the end of the following year; moreover, as regards the proceedings instituted under the Convention on Human Rights, Article 65 (2) makes it quite clear that denunciation does not affect any duties or obligations arising out of events which may have occurred before the denunciation becomes effective. Consequently, the Committee of Ministers adopted a resolution in which they took note of the Greek declarations and drew the conclusion that Greece would cease to participate in the work of the Council of Europe immediately.

However, the Committee of Ministers was still required by Article 32 of the Convention to take a decision on the report of the Commission. This they proceeded to do at their next session in April 1970. They endorsed the opinion of the Commission and decided that Greece had violated ten articles of the Convention on Human Rights and the First Protocol; at the same time they expressed the hope that democratic liberties would be restored in Greece in the near future, that she would then resume her membership of the Council of Europe, and they decided to 'follow developments in Greece in this respect'.[19]

Happily the situation in Greece was remedied with the restoration of democratic government in 1974, after which Greece resumed its membership in the Council of Europe and ratified once more the Convention of Human Rights.

(b) The Northern Ireland case Physical maltreatment was also one of the issues raised in the case of *Ireland* v. *United Kingdom*. The Irish government lodged this application in December 1971 and filed two supplementary memorials in March 1972. The Commission decided to treat the first supplementary memorial as part of the original application, but to register the second as a new application.

The government referred to the Civil Authorities (Special Powers) Act, Northern Ireland, 1922, and the connected statutory rules, regulations and orders and submitted that this legislation was in itself a failure by the United Kingdom to comply with the obligation in Article 1 of the Convention to secure to everybody within its jurisdiction the rights and freedoms defined in Section I of the Convention.

The application further referred to the taking into custody of persons on or after 9 August 1971 under the Special Powers Act and alleged that they were subjected to treatment which constituted torture and inhuman and degrading treatment and punishment contrary to Article 3 of the Convention. The Irish government also claimed that internment without trial, as carried out in Northern Ireland subsequent to 9 August 1971, constituted a violation of Article 5 (the right to liberty and security of the person) and Article

6 (the right to a fair trial). In addition the applicant government alleged that the powers of detention and internment were exercised in a discriminatory manner, contrary to Article 14 of the Convention.

On the question of torture or inhuman treatment the Irish government complained particularly about the methods of interrogation used by the British security forces in Northern Ireland, including hooding, noise, standing against a wall, deprivation of sleep and limited diet. In this respect the British government was a victim of its own good faith. The Home Secretary had appointed in 1971 a committee of enquiry to look into allegations of brutality in Northern Ireland in the course of procedures known as 'interrogation in depth'; in its report, known as the 'Compton report', the committee described in detail the techniques used by the security forces. As the result of a further report of Privy Counsellors, known as the 'Parker report', the Prime Minister announced in the House of Commons on 2 March 1972 that the government had decided that the use of the techniques in question would be discontinued. This action to stop the use of the methods of interrogation in question was commendable in itself, but it put a powerful argument in the hands of the Irish government, because it could quote official British sources as to the methods utilised, the criticism of them by, among others, a former Lord Chancellor, the decision of the Prime Minister to stop their use and the possibility (even if remote) of further recurrence to them in future.

On 1 October 1972 the Commission declared the first application admissible, but decided to strike the second application off the list. Examination of the merits then began. After an exchange of memorials, hearings on the merits took place in October 1973, and again in December that year. Witnesses proposed by the Irish government were heard by three delegates of the Commission in December 1973 and February 1974 and those proposed by the British government on several occasions in 1974, some of them, for reasons of security, at an air force base at Stavanger in Norway, others in London in February 1975. In fact, 118 witness were heard by the delegates of the Commission in the course of this case.

The Commission sent its report to the Committee of Ministers in February 1976.[20] It expressed the opinion that the measures for detention without trial were not in violation of the Convention, as being 'strictly required by the exigencies of the situation' and therefore covered by the derogation made by the British government under Article 15; moreover, that the powers of detention and internment had not been applied in a discriminatory manner. On the other hand, the Commission considered that the use of the five techniques known as 'interrogation in depth' constituted a violation of Article 3 of the Convention prohibiting torture and inhuman treatment.

In March 1976 the Irish government referred the case to the European Court of Human Rights – the first and (at least until 1980) the only inter-State case to be referred to the Court. Oral hearings took place in two stages in the following year and the Court's judgment was given in January 1978.[21]

In its judgment the Court made a distinction between torture, on the one hand, and inhuman and degrading treatment, on the other. It held that the techniques of interrogation which had been used in Northern Ireland constituted inhuman and degrading treatment in violation of Article 3 of the Convention, but that they did not occasion suffering of the degree of intensity and cruelty implied by the word torture. The Court agreed with the Commission that the measures of detention and internment without trial were covered by the derogation made under Article 15 of the Convention and that these measures had not been exercised in a discriminatory manner.

(c) **Some individual applications** By 1980 the European Commission on Human Rights had been at work for twenty-five years and had declared admissible more than 200 individual applications. About a dozen of them had formed the object of a friendly settlement within the meaning of Article 28 of the Convention, and as many more had been settled by some informal arrangement.[22]

The remainder, apart from some cases still under examination, had formed the object of reports to the Committee of Ministers under Article 31 of the Convention. Many of these cases had been decided by the Committee of Ministers and more than thirty had been referred to the Court. As already explained, a case may be referred to the Court only if the respondent government has accepted its jurisdiction either in general terms (Article 46) or on an *ad hoc* basis (Article 48). But all governments which have accepted the right of individual petition have also accepted the compulsory jurisdiction of the Court. Consequently, it is always possible for a case which has its origin in an individual petition to be referred to the Court.

It is for the Commission or the government concerned to decide, within a period of three months after the transmission of the Commission's report to the Committee of Ministers, whether or not the case should go to the Court. There are no official texts laying down criteria on which this decision should be based. Generally speaking, however, one may say that if the Commission is unanimous or nearly unanimous in expressing the opinion that no violation has occurred, the tendency is to leave the case with the Committee of Ministers. In such cases the Committee has always confirmed the Commission's opinion. On the other hand, the tendency is that either the Commission or the government concerned – or frequently both of them – will refer a case to the Court in the following circumstances: if the Commission is narrowly divided in its opinion, if the Commission considers that a violation has occurred, or if the case raises an important question of interpretation of the Convention.

As a result, if we wish to obtain a general view of the application of the Convention but have to be selective in doing so, we can find the more interesting examples in the case law of the Court. And since we cannot, for reasons of space, examine that case law in detail, we will limit ourselves to a brief indication of the principal issues which arose in the thirty-one cases arising out of individual applications which had been decided by the Court by the end of 1980.[23]

The first case considered by the Court was the *Lawless case*, decided in 1961. It concerned the detention without trial in Ireland of a suspected member of the Irish Republican Army in the exercise of special powers conferred by the Offences against the State Act, 1940. The Irish government had made a derogation under Article 15 of the Convention, claiming the existence of a state of emergency. The Court held that the derogation was justified and there was no violation.[24]

The *De Becker case*, 1962, concerned penalties imposed in Belgium on a journalist convicted of collaboration with the occupying forces during the war. The Belgian law having been amended during the proceedings, the Court decided to strike the case off its list.[25]

The *Case relating to certain aspects of the laws on the use of languages in education in Belgium*, 1968, commonly known as the 'Belgian linguistic case', concerned the compatibility with the

Convention of legislation on the use of languages in schools, which required the teaching of children of French-speaking parents living in Dutch-speaking areas to be performed in the Dutch language. In general, the Court found the Belgian legislation compatible with the Convention, though in one limited respect there was discrimination – and therefore a violation – as regards certain children living in the Brussels periphery.[26]

Five cases arising out of individual applications brought against the Federal Republic of Germany (*Wemhoff*) and against Austria (*Neumeister, Stögmuller, Matznetter, Ringeisen*) concerned prolonged periods of detention on remand awaiting trial – in several cases for two years, in one case for three years. The Court decided on the facts that there was no violation as regards *Wemhoff* and *Matznetter*[27] but that there was violation in the cases of *Neumeister, Stögmuller* and *Ringeisen*.[28] Subsequently, on requests for 'just satisfaction' Neumeister was awarded his costs[29] and Ringeisen a substantial sum as compensation.[30] As a result of these cases both the Federal Republic of Germany and Austria amended their law on detention pending trial.

The *Delcourt case*, 1970, raised the question whether the presence of a member of the Attorney-General's department during the deliberations of the Belgian Supreme Court violated the principles of a fair trial. The Court held that there was no violation.[31]

The case of *De Wilde, Ooms and Versyp*, 1971, concerned the Belgian law on vagrancy. The Court held that there was violation of the Convention because the applicants, detained as vagrants, had no right of appeal to a court of law.[32] On the other hand, their request for compensation was rejected.[33] As a result of the judgment, Belgium amended its law on vagrancy.

The *Golder case*, 1975, concerned the right of access to a court of law. The applicant, condemned in the United Kingdom for a criminal offence to a term of imprisonment, wished to see a lawyer with a view to bringing a civil action against one of the prison warders. Permission to do so was refused. The Court found a violation of the Convention, because the right to a fair trial implies necessarily the right of access to a court.[34] Subsequently the Home Secretary announced to Parliament a change in the prison rules in order to comply with the judgment.

The scope of trade union freedoms was considered by the Court of Human Rights in three cases decided in 1975 and 1976. In the

National Union of Belgian Police and the *Swedish Engine Drivers' Union* cases the Court decided that the recognition of the right to form and join trade unions did not imply an obligation on the State to negotiate with those unions about matters of concern to their members.[35] In the *Schmidt and Dahlström case* the Court held that the refusal to give retroactive effect to a wage settlement to members of a union which had taken strike action was not a violation of the Convention.[36]

The question whether the rules in the Convention about the right to a fair trial apply to disciplinary proceedings in the armed forces was raised in the case of *Engel and others*, which concerned the Netherlands and was decided in 1976. On the question of principle the Court gave a positive answer, but nevertheless distinguished certain forms of disciplinary measures in the armed forces from deprivation of liberty as generally understood. Certain minor violations, however, were established.[37] One of the applicants received a token indemnity and certain amendments were introduced into the law and practice of military discipline in the Netherlands.

Compulsory sex education in schools in Denmark was the theme of the case of *Kjeldsen, Busk Madsen and Pedersen*, also decided in 1976. The Court held that the Danish legislation on this subject, according to which information was given to schoolchildren in an objective and critical manner, was not in breach of the Convention.[38] At the same time, in the *Handyside case*, the Court decided that the conviction of the applicant in the United Kingdom for publication of an obscene book (the 'Little Red Schoolbook') containing sexual information for children, on the ground that it tended to deprave and corrupt them, was not in violation of the Convention.[39]

An important case concerning freedom of expression in the United Kingdom was the *Sunday Times case*, decided in 1979. The applicants claimed that a court order prohibiting the publication of an article concerning 'thalidomide children' (children who were born deformed by reason of their mothers having taken thalidomide as a tranquilliser during pregnancy) constituted a violation of the right of freedom of expression. The order had been made on the ground that the article in question might prejudice the court proceedings then pending against the manufacturers of the drug. The Court of Human Rights decided that there was violation of the Convention and subsequently ordered payment of a substantial sum to the applicants for their costs.[40]

Judicial proceedings and related matters have formed the subject of a number of other cases decided by the Court of Human Rights in recent years. The *König case* concerned prolonged proceedings before administrative tribunals in the Federal Republic of Germany, which constituted a violation of the Convention.[41] The case of *Luedicke, Belkacem and Koç* involved the obligation to provide free interpretation for the defendant in a criminal case if he does not understand the language used in court. The requirement that the applicants should reimburse the cost of interpretation, also in the Federal Republic, constituted a violation.[42] In the *Winterwerp case* there was violation by the Netherlands by reason of the absence of a recourse to a court for a person confined to a psychiatric hospital.[43] In the *Airey case* there was a violation because the prohibitive costs of obtaining a judicial separation in Ireland meant in practice that the applicant was deprived of the right of access to a court.[44] On the other hand, in the *Schiesser case* it was decided that the applicant's detention in Switzerland by order of the district attorney, on suspicion of having committed a series of aggravated thefts, was not in violation of the Convention.[45] In the *Tyrer case* the Court held that the punishment of birching ordered by a court in the Isle of Man was in violation of the prohibition in the Convention of degrading punishment.[46]

Quite different issues were raised in two other recent cases. *Klass and others* concerned the clandestine control of correspondence and telephone calls in the Federal Republic of Germany. While such action clearly interferes with the right to respect for correspondence and for private life, the Court held that, in the circumstances, it was justified in the interests of safeguarding national security and preventing disorder or crime.[47] Moreover, in the *Marckx case*, the Court held that the provisions of the Belgian law relating to children born out of wedlock, particularly as regards rights of inheritance, discriminated against them, as compared with legitimate children, and therefore violated the Convention.[48]

Finally, the first two cases concerning Italy to come before the Court were decided in 1980. The *Guzzardi case* related to a court order confining the applicant to compulsory residence on an island off the coast of Sardinia, in accordance with a law designed to combat the Mafia. He claimed that this constituted a deprivation of liberty inconsistent with the Convention. The Court decided there was a violation.[49] The *Artico case* raised the question of legal aid before the Italian Court of Cassation. The applicant had applied for legal aid and the Court of Cassation had assigned a lawyer to handle his case, but the latter had withdrawn from the proceedings. Again, the Court of Human Rights decided there was violation of the Convention.[50]

These summary indications cannot, of course, give any idea of the extraordinarily rich case law of the European Commission and Court of Human Rights, but they will, it is hoped, permit the reader to have some idea of the actual operation of the European Convention. Several aspects seem worthy of comment. First, one must pay tribute to the real co-operation of the governments with the Commission and the Court, without which the system could not function effectively. Secondly, it is interesting to note the great variety of problems which have arisen – and innumerable other questions have been raised in applications brought before the Commission which we have not mentioned[51] – involving nearly all the rights and freedoms protected by the Convention and its Protocols. Thirdly, one must observe that few States, if any, are immune from the necessity of occasional scrutiny to control whether their judicial and other authorities are complying completely with the obligations they have accepted under international treaties for the protection of human rights. All the sixteen States which have accepted the right of individual petition have seen cases against them brought before the Commission of Human Rights, and ten out of sixteen have had such cases referred to the Court. No administration is free from the possibility of error, even in countries which, when we look around the world, appear to be among those with the best record for the administration of justice and the protection of civil liberties.

These reflections would seem to justify two conclusions: that a system of international control such as the European system is both necessary and desirable, even for States which respect the rule of law and possess constitutional guarantees of human rights and fundamental freedoms; secondly, that – as has been often stated – the system established by the European Convention is the most effective that has yet been introduced anywhere in the world.

When the European Convention had been in force for twenty-five years, the Committee of Ministers of the Council of Europe reaffirmed the importance it attached to the Convention and its confidence in the Commission and the Court, and decided to give priority to the work of exploring the possibility of extending the list of rights protected, notably by including rights in the social, economic and cultural fields.[52] This work is under way.

But if there are grounds for satisfaction, there is an important corollary which we should not forget. The European system has been able to function effectively because the governments concerned have been willing to co-operate with the Strasbourg organs, and the States to which the sytem applies are genuinely desirous of securing the effective exercise of human rights on their territories. The problems which come before the European Commission and Court, important as they may be for the individuals concerned, are – with few exceptions – of only marginal concern to the international community when compared with the massive and flagrant violations which occur in other parts of the world. The systematic torture of political prisoners, massive arrests of persons who then 'disappear', confinement of dissidents to psychiatric institutions, imprisonment of human right activists, these and other practices which are current in many countries pose problems which are immeasurably more serious than those which constitute the day-to-day business of the European organs.

One may easily believe that a member of the Inter-American Commission on Human Rights would be suitably impressed by the functioning of the European system, but that he would be entitled to reflect that it has comparatively little relevance to the problems of massive violations in certain Latin American countries with which his Commission has to deal. And what is true for Latin America applies with even greater force in certain other regions of the world. To draw an analogy which is not as flippant as might at first appear, it is excellent to have a first-class referee in a football match where all the players intend to respect the rules of the game, but the referee can do very little when there is no agreement among the players as to which rules should be applied. Much work remains to be done in achieving consensus on the rules before we can hope to see a pattern of regional arrangements for the protection of human rights comparable to the European system established in other parts of the world.

5. Comparison of the European Convention with the United Nations Covenant on Civil and Political Rights

The member States of the Council of Europe which are also members of the United Nations participated in the elaboration of the UN Covenants and voted for their adoption in 1966. It was therefore only natural that the parties to the European Convention should compare the United Nations Covenant on Civil and Political Rights with the European text and examine the question of ratification of the former in the light of their experience of the latter. Such an examination was necessary not only in order to consider *in abstracto* the nature of the obligations which States will assume by ratifying the United Nations Covenant, but also in order to determine questions of practical importance, such as which rules will apply in the internal law of States that accept the direct applicability of treaties which they have ratified; and which international forum will be competent to adjudicate in cases of alleged violation of rights that are protected both by the United Nations Covenant and the European Convention.[53]

The problems which arise concern all States which are parties to the European Convention. Since it is a common problem, it was natural that a joint study should be undertaken. Measures which will provide a solution to the problems raised for one State will do so equally for another. Consequently, it was desirable that a common attitude should be adopted, if possible, by the parties to the European Convention as regards ratification of the United Nations Covenant and as regards any special arrangements which might be necessary to safeguard the European system. As a result, the Committee of Ministers of the Council of Europe decided that such a study should be undertaken. The task was entrusted to the body which was then known as the Committee of Experts on Human Rights, consisting for the most part of lawyers from the government departments (usually the Foreign Ministry or the Ministry of Justice) dealing with human rights matters. It has since been upgraded and is now entitled the Steering Committee on Human Rights.

The problems which arise may be divided broadly into two categories: those which concern the rights guaranteed and those relating to the machinery for their enforcement – or, in other words, questions of substance and questions of procedure. It is proposed to consider these separately.[54]

(a) The enumeration and definition of the rights guaranteed
As we have seen above, the European Convention and its Protocols protect nineteen separate rights, and the United Nations Covenant on Civil and Political Rights protects twenty-three. As might be

expected, a number of the rights protected by the two instruments are the same and their definitions are substantially similar. This is all the more natural since work on the Covenant had already begun before the European Convention was prepared; as a result, those who worked on the drafting of the latter in the spring of 1950 had available – and made use of – the work already done at that stage by the United Nations Commission on Human Rights.

But if many of the definitions are substantially the same, there are other cases where the same rights are included but the definitions differ considerably, and these differences may have considerable importance for States which are – or may become – parties to both instruments. It is necessary for them to consider whether the obligations they will assume under the United Nations Covenant are more or less extensive than those already assumed under the European Convention and, if they are more extensive, whether their national law is in conformity therewith.

A third category is constituted by those rights which are provided for in the United Nations Covenant but not in the European Convention, or vice versa. This might seem a simple situation where no problem would arise. But, as will be seen, it is less simple than would at first appear, because in some cases rights which are not expressly included in the Convention are implicitly covered by other provisions; in other cases they are covered by other Conventions concluded under the auspices of the Council of Europe to which many of the same States are parties.

(i) *Rights included in both instruments in substantially similar terms* Eleven rights are included in both instruments in substantially similar terms. They are the following (the reference given in each case being to the article in the United Nations Covenant by which the right is protected):

Article   7. Freedom from torture and inhuman treatment.
  8. Freedom from slavery, servitude and forced labour.
  9. The right to liberty and security of the person.
 11. Freedom from imprisonment for failure to fulfil a contractual obligation.
 12. The right to freedom of movement.
 15. Protection against retroactivity of the criminal law.
 17. The right to privacy.

18. The right to freedom of thought, conscience and religion.
19. The right to freedom of expression.
21. The right of peaceful assembly.
22. The right to freedom of association.

When it is said that these rights are defined in substantially similar terms, this is not meant to conceal the fact that in some cases there are differences in the definitions which may have some importance. Thus, as regards the right to liberty and security of the person, Article 9 of the United Nations Covenant prohibits 'arbitrary arrest or detention', while Article 5 of the European Convention prohibits arrest or detention except in six sets of circumstances which are specifically defined (after conviction by a competent court, for non-compliance with the lawful order of a court, etc.). The question therefore arises whether there is a correspondence between the prohibition of 'arbitrary arrest or detention' and the more carefully defined European formula. It appears that 'arbitrary' is intended to mean 'unlawful and unjust'[55] and that it would thus prohibit arrest or detention which might be permitted under some systems of law but which, by international standards, would not be considered 'just'. This could hardly be the case, however, with the six cases permitted by Article 5 of the European Convention, so that, even though the two definitions are not identical, no conflict should arise.

As another example, the United Nations text (Article 9, paragraph 2) requires that a person arrested shall be informed of the reasons 'at the time of his arrest', while the European requirement is that he should be informed 'promptly'. The requirement of the Covenant may be considered as imposing a stricter obligation; nevertheless, it appears that the intention – and the consequential obligation – is much the same, so that the conclusion seems justified that these rights are defined in 'substantially similar terms'.

(ii) Rights with regard to which there are important differences in the definitions This concerns four rights:

The right to life (Article 6).
The right to a fair trial (Article 14).
The right to marry (Article 23).

Political rights (Article 25).

The right to life. Article 6 of the Covenant protects the right to life. Its first paragraph reads 'Every human being has the inherent right to life. This right shall be protected by law. No one shall be arbitrarily deprived of his life.' Once again we find that the United Nations text uses the word 'arbitrarily', which was proposed but rejected during the drafting of the European Convention on the ground that it was too general or vague. The European text states explicitly that 'no one shall be deprived of his life intentionally save in the execution of a sentence of a court following his conviction of a crime for which this penalty is provided by law'. It continues by permitting restrictions on the right in the case of death resulting from the use of force which is no more than absolutely necessary in three cases: in defence against unlawful violence; in order to effect arrest or prevent escape; for the purpose of quelling a riot or insurrection.

As in the case of liberty and security, it would appear that the intention and the effect of the two texts are similar, and that the restrictions permitted under the Convention could not be considered 'arbitrary' within the meaning of the Covenant.

The more important differences are found in the subsequent paragraphs of Article 6 of the Covenant. They are clearly conceived with the conception that the death penalty should be restricted as far as possible and eventually abolished. Paragraph 2 begins, 'In countries which have not abolished the death penalty, sentence of death may be imposed only for the most serious crimes . . .' and paragraph 6 states that 'Nothing in this article shall be invoked to delay or to prevent the abolition of capital punishment by any State Party to the Covenant'. In this respect the Covenant is distincly more progressive than the European Convention, and one may wonder whether the reintroduction of the death penalty, when it has once been abolished, would be consistent with the Covenant. There are two references to the Genocide Convention, though these hardly constitute a difference of substance with the European text, since genocide is clearly incompatible with the provisions of the latter. A further difference is that the Covenant prohibits the death penalty for persons under eighteen years of age and for pregnant women; it also provides for the right to seek pardon or commutation of the sentence. There are no corresponding provisions in the European Convention, even though the practice of European

States is generally in conformity with the requirements of the Covenant. On the whole, therefore, the United Nations text reflects a more liberal spirit than the European Convention and one may hope that its provisions will be widely accepted.

The right to a fair trial. The second article where one notes important differences from the European text is perhaps (to judge by the European experience and from history) the most important of all: the right to a fair trial or to 'due process of law'. Article 14 of the Covenant starts off with the general affirmation 'All persons shall be equal before the courts and tribunals'. This is, of course, unexceptionable as a general principle, but is not found in the European Convention.

The main statement of the right is rather similar in the two instruments. Article 14 of the Covenant provides:

In the determination of any criminal charge against him, or of his rights and obligations in a suit at law, everyone shall be entitled to a fair and public hearing by a competent, independent and impartial tribunal established by law.

There are, however, three differences between this text and the corresponding sentence in Article 6 of the European Convention. First, the United Nations text uses the expression 'rights and obligations in a suit at law' whereas the Convention speaks of 'civil rights and obligations'. But it seems clear that these two different formulations are intended to have the same meaning, because the French versions are identical in the two instruments (*droits et obligations de caractère civil*).[56]

The second difference in the two statements of the right to a fair trial is that the European text includes, while the United Nations text omits, a provision to the effect that the hearing must be 'within a reasonable time'. A later paragraph (paragraph 3 of Article 14) of the United Nations text provides that a trial on a criminal charge must take place 'without undue delay', so that both instruments contain this guarantee in criminal matters, but only the European Convention as regards civil proceedings.

The third difference is that while both texts provide for hearing by 'an independent and impartial tribunal established by law', the United Nations text adds the requirement that the tribunal shall be 'competent'. The intention was to make it clear that all persons should be tried by courts whose jurisdiction has been previously established by law and thus avoid arbitrary proceedings; but since this notion is already included or implied in 'independent . . . tribunal established by law' this difference also appears of minor importance.

The second paragraph of Article 14 states the presumption of innocence in terms which are almost identical with those used in the European Convention.

The third paragraph sets out the rights of the defence in criminal proceedings. It is generally similar to Article 6 (3) of the European Convention.

The United Nations Covenant then continues with four further paragraphs setting out additional provisions regarding the right to a fair trial: paragraph 4 protecting the special position of juveniles; paragraph 5 on the right of a convicted person to appeal; paragraph 6 on the right to compensation for miscarriage of justice; and paragraph 7 expressing the principle of *ne bis in idem*. None of these points is covered in the European Convention, except that Article 6 thereof contains a provision which authorises an exception to the general rule about the publicity of trials 'where the interests of juveniles . . . so require'.

The right to marriage. Article 23 of the Covenant proclaims the right to marry and found a family. In one respect it is less positive than the corresponding article in the European Convention, because it states that the right 'shall be recognised', whereas Article 12 of the Convention provides that men and women of marriageable age 'have the right to marry and to found a family'. In other respects, however, the provisions of the United Nations Covenant are more far-reaching.

In the first place it starts with a general affirmation of principle, comparable to that in a number of national constitutions: 'The family is the natural and fundamental group unit of society and is entitled to protection by society and the State'. Secondly, the European text affirms the right 'according to the national laws governing the exercise of this right', and thus incorporates by reference the restrictions on the right permitted by national law (e.g. in case of insanity or hereditary disease, as regard detained persons, or members of the armed forces). There is no corresponding provision permitting restrictions in the Covenant. Thirdly, the United Nations text continues, 'no marriage shall be entered into without the free and full consent of the intending spouses', which is an additional guarantee not found in the Convention, though it is no doubt secured in fact by the reference to national law. Fourthly – and this is the most important point – the Covenant provides, in paragraph 4 of Article 23, for 'equality of rights and responsibilities of spouses as to marriage, during marriage and at its dissolution'. There is nothing comparable in the European Convention, and it may be difficult for many States to give effect to this provison, since many systems of law do not provide for complete equality in matters of civil status (the nationality or domicile of the wife often follows that of the husband) or as regards maintenance (where there is an obligation on the husband to support the wife but not vice versa).

Political rights. Here again Article 25 of the Covenant is considerably more extensive than Article 3 of the First Protocol to the European Convention. The latter text provides:

The High Contracting Parties undertake to hold free elections at reasonable intervals by secret ballot, under conditions which will ensure the free expression of the opinion of the people in the choice of the legislature.

This constitutes an undertaking of States and not an enforceable right of individuals. The United Nations text, on the other hand, provides that 'every citizen shall have the right and the opportunity without . . . distinction . . . and without unreasonable restrictions' to exercise certain activities; these are:

(a) To take part in the conduct of public affairs, directly or through freely chosen representatives.
(b) To vote and to be elected at genuine periodic elections . . .
(c) To have access, on general terms of equality, to public service in his country.

The Covenant thus contains several provisions not included in the Convention. As regards the right to vote, it is more positive in form and of wider application; it would seem not to be limited to the election of the legislature but also to cover, for example, local elections. The right 'to take part in the conduct of public affairs . . . through freely chosen representatives' is harder to understand. If it means the right to vote, there is no problem; but this is covered by the following paragraph, so it presumably means something else. Does it then refer to the 'conduct of public affairs' by the executive branch of the government? In most countries the citizen does not directly elect the members of the executive – and the same would apply *a fortiori* to the judiciary; its content therefore remains somewhat obscure. The third paragraph, on access to the public service on general terms of equality, is also something new

compared with the European Convention; it is not mentioned
therein and the European Commission has rejected as inadmissible
applications alleging violation of this right. It will therefore be
interesting in future years to follow the manner in which the article
is interpreted.

*(iii) Rights included in the Covenant but not in the Convention or
vice versa* Eight rights are included in the United Nations Covenant
but not in the Convention, and three are found in the European
system but not in that of the United Nations.

The first article of both Covenants proclaims that 'All peoples
have the right of self-determination'. This involves the right to
determine freely their political status, to pursue freely their
economic, social and cultural development and to dispose freely of
their natural wealth and resources. States parties to the Covenant
undertake to promote the realisation of this right.

Once more we are confronted with what is clearly a statement of
political principle rather than an enforceable right. Indeed, the
Third Committee of the General Assembly hesitated for a long time
about the inclusion of this article, which had not been proposed by
the Human Rights Commission. Its distinct character is evidenced
by the fact that it is put at the beginning of each Covenant, as a
single article constituting Part I, and not in sequence with the other
rights protected.

The main difficulty arises from its vague and general character.
What is meant by 'all peoples'? Who has the right to self-
determination? Where is the borderline between a 'people' and a
minority? Clearly there is matter here for plenty of speculation and
probably for much argument.

A later article, which is the last in Part III of the Covenant
(Article 27), relates to 'ethnic, religious or linguistic minorities'.
Persons belonging to such minorities 'shall not be denied the right,
in community with the other members of their group, to enjoy their
own culture, to profess and practise their own religion, or to use
their own language'. This article raises some of the same problems,
though it will be observed that the rights are conferred on the
'persons belonging to such minorities' and not on the minority
groups as such.

While there is no corresponding article in the European
Convention, the Consultative Assembly of the Council of Europe
proposed at one stage that a provision on the rights of minorities

should be included in the Fourth Protocol, which was then being drafted.[57] The text then proposed went further than Article 27 of the Covenant, because in addition to the three rights included there relating to culture, language and religion it added a fourth, 'to establish their own schools and receive teaching in the language of their choice'. But the governments did not feel able to accept this proposal[58] and the Fourth Protocol was completed without any reference to the rights of minorities. The Covenant text is therefore the most positive that we have on this subject; we may consider that it represents a modest step in the right direction.

Another provision of the Covenant which has no counterpart in the European Convention is Article 10, which provides that 'All persons deprived of their liberty shall be treated with humanity and with respect for the inherent dignity of the human person'; it continues by providing for the separation of accused persons from convicted persons and of juveniles from adults, and concludes that the essential aim of the penitentiary system shall be the reformation and social rehabilitation of prisoners. The principles to be observed in the treatment of prisoners correspond largely to those set out in the Standard Minimum Rules for Prisoners adopted by the United Nations World Congress on the Prevention of Crime and Treatment of Offenders in 1955, many of which have been further elaborated in Council of Europe texts in subsequent years.

It will suffice to mention briefly the other articles of the Covenant protecting rights not included in the European Convention and its Protocols. They are:

Article 13, which contains certain procedural safeguards for an alien who is under threat of expulsion. There is no corresponding provision in the European Convention, and a proposal to include such a provision was rejected when the Fourth Protocol was being drafted.

Article 16, on 'the right to recognition everywhere as a person before the law', and Article 26, on equality before the law and the right to the equal protection of the law. Once more we are confronted with provisions which are excellent statements of political principle but which perhaps lack the precision necessary for legal texts.

Article 20 of the Covenant provides categorically that 'any propaganda for war shall be prohibited by law', and continues by requiring a similar prohibition of 'any advocacy of national, racial or religious hatred that constitutes incitement to discrimination'.

The Convention on the Elimination of All Forms of Racial Discrimination of 21 December 1965 covers some of the same ground, but the text of the Covenant is wider in scope because it also includes 'national . . . or religious hatred'.

Article 24 deals with the rights of the child, which include the right to special measures of protection without discrimination, the requirement of registration immediately after birth, the right to a name and the right to acquire a nationality.

Finally, we must note three rights which are protected by the European system but not in the United Nations Covenant. The first of these is the right to property, which is protected by Article 1 of the First Protocol to the European Convention. Even though this text was carefully drafted so as to make it acceptable to socialist governments which were engaged in the nationalisation of certain forms of private property, and even though the right of property was included (as Article 17) in the Universal Declaration in 1948, no similar provision was found acceptable in the forum of the United Nations.[59] Secondly, the Fourth Protocol to the European Convention contains in its Article 3 a prohibition of exile in the terms: 'no one shall be expelled . . . from the territory of the State of which he is a national'. Thirdly, the Fourth Protocol to the European Convention also prohibits, in its Article 4, the collective expulsion of aliens; admittedly, this is an exceptional measure which would rarely have practical importance, though there may be countries in the world which would be glad to see such practices prohibited by the United Nations Covenant.

(b) The machinery of international control The major problem for European States which are parties to the European Convention and have ratified or are thinking of ratifying the United Nations Covenant and its Optional Protocol is that relating to the 'measures of implementation' or system of international control.

The coexistence of the two sets of provisions in the two instruments raises the question whether a State which has ratified both instruments and made a declaration under Article 41 of the U.N. Covenant and which wishes to bring a case against another State which has also done so can choose between the two systems or use them both in turn.

This problem was envisaged when the texts were drafted. Article 44 of the Covenant provides that its provisions shall not prevent States parties from having recourse to other methods of settlement of disputes, which would clearly include those provided for in the European Convention. The corresponding provision in the European Convention (Article 62) does not permit, except by special agreement, the submission of a dispute arising out of the interpretation or application of the Convention to a means of settlement other than those provided for in the Convention.

It therefore follows that European States which are parties to the European Convention should utilise the European machinery for their disputes on human rights matters rather than refer them to the United Nations, and that this would be quite in conformity with Article 44 of the Covenant. It would also be consistent with the principle set out in Article 33 of the United Nations Charter, which approves the regional settlement of disputes in preference to the invocation of United Nations procedures. This general statement that European States should utilise the European machinery in preference to that established by the Covenant should be limited, however, in two respects: first it applies only to disputes about the alleged violation of a right which is included in substantially similar terms in both instruments; secondly, it will only apply to the disputes of the European States *inter se* and should not prevent them from accepting the United Nations machinery for the settlement of disputes with other States.

This conclusion as regards the procedure for dealing with inter-State disputes was proposed by the Committee of Experts on Human Rights to the Committee of Ministers of the Council of Europe, and approved by the latter body in a resolution adopted in 1970.[60]

Different problems again arise when we come to consider applications or 'communications' by individuals alleging violation of their rights.

The coexistence of the two sets of implementation measures will evidently raise certain problems for those States which have accepted the procedure of Article 25 of the European Convention and also ratified the United Nations Optional protocol, particularly the question whether an individual applicant can choose between the two systems or use both of them in turn.

Article 5, paragraph 2, of the Optional Protocol provides that:

The Committee shall not consider any communication from an individual unless it has ascertained that:
(a) the same matter is not being examined under another procedure of international investigation or settlement;

Article 27, paragraph 1 (b) of the European Convention states:

The Commission shall not deal with any petition submitted under Article 25 which:

. . .

(b) is substantially the same as a matter which has already been examined by the Commission or has already been submitted to another procedure of international investigation or settlement and if it contains no relevant new information.

From these texts it would appear that the European Commission would be altogether prevented from considering a complaint previously lodged with the United Nations Committee (unless new evidence has been produced); on the other hand, the UN Committee could not consider an application already lodged with the European Commission while the European procedure continued, but would be free to do so once the European procedure was terminated.

Since the underlying object of both instruments is to secure the protection of the rights of the individual, it should be accepted that a person who believes that his rights have been violated should have a choice between the European procedure and the United Nations procedure and should be allowed to use that which he considers most favourable to his case. On the other hand, it is more difficult to accept that he should be able to use both procedures in turn. Of course, if he makes a mistake and addresses himself to the wrong forum – for example, by complaining to the European Commission of the violation of a right which is not protected by the European Convention but is included in the United Nations Covenant – then he should be allowed to correct his mistake and make a new application to the right forum. But, in the case of a right which is, in substance, guaranteed by both instruments, there are reasons of public policy which militate against the acceptance of a series of successive international remedies.

Our conclusion, then, is that an individual applicant who wishes to bring a case against a State which has accepted the two optional procedures under Article 25 of the European Convention and the Protocol to the United Nations Covenant should have the right of choice between the two methods of bringing his case before an international organ but, except in the case of an honest mistake as to the appropriate forum, should accept the consequences of his decision and not have the possibility of going from one forum to the other. This would apply in both directions. The attempt to 'appeal' from the United Nations Committee to the European Commission already seems to be barred by Article 27 (1) (b) of the European Convention. An attempt to 'appeal' from the European organs to the United Nations Committee is at present barred by Article 5 (2) of the Optional Protocol for as long as the European proceedings continue, but not thereafter. What is required, therefore, is a suitable provision to extend the scope of Article 5 (2) so as to give it the same effect as Article 27 (1) (b). It would appear that this might be done either by a reservation when ratifying the Optional Protocol or by a declaration of interpretation; the method of doing so is a question of legal technique which it is not proposed to examine here.

This solution was proposed to the Committee of Ministers of the Council of Europe by the Committee of Experts on Human Rights, which drew up a text that could be used either as a reservation or as a declaration of interpretation. The Ministers agreed with the conclusions of the Committee of Experts and transmitted their text to the member governments of the Council of Europe so that they could use it, if they wished, when ratifying the Optional Protocol to the UN Covenant.[61] Several of them have in fact done so.

Even in the absence of any formal texts of this sort, one can also imagine a simpler method of harmonising the two systems by agreement between the European Commission and the United Nations Committee. It should be possible to devise a system whereby the two organs would agree that cases which could more appropriately be considered by either of them would be automatically transferred to that organ if initially directed to the other, and whereby the principle of *ne bis in idem* would be equally recognised. Such provisions could then be incorporated in the rules of procedure of both the United Nations Committee and the European Commission.

Whatever procedure is adopted, it should not be beyond the wit of man — and, more particularly, of lawyers — to work out adequate measures of harmonisation of the two systems, the European and the universal, the more so as the fundamental objective of both of them is the same: the better protection of the rights of the common man and of the rule of law throughout the world.[62]

II. THE HELSINKI AGREEMENT AND HUMAN RIGHTS[63]

The 'Conference on Security and Co-operation in Europe' was

formally opened at Helsinki on 3 July 1973 and continued at Geneva from 18 September 1973 to 21 July 1975. It was concluded at Helsinki on 1 August 1975. The thirty-five participants included all European States from East and West, irrespective of their size, except Albania, and also the United States and Canada. The Holy See and three 'mini-States' (Liechtenstein, Monaco, San Marino) participated on a basis of equality with the U.S.A. and the U.S.S.R.[64]

The final session in Helsinki from 30 July to 1 August 1975 was attended by the heads of state or of government of nearly all the participating States; the Final Act was signed on 1 August 1975. It comprised four sections concerning respectively: (1) Questions relating to Security in Europe; (2) Co-operation in the fields of Economics, of Science and Technology and of the Environment; (3) Co-operation in Humanitarian and other fields; (4) the 'Follow-up' to the Conference.[65]

1. The Final Act

The first thing to be noted about the Final Act of the conference is that it is not a treaty but a declaration of intentions. It does not use the standard formulation of a treaty, containing undertakings of States. It says, 'The High Representatives of the participating States have solemnly adopted the following,' and then continues, 'The participating States will respect each other's sovereign equality . . .'; 'The participating States regard as inviolable all one another's frontiers . . .'; 'The participating States will respect the territorial integrity of each of the participating States' and so on.

At first sight it may seem that there is little difference between an undertaking by States to do certain things and a statement that they will do certain things. But the difference is more than a lawyer's quibble. There are at least two important differences between a legal undertaking and a declaration of intention. First of all, on the domestic constitutional plane, a treaty is not binding in most countries unless it is ratified by the legislature; but the Helsinki Final Act did not require ratification and was not submitted to the various national parliaments for this purpose. Secondly, on the international plane, non-observance of a treaty constitutes a breach of international law and can, in many cases, form the object of proceedings before the International Court of Justice; no such consequences result from the non-observance of a declaration of intention.

This does not mean that the Helsinki Final Act is unimportant or that it should not be observed. Of course it should. It sets out moral and political obligations of States, but these are something less than obligations binding in international law. As a result, it is inaccurate, from a legal point of view, to speak of the 'Helsinki Agreement'; but since the expression has come into current use, and is more convenient than the full title 'Final Act of the Conference on Security and Co-operation in Europe', there is no harm in adopting it so long as we understand that the word 'agreement' is used in its popular, but not in its legal, sense.

The second thing to be noted about the Final Act is that it is concerned in the first place, and principally, with international security and relations between States. For various reasons which are generally well known it was not possible to conclude a peace treaty after the end of the Second World War; during the period of the 'Cold War' it was evident that no mutually satisfactory definition of relations between East and West was possible. But after some years of 'détente', of the new 'Ostpolitik' of Chancellor Willy Brandt, the agreement between the two Germanies and the admission of both of them to the United Nations, some new arrangements for 'peaceful coexistence' between East and West seemed possible. The Soviet Union had been seeking for years the recognition by the other powers of its Western frontiers as established after the end of the war, and Mr Brezhnev had made this a central issue of his foreign policy; but there was little that the Western powers were likely to receive in return. They had no territorial claims to make — apart from the Germans, who knew in advance that the reunification of Germany was not to be expected — and they recognised that any fundamental political changes in the direction of liberalisation were excluded. What they tried to obtain, therefore, was certain modest concessions as regards respect for human rights and freedom of movement and of information between East and West, in the hope that this could be the beginning of a gradual liberalisation of authoritarian regimes.

This leads us to the third preliminary point, which concerns the human rights provisions of the Final Act. Since the latter is concerned with relations between States and the interests of States, the provisions concerning human rights do not seek to protect the individual as such; the interests of individual human beings are rather incidental to reasons of state. The Final Act does not follow the method of the Universal Declaration or of the U.N. Covenants in providing that 'Everyone has the right to . . .' a certain number of fundamental rights and freedoms; rather, it provides that 'The participating States will respect human rights and fundamental freedoms . . .'. Thus, in accordance with the whole philosophy of the Final Act, it is the action of States which is aimed at, and not the situation or behaviour of individuals as such.

The first three sections of the Final Act are commonly known as three 'baskets'. The most important for our purpose is 'Basket I', which starts off with a *Declaration on Principles guiding Relations between Participating States*. This sets out ten principles which are so fundamental that it will be convenient to list them. They are the following:

1. Sovereign equality, respect for the rights inherent in sovereignty.
2. Refraining from the threat or use of force.
3. Inviolability of frontiers.
4. Territorial integrity of States.
5. Peaceful settlement of disputes.
6. Non-intervention in internal affairs.
7. Respect for human rights and fundamental freedoms, including freedom of thought, conscience, religion or belief.
8. Equal rights and self-determination of peoples.
9. Co-operation among States.
10. Fulfilment in good faith of obligations under international law.

Each of these principles is explained in some detail in the Final Act. It is perhaps significant that Principle No. 7 concerning human rights and fundamental freedoms has the longest explanatory text of them all, running to eight paragraphs. It makes four principal points. First, 'The participating States will respect human rights and fundamental freedoms'; particular mention is made of freedom of thought, conscience, religion or belief. Secondly, the participating States say that they will '*promote and encourage* the effective exercise of civil, political, economic, social, cultural and other rights and freedoms'. It should be noted that this very widely drawn reference to 'civil, political, economic, social, cultural and other rights and freedoms' is preceded by the words 'promote and encourage'. It is thus distinctly less than an affirmative statement that the participating States will 'respect' these rights and freedoms. It recalls Article 1 (3) and Article 55 of the Charter of the United Nations, which speak of 'promoting and encouraging respect' for human rights and fundamental freedoms and thereby contain an expression of intention for the future but not an immediate obligation.

The third principal point in the text is that it contains a statement that the participating States will respect the rights of national minorities, which recalls Article 27 of the Covenant on Civil and Political Rights. The fourth is that there are two references to the human rights work of the United Nations. The sixth paragraph states that the participating States will endeavour 'jointly and separately, including in co-operation with the United Nations, to promote universal and effective respect' for these rights and freedoms – which recalls (and substantially repeats) Article 56 of the Charter. Finally, in the eighth paragraph, the participating States say that they 'will act in accordance with the purposes and principles of the Charter of the United Nations and with the Universal Declaration of Human Rights'. This paragraph continues by referring specifically to their 'obligations as set forth in the international declarations and agreements in this field, including inter alia the International Covenants on Human Rights, by which they may be bound'.

To summarise, then, we see that the 'Declaration on Principles guiding Relations between Participating States' includes respect for human rights among those basic principles, alongside other principles such as the inviolability of frontiers, the peaceful settlement of disputes and refraining from the use of threat of force. Principle No. 7 is wide in its scope, because the second paragraph refers to the effective exercise of all categories of rights and freedoms, but limited in its effect, because (like the Charter) it contains rather expressions of intention to 'promote and encourage' than affirmative statements of a determination to 'respect' human rights. Some of its provisions would appear to be tautologous, as reaffirming existing obligations; but this is not a criticism, because the constant reaffirmation of the obligation to respect human rights may help to impress that obligation more securely in the conscience both of governments and of the general public.

'Basket III' is also relevant to our purpose, but may be summarised more briefly. It is entitled *Co-operation in Humanitarian and other Fields* and contains four sections. The first relates to 'human contacts' and deals *inter alia* with reunification of families, marriages between citizens of different States, travel, tourism, meetings of young people and sport. The second section – which, if effectively implemented, could be of great importance for the future – concerns the free flow of information. The participating States 'make it their aim to facilitate the freer and wider dissemination of information of all kinds' and set out a number of steps to be taken for this purpose, relating severally to oral information, printed information, and filmed and broadcast information. These include measures 'to facilitate the improvement of the dissemination on their territory of newspapers and printed publications . . . from the other participating States', and measures 'to improve the conditions under which journalists from one . . . State exercise their profession in another . . . State'. Basket III finishes with two short sections about co-operation and exchanges in the fields of culture and education.

2. Post-Helsinki developments

The signature of the Final Act of the conference was much more widely acclaimed, and its contents more widely publicised, in the East than in the West. This was no doubt for the reason already mentioned, that is to say that the Soviet Union had a greater interest in the successful conclusion of the conference, because it constituted an official acceptance by the West of her territorial acquisitions during the Second World War. What had been agreed by three powers at Yalta – and a good deal more than that – had now been accepted as permanent, thirty years later, by the whole of Europe, plus the United States and Canada. This was a real achievement for Soviet diplomacy.

One might have thought that it would mark the beginning of a new era of *détente* and co-operation in Europe. Such hopes, however, have so far been largely disappointed.

What did change was public opinion, at least in certain intellectual circles, in Eastern Europe. The publicity given to the Final Act led many people to believe that its provisions on human rights would be implemented and that an era of liberalisation was about to begin. The well-informed knew that all the East European States had ratified the United Nations Covenants (except Poland, which did so subsequently) and thus accepted binding obligations in international law to respect human rights. With these two significant developments, it was hardly surprising that politically conscious individuals looked to their governments to allow a freer flow of information and greater liberty of expression – even if they were not so foolhardy as to expect the right to form a political opposition.

The most striking example of this was in Czechoslovakia, where nearly five hundred intellectuals and others subscribed to a human rights manifesto which they called 'Charter 77'. It took as its point of departure the ratification by Czechoslovakia, and the publication in the 'Czechoslovak Register of Laws' on 13 October 1976, of the two United Nations Covenants on Human Rights and the reaffirmation of the Covenants in the Final Act of the Helsinki conference. The Charter welcomed accession to those agreements, but continued, 'Their publication, however, serves as a powerful reminder of the extent to which basic human rights in our country exist, regrettably, on paper alone.' A series of examples were then given in the Charter of various rights which are proclaimed and supposed to be protected by the Covenants but in fact are systematically violated in Czechoslovakia; they include: freedom of expression, freedom of information, freedom of religion, freedom of association, the right to form trade unions, the right to privacy and the right to leave any country including one's own.

'Charter 77' evoked considerable support in other Eastern European countries. In Yugoslavia Milovan Djilas, a former leader of the Communist party, appealed to West European Communist parties to support the Charter and the movement for human rights not only in Czechoslovakia but also in his own country, where he said that, on a proportional basis, there were as many political prisoners as in the Soviet Union. Similar repercussions were observed in East Germany, in Poland and in Roumania.

But the most important reaction was no doubt that in the Soviet Union itself. A committee was established to supervise the application of the Helsinki Agreement, under the chairmanship of Youri Orlov; the detention of Alexander Guinzbourg led to the signature of a manifesto by 248 supporters; Andrei Sakharov, who had formed the Soviet Committee on Human Rights nearly ten years earlier, continued his struggle in unprecedented ways, including an American television interview, a personal letter to President Carter and a letter to all the heads of state or of government who signed the Helsinki Agreement; President Carter replied, 'You may be assured that the American people and our government will maintain their firm engagement to promote respect for human rights not only in our country but also abroad.'

Sakharov was constantly harassed and in 1980 exiled to Gorkhi. Vladimir Boukovski, having been liberated and exiled in December 1976, after twelve years in prison, in exchange for the Chilean Communist leader Luis Corvalan, was received by President Carter in February and testified to a Congressional committee that none of the human rights provisions of the Helsinki Agreement was respected in the U.S.S.R. Andrei Amalrik, a dissident historian exiled in 1976, spoke to the press in Paris as a representative of the committee on the application of the Helsinki Agreement in the same sense as Boukovski in Washington; in 1980 he was killed in a car accident on his way to attend the second 'follow-up' conference in Madrid.

This brief summary of some well known developments (which does not pretend to be complete) shows that the Helsinki Agreement – or, more specifically – its human rights provisions – has had an effect in Eastern Europe far surpassing the expectations of some of its authors in highlighting the fact that the principles proclaimed have remained largely a dead letter in the Communist countries.

The Soviet Union has, of course, retorted that the Western reaction to these events constitutes an improper interference in its internal affairs, which itself is contrary to the Helsinki Agreement. The Russian point of view, even if one does not share it, is not to be dismissed out of hand. The sixth principle in the 'Declaration on Principles guiding Relations between Participating States' is non-intervention in internal affairs. This is explained in part as follows:

The participating States will refrain from any intervention, direct or indirect, individual or collective, in the internal or external affairs falling within the domestic jurisdiction of another participating State, regardless of their mutual relations.

We therefore have to ask whether acts such as President Carter's letter to Andrei Sakharov or the hearing of Vladimir Boukovski by a Congressional committee (or many proposals made to the U.N. Commission on Human Rights) constitute an 'intervention, direct or indirect ... in the internal affairs falling within the domestic jurisdiction' of the Soviet Union. This brings us back to the problem discussed in the preceding chapter (section III (1)) whether procedures permitting the United Nations to consider complaints of violation of human rights would violate Article 2, paragraph 7, of the Charter, which contains a prohibition 'to intervene in matters which are essentially within the domestic jurisdiction of any State . . .'. One can only repeat that when States have accepted international obligations with regard to particular matters, those matters cease to be exclusively within their domestic jurisdiction.

3. The 'follow-up' conferences

The 'Fourth Basket' of the Helsinki Final Act concerns the follow-up to the conference. It starts with a declaration by the participating States of their resolve 'to pay due regard to and implement the provisions of the Final Act', unilaterally, bi-laterally and multilaterally. They then declare their intention of continuing the multilateral process begun at the conference by further exchanges of views on the implementation of the Final Act, and on improving security and further developing co-operation and *détente* in Europe. The first follow-up meeting took place in Belgrade, from 4 October 1977 to 8 March 1978; the second in Madrid, beginning on 11 November 1980.

Little was achieved at the Belgrade meeting in the field of human rights. It was reported that there was a 'full and frank review' of all aspects of the Helsinki Final Act, which included detailed discussion of human rights, comprising an examination of the extent to which specific countries had complied with the provisions of the Final Act and discussion of individual cases. In this way participating States were informed, officially and in some detail, of what other participants thought of their human rights record. But when it came to conclusions, there was complete lack of agreement.

It was widely expected before the Belgrade conference met that it would put on record the progress made in the implementation of what had been agreed at Helsinki, so that the concluding document would constitute something in the nature of a balance sheet of action taken by governments to promote security and co-operation in Europe since 1975. But the balance sheet, if drawn up, would have been largely negative. Under the agreed rules of the conference, the concluding document had to be adopted by consensus. The Soviet Union refused to accept that there should be any mention of human rights at all At one stage it looked as if the conference would break up without adopting any conclusions. Finally, the Western powers accepted a brief compromise text, which recorded *inter alia* that 'It was recognised that the exchange of views constitutes in itself a valuable contribution towards the achievement of the aims set by the C.S.C.E., although different views were expressed as to the degree of implementation of the Final Act reached so far'. The omission of any specific reference to human rights was the price paid in order to enable the Helsinki process to continue by holding a further conference in Madrid in 1980.

When that year opened, the international atmosphere was sombre. *Détente* had been thwarted by the Soviet invasion of Afghanistan in December 1979, which was promptly condemned not only by the Western powers but also by the non-aligned countries. In the spring of 1980 serious doubts were felt in many quarters as to whether it was possible or desirable to hold the Madrid conference at all. (The partial boycott of the Olympic Games in Moscow was another symptom of the same reaction.) Yet preparations for the conference continued, since none of the intended participants wished to assume the responsibility for a rupture.

There was indeed a good case to be made for attempting to continue the Helsinki process, in spite of the difficulties. The Final Act had provided for a continuing process of review, and without that the C.S.C.E. would have lost most of its purpose. As one authority put it, 'The whole point of the Helsinki Accords is mutual monitoring, not mutual evasion of difficult problems.'[66] However hard it might be for the West to secure recognition of this fact, it was better to go on trying than to give up the attempt altogether. 'Indeed, despite and because of the many breaches of the Final Act, its provisions should be reaffirmed.'[67] At the same time, this process should not be undertaken in a self-righteous spirit. As one high-level group in the United States put it, the review should include 'consideration of the ways in which we are perceived by others, critical examination of our own record of compliance and acknowledgement of our shortcomings. We should reiterate our concern with social and economic as well as civil and political rights, yet make clear that one set of rights cannot be traded off against the other'.[68]

The Madrid conference very nearly did not open at all. After nine weeks of preliminary discussions, agreement had not been reached on the agenda by 10 November, the eve of the official opening. Once more a last-minute compromise was reached, permitting heads of delegations to make their opening speeches despite the absence of an agenda; the six weeks until Christmas were to be devoted to a review of the application of the Final Act, and six weeks in the new year to the discussion of further measures designed to encourage security in Europe and political *détente*.

The conference was originally scheduled to finish by mid-March 1981, but by that time no agreement was in sight either on matters of substance or on a final communiqué. The proceedings dragged on into the summer months, but still with no significant progress in securing the more effective observance of the human rights provisions of the Helsinki Final Act. The delegations still hoped that some useful result would emerge and refused doggedly to abandon the attempt, so the conference adjourned again until the autumn. Nevertheless, one is forced reluctantly to the conclusion that from the human rights point of view the Conference on Security and Co-operation in Europe has so far achieved very little.

NOTES

1   The negotiations are described more fully in A. H. Robertson, 'The European Convention for the Protection of Human Rights', *British Yearbook of International Law*, 1950, p. 145; and in *Human Rights in Europe*, second edition, Manchester University Press, 1977, pp. 1–21.

2   Many books have been published on the Convention. Those in English are: S. Castberg, *The European Convention on Human Rights*, Leyden, 1974; J. E. S. Fawcett, *The Application of the European Convention on Human Rights*, Oxford, 1969; F. G. Jacobs, *The European Convention on Human Rights*, Oxford, 1975; C. Morrison, *The Developing European Law of Human Rights*, Leyden, 1967; A. H. Robertson, *Human Rights in Europe* (cited *supra*, n. 1); L. Sohn and T. Buergenthal, *International Protection of Human Rights*, New York and Indianapolis, 1973, chapter VII; G. L. Weil, *The European Convention on Human Rights*, Leyden, 1963. For other books and articles about the Convention see the bibliography published annually in the *Yearbook of the Convention on Human Rights*; a separate bibliography with annual supplements is published by the Directorate of Human Rights of the Council of Europe. For primary sources see 'Note on sources' in *Human Rights in Europe* (*supra*, n. 1), pp. xv–xvii. The text of the Convention and Protocols may be found in many books and collections, including the following: *Yearbook of the European Convention on Human Rights*, I, 1955–57, p. 4; *European Yearbook*, I, 1955, p. 317; Council of Europe, *Conventions and Agreements*, I, 1949–61, p. 21; *idem*, *Human Rights in International Law – Basic Texts*, 1979, p. 3; Ian Brownlie, *Basic Documents on Human Rights*, Oxford, 1971, p. 338;

Human Rights in Europe (*supra*, n. 1), p. 294.

3   In a number of member States the normative provisions of the Convention are directly applicable in national law and can be applied by national courts – see H. Golsong, 'The European Convention on Human Rights before domestic courts', *B.Y.I.L.*, 1962, p. 445; T. Buergenthal, 'The effect of the European Convention on Human Rights on the internal law of member States', *I.C.L.Q.*, supplement No. 11, 1965, p. 79; *Human Rights in National and International Law*, Manchester, 1967, particularly the reports of Professors Sørensen, Verdross and Ganshof van der Meersch; Fawcett, *op. cit.* n. 2, pp. 5–18; *Human Rights in Europe* (*supra*, n. 1), pp. 26–31.

4   Consultative Assembly, *Official Reports*, 7 September 1949, p. 127.

5   The presidents have been: Professor Sir Humphrey Waldock (1957–62); Mr Sture Petren (1962–7); Professor Max Sørensen (1967–72); Professor J. E. S. Fawcett (since 1972).

6   Further information on these cases (except the last two) may be found in *Human Rights in Europe* (*supra*, n. 1) at p. 148 and the references there given. The Greek case and the Northern Ireland case are summarised in section 4 of this chapter.

7   Professor Torkel Opsahl of Norway, who is the only member of both bodies, has compared them in an article 'The protection of human rights in the Council of Europe and in the United Nations', *European Yearbook*, XXIV, 1978, pp. 92–118. For the citation in the text see *Yearbook of the European Convention on Human Rights*, IV, 1961, p. 196, Cf. J. E. S. Fawcett, *op. cit.* n. 2, pp. 312–13.

8   *Human Rights in Europe* (*supra*, n. 1), pp. 177–8.

9.   *Ibid.*, pp. 179–84.

10   The functions and procedure of the Commission are described in greater detail in *ibid.*, pp. 139–92.

11   Austria, Belgium, Cyprus, Denmark, France, the Federal Republic of Germany, Greece, Iceland, Ireland, Italy, Liechtenstein, Luxembourg, Malta, the Netherlands, Norway, Portugal, Spain, Sweden, Switzerland, Turkey and the United Kingdom.

12   The functions and procedure of the Committee of Ministers under the Convention on Human Rights are described more fully in *Human Rights in Europe* (*supra*, n. 1), pp. 237–67.

13   The Presidents of the Court have been: Lord McNair (1959–65), M. René Cassin (1965–68), Professor Henri Rolin (1968–71), Professor Sir Humphrey Waldock (1971–74), Professor Balladore-Pallieri (1974–80), M. Gerard Wiarda (elected in 1981). The functions and procedure of the European Court of Human Rights are described in greater detail in *ibid.*, pp. 193–236.

14   The *Yearbook of the European Convention on Human Rights* (cited below as *Yearbook*) is the official publication which contains the basic texts and the more important decisions of the three organs. The first two volumes covered the years 1955–59. Since 1960 it has been published annually; twenty-two volumes had been published by 1980. An extra volume was published in 1969 (XII *bis*) containing the report of the Commission and the decision of the Committee of

Ministers in the *Greek case*. The Court publishes two separate series: *Publications of the European Court of Human Rights, Series A: Judgments and Decisions,* and *Series B: Pleadings, Oral Arguments and Documents.* The Commission publishes its own series of *Decisions and Reports* (nineteen volumes by 1980).

15 The case law is summarised in several of the books mentioned in n. 2, particularly those of Fawcett, Jacobs and the present author.

16 *Yearbook*, XI, 1968, pp. 690–728.

17 *Yearbook*, XII *bis: the Greek case.*

18 Recommendation 547, *Texts adopted by the Assembly,* January 1969; *Yearbook of the Convention,* XII, 1969, p. 126.

19 See n. 17 above.

20 *Yearbook*, XIX, 1976, p. 512.

21 *Publications of the Court, Series A,* No. 25 (1978).

22 A very convenient, though unofficial, source of information on the case law of the Commission is *Stock-taking on the European Convention on Human Rights,* published periodically by the Commission's Secretary. In the 1979 edition (reference DH(79)1) the cases of friendly settlement are summarised at pp. 34–45, the informal arrangements at pp. 46–56.

23 In compiling this summary I have been much assisted by an information document produced by the Registrar of the Court – *The European Court of Human Rights: its organisation and working,* document B(81)3 of 27 January, 1981; also by the Secretary of the Commission's document *Stock-taking,* cited in the previous note.

24 *Publications of the Court, Series A: Judgments and Decisions* (cited below as *Series A*), Nos. 1, 2 and 3, 1960–61. Most of the cases summarised in the text are recounted more fully in *Human Rights in Europe (supra,* n. 1), where the page references may be found in the Table of Cases.

25 *Series A,* No. 4.

26 *Series A,* Nos. 5 and 6.

27 *Series A,* Nos. 7 (1968), and 10 (1969).

28 *Series A,* Nos. 8 (1968), 9 (1969) and 13 (1971).

29 *Series A,* No. 17 (1974).

30 *Series A,* Nos. 15 (1972), and 16 (1973).

31 *Series A,* No. 11 (1970).

32 *Series A,* No. 12 (1970–71).

33 *Series A,* No. 14 (1972).

34 *Series A,* No. 18 (1975).

35 *Series A,* Nos. 19 (1975) and 20 (1976).

36 *Series A,* No. 21 (1976).

37 *Series A,* No. 22 (1976).

38 *Series A,* No. 23 (1976).

39 *Series A,* No. 24 (1976).

40 *Series A,* Nos. 30 (1979) and 38 (1981). The sum awarded was £22,626.

41 *Series A,* No. 27 (1978). The applicant was awarded nearly DM40,000 as 'just satisfaction'.

42   *Series A*, No. 29 (1978).
43   *Series A*, No. 33 (1979).
44   *Series A*, No. 32 (1979).
45   *Series A*, No. 34 (1979).
46   *Series A*, No. 26 (1978).
47   *Series A*, No. 28 (1978).
48   *Series A*, No. 31 (1979).
49   *Series A*, No. 38 (1980). The applicant was awarded 1 million lire compensation.
50   *Series A*, No. 37 (1980). The applicant was awarded 3 million lire compensation. In November 1980 the Court also gave its decision in the *Van Oosterwijck case*, which concerned the absence in Belgian law of any provision permitting account to be taken of a change of sex. The Court held that there had been a failure to exhaust domestic remedies and that it was therefore unable to take cognisance of the merits of the case. At the beginning of 1981 eight other cases were pending before the Court.
51   See the Secretary of the Commission's document *Stock-taking*, cited in n. 22 above.
52   *Declaration on Human Rights* of 27 April 1978, *Yearbook*, XXI, 1968, p. 82.
53   By 1 January 1981 the following States parties to the European Convention had also ratified the U.N. Covenant on Civil and Political Rights: Austria, Cyprus, Denmark, France, the Federal Republic of Germany, Iceland, Italy, Netherlands, Norway, Portugal, Spain, Sweden, United Kingdom. Belgium, Ireland and Luxembourg had signed but not ratified it.
54   Some of the matters examined in this section were discussed in greater detail in the first edition of this book at pp. 80–110. The report of the Committee of Experts comparing the rights protected in the two treaties was published by the Council of Europe as doc. H(70)7, September 1970. The decisions of the Committee of Ministers are published in *Yearbook*, XIII, 1970, pp. 70–6.
55   Report of the Secretary-General of the United Nations on the draft Covenants, doc. A/2929 of 1 July 1955, Chapter VI, para. 3.
56   For the legislative history of this provision and the important case law of the European Commission and Court see A. H. Robertson, *Human Rights in Europe*, 1977, pp. 68–72.
57   Recommendation 285 of 28 April 1961. For the work of the Council of Europe on the subject of minorities see H. Lannung, 'The rights of minorities', in *Mélanges offerts à Polys Modinos*, Paris, 1968, pp. 184–95.
58   *Sixteenth Report of the Committee of Ministers* (1965), paragraphs 301–2. The 'Case relating to certain aspects of the use of languages in schools in Belgium' was then under consideration by the European Commission of Human Rights.
59   The Commission on Human Rights found it impossible to agree on a text and, at its tenth session in 1954, adjourned consideration of the question *sine die* – doc. A/2929, 1955, Chapter VI, paragraph 195.

60   *Yearbook*, XIII, 1970, pp. 70–6. By 31 December 1980 the following
parties to the European Convention had accepted the optional
procedure for inter-State cases under Article 41 of the U.N.
Covenant: Austria, Denmark, Federal Republic of Germany,
Iceland, Italy, Netherlands, Norway, Sweden, United Kingdom.

61   *Ibid.* By 31 December 1980 the following parties to the European
Convention had ratified the Optional Protocol: Denmark, Iceland,
Italy, Netherlands, Norway, Sweden.

62   A quite distinct problem of 'coexistence' concerns the relationship
between the system established by the European Convention on
Human Rights and the provisions affecting human rights of
Community law, i.e. the legal system instituted by the Treaty of
Rome, 1957, establishing the European Economic Community. For
discussion of this problem see A. H. Robertson, *Human Rights in
Europe*, 1977, pp. 286–291, and 'Human rights and Community
law', in *Mélanges dédiés à Robert Pelloux*, Lyon, 1980, pp. 281–97,
and the references there given.

63   This section is based on a lecture delivered at the University of Notre
Dame, Indiana, in 1977, which was subsequently published in
Human Rights and American Foreign Policy, ed. Donald P.
Kommers, Notre Dame, 1978, pp. 130–149. See also: *Human Rights,
International Law and the Helsinki Accord*, ed. Thomas
Buergenthal, New York, 1977.

64   In addition, statements were made to the conference by
representatives of Algeria, Egypt, Israel, Morocco, Syria and
Tunisia. One section of the Final Act relates to 'Security and Co-
operation in the Mediterranean'.

65   The full text of the Final Act, which is very long (about 80,000
words), may be found in various official publications. Extensive
extracts are given in *Keesing's Contemporary Archives*, 1–7
September 1975, pp. 27, 301–8; and in *European Yearbook*, XXIII,
1977, pp. 211 ff.

66   Lord Caccia, 'The East–West balance that must be achieved in
Madrid', *The Times*, 19 November 1980.

67   *Ibid.*

68   *The Road to Madrid: Recommendations for United States Human
Rights Policy*, report of a meeting organised by the Aspen Institute
for Humanistic Studies in New York, November 1978, pp. 5–6.

Chapter four

THE AMERICAN CONVENTION ON HUMAN RIGHTS

1. The origin and history of the Convention

The origins of the movement for Latin American unity can be traced back to the early years of the nineteenth century, when the Latin American republics attained their independence. By 1825 this had been recognised by the United States and then by Britain, while the proclamation of the Monroe doctrine prevented European intervention in American affairs.

As early as 1822 Simon Bolivar proposed a 'meeting of plenipotentiaries of the Americas' with a view to establishing a confederation of the newly independent republics. As a result of further proposals which he made in December 1824, the 'First Congress of American States' was held in Panama in June and July 1826; it produced a 'Treaty of Perpetual Union, League and Confederation' between the participating States, but this ambitious project never entered into force, because it was ratified only by Colombia. Subsequently, the 'First International American Conference', held at the invitation of the United States and attended by seventeen American republics, was held in Washington from October 1889 to April 1890. It was on this occasion that the International Union of American Republics was founded, commonly known as the *Pan American Union*. Its principal functions were to promote economic co-operation and the peaceful settlement of disputes; arrangements were made at this initial stage for the collection and publication of statistics and reports on production, trade and customs regulations.

From the beginning of the twentieth century until the outbreak of the Second World War eight conferences of American States were held at irregular intervals, but with increasing frequency, in various Latin American capitals. This period also saw the opening of the 'House of the Americas' in Washington in 1910, as the headquarters of the Pan American Union. During the Second World War three meetings of consultation of the Foreign Ministers took place, in 1939, 1940 and 1942, to discuss the problems which confronted the American republics resulting from the war, in an attempt to safeguard them against subversion in what came to be known as 'the political defence of the hemisphere'. The third of these meetings recommended to all the American republics the severance of diplomatic relations with the Axis powers.

The Inter-American Conference on Problems of War and Peace held in Mexico in February and March 1945 considered, among other things, the organisation of the Inter-American system in the post-war world; its conclusions played an important part in leading to the adoption at the San Francisco conference a few months later of Chapter VIII of the U.N. Charter on 'Regional arrangements'. The Inter-American Conference in Rio de Janeiro in 1947 was principally devoted to the subject of the maintenance of continental peace and security; the Inter-American Treaty of Reciprocal Assistance, signed in Rio on 2 September 1947, is still the basic instrument of collective security of the Inter-American system.

At Bogotá in 1948, at the ninth Inter-American Conference, the American States undertook a review of their methods of co-operation and reorganised the whole system. The 'Charter of Bogotá' adopted on this occasion furnished the new constitutional instrument that was required and thereby established the *Organisation of American States*.

The Charter proclaimed expressly in its first article that the O.A.S. is a regional agency within the United Nations. It continued by proclaiming the essential purposes of the Organisation, which include: to strengthen peace and security, to ensure the peaceful settlement of disputes, to provide for common action in the event of aggression, and to promote economic, social and cultural development.

There followed two important chapters on 'Principles' and 'Fundamental Rights and Duties of States'. These reaffirm the principles of international law and of fundamental human rights, declaring that an act of aggression against one constitutes aggression against all American States, and reassert the principle of non-intervention to which so much importance is attached by the American republics. The Charter then contained separate chapters on the pacific settlement of disputes, on collective security, and on economic, social and cultural standards.[1]

Another text of importance adopted at Bogotá in 1948, which concerns us more directly, was the *American Declaration on the*

Rights and Duties of Man. While it is, for the most part, on rather similar lines to the Universal Declaration of the United Nations, it is noteworthy that it was adopted on 2 May 1948, that is to say, seven months before the Universal Declaration, and that it contained ten articles setting out the duties of the individual citizen in addition to twenty-eight articles proclaiming his rights.

The ninth Inter-American Conference at Bogotá gave new life, as well as new institutions, to the Organisation of American States. The Inter-American Conference was established as the supreme policy-making organ. New councils (Economic and Social, Cultural, Juridical) got organised and started their work; the existing Council of Permanent Representatives in Washington continued as the organ of direction for current business.

A meeting of consultation of the Ministers for Foreign Affairs held at Santiago in 1959 took new initiatives regarding human rights. The Ministers adopted a 'Conclusion' containing the following statement:

That eleven years after the American Declaration of the Rights and Duties of Man was proclaimed, the climate in the hemisphere is ready for the conclusion of a Convention – there having been similar progress in the United Nations Organisation and in the union known as the Council of Europe in the setting of standards and in the orderly study of this field, until today a satisfactory and promising level has been reached.

The same conclusion charged the Inter-American Council of Jurists to prepare a draft Convention on Human Rights and a draft Convention on the creation of an Inter-American Court for the Protection of Human Rights and of other appropriate organs. It also resolved to create an Inter-American Commission on Human Rights of seven members elected as individuals by the Council of the O.A.S. from panels of three candidates presented by the governments. The Inter-American Council of Jurists met in Santiago later in the year and prepared a draft Convention, which was largely based on the European model.

This draft Convention was considered at the Second Special Inter-American Conference held in Rio de Janeiro in 1965. In fact the conference considered three drafts: that prepared by the Inter-American Council of Jurists in 1959, and two revised drafts presented by Chile and by Uruguay in order to take account of developments since 1959, particularly the European Social Charter of 1961 and the three Protocols to the European Convention of 1963. The Chilean text added a striking innovation in its Article 19, designed to prevent military *coups d'état*: the right of the electorate to be represented and governed by their legally elected representatives; the Uruguayan draft gave particular attention to economic and social rights. It was soon evident, however, that the competent committee of the Rio conference could not produce a new draft Convention during the few days at its disposal. It was therefore agreed that the three drafts should be referred to the Council of the Organisation and that the latter, after hearing the views of the Inter-American Commission on Human Rights, should produce a new draft Convention. This would then be sent to the governments for their comments; thereafter the Council would call a specialised conference to produce a final text and open it for signature.

The Rio conference also adopted its *Resolution XXII* to the effect that, pending the conclusion of the new Convention on Human Rights, the existing Commission on Human Rights should be authorised to consider individual complaints of violation of certain basic rights: the right to life and liberty, freedom of opinion and expression, the right to a fair trial, protection from arbitrary arrest, due process of law, equality before the law without discrimination and freedom of religion. The Commission would have the right, when considering such complaints, to request information from and make recommendations to governments and, in certain cases, to publish reports on the action taken.

A Third Special Inter-American Conference was held in Buenos Aires from 15 to 25 February 1967, with the object of revising the Charter of the Organisation of American States. Most of its decisions do not concern the subject matter of this book[2] but one of them related to the Inter-American Commission on Human Rights.

The Inter-American Commission, which, as we have seen, was originally created by simple resolution of the Foreign Ministers at Santiago in 1959, becomes in the amended Charter a statutory organ of the O.A.S. 'whose principal function shall be to promote the observance and protection of human rights and to serve as a consultative organ of the Organisation in these matters'. The revised Charter goes on to say that the structure, competence and procedure of the Commission will be determined in an Inter-American Convention on Human Rights; pending the conclusion of the new Convention, the existing Commission on Human Rights would discharge the functions set out in the Charter (Article 150).

In accordance with the decisions taken at Rio de Janeiro in 1965, the Council of the O.A.S. requested the Inter-American Commission on Human Rights to examine the various drafts for the proposed Convention and submit its own proposals in the matter. This was duly done. In the meantime the General Assembly of the United Nations, in December 1966, approved the text of the U.N. Covenants. The Council of the O.A.S. then consulted its member governments on the question whether they wished to go ahead with the preparation of a separate Inter-American Convention now that the U.N. Covenants had been completed. The majority of member governments replied in the affirmative. Accordingly, on 2 October 1968 the Council of the O.A.S. submitted to member governments the revised draft Convention prepared by the Inter-American Commission on Human Rights, inviting their comments. When these had been received a Specialised Conference on Human Rights was held in San José, Costa Rica, from 7 to 22 November 1969 to produce the final text and to proceed to its signature.

Nineteen of the twenty-four member States of the O.A.S. were represented at the conference, the absentees being Bolivia, Barbados, Haiti, Jamaica and, of course, Cuba. There were observers from various non-member States and from certain international organisations, including the United Nations, UNESCO, the I.L.O. and ODECA. The members of the Inter-American Commission on Human Rights also attended, and three 'special advisers' who were invited to attend the conference as expert consultants on account of their knowledge of the European Convention and of the system instituted thereby.[3]

The American Convention on Human Rights, otherwise known as 'the Pact of San José', was drafted at this conference and signed on 22 November 1969.[4] It entered into force on 18 July 1978, on the deposit of the eleventh instrument of ratification. By 31 December 1980 it had been ratified by Bolivia, Colombia, Costa Rica, Dominican Republic, Ecuador, El Salvador, Grenada, Guatemala, Haiti, Honduras, Jamaica, Nicaragua, Panama, Peru and Venezuela. Mexico acceded in March 1981.

2. The rights protected

The undertaking of the States in Article 1 of the American Convention is 'to ensure to all persons subject to their jurisdiction the free and full exercise' of the rights and freedoms recognised therein; the limitation 'within their territory' (found in the U.N.

text) is not included in the American Convention. The obligation is very similar to that contained in the U.N. Covenant, that is to say that it is intended, in principle, to be of immediate application; but Article 2 provides that contracting parties will adopt such legislative or other measures as may be necessary in cases where the rights and freedoms are not already ensured in their domestic law.

Twenty-six rights and freedoms are protected by the American Convention. Twenty-one of these are included in the U.N. Covenant on Civil and Political Rights. They are:

The right to life.
Freedom from torture and inhuman treatment.
Freedom from slavery and servitude.
The right to liberty and security.
The right to a fair trial.
Freedom from retroactivity of the criminal law.
The right to respect for private and family life.
Freedom of conscience and religion.
Freedom of thought and expression.
Freedom of assembly.
Freedom of association.
Freedom to marry and found a family.
Freedom of movement.
The right to free elections.
The right to an effective remedy if one's rights are violated.
The right to recognition as a person before the law.
The right to compensation for miscarriage of justice.
The right to a name.
The rights of the child.
The right to a nationality.
The right to equality before the law.

The five rights and freedoms included in the American Convention but not in the United Nations Covenant are:

The right of property.
Freedom from exile (though the Covenant provides in Article 12 that 'No one shall be *arbitrarily* deprived of the right to enter his own country').
Prohibition of the collective expulsion of aliens.
The right of reply.

The right of asylum.

On the other hand, the provision in the U.N. Covenant on the rights of minorities (Article 27) has no counterpart in the American Convention.

When we come to compare the provisions of the latter with those of the European Convention and its Protocols, we find that the principal rights included in the American but not in the European text are: the right of reply, the rights of the child, the rights to a name and to a nationality and the right of asylum. On the other hand, the right to education (found in the First Protocol to the European Convention) is not, as such, protected by the American text.

The definition of the rights used in the American Convention are generally closer to those of the United Nations Covenant on Civil and Political Rights than to the European Convention, though there are not a few differences, which in several cases are due to following the European model. Many articles provoked long and lively discussion at the San José conference, for example those on the right of property, on the right of asylum, on the rights of illegitimate children and on the prohibition of propaganda for war (which is included, as an exception, in the article on freedom of expression). A departure from the earlier texts is the provision in Article 4 on the right to life: 'This right shall be protected by law, and, in general, from the moment of conception', which means that, as a general rule, abortion is a violation of fundamental rights. On a number of occasions delegates maintained that it would be better to follow more closely the United Nations texts and thus avoid conflicting definitions at the regional and universal levels. Generally however, this argument was rejected, on the ground, *inter alia*, that if the American States had decided to go ahead with the conclusion of their own Convention after the U.N. Covenants had been completed, then it was appropriate to introduce any modifications that were desirable in the light of circumstances prevailing in the American republics.

Two of the most important rights guaranteed in the U.N. Covenant and in the two regional Conventions (American and European) are the right to liberty and security, including freedom from arbitrary arrest, and the right to a fair trial. The draft Convention submitted to the San José conference contained texts defining these rights which were less satisfactory in affording protection than Articles 9 and 14 of the U.N. Covenant and Articles 5 and 6 of the European Convention. The 'special advisers' drew attention to these differences, and the conference agreed to change the texts in the American Convention. As a result, Article 7 (5) now provides that 'any detained person shall be brought promptly before a judge . . . and shall be entitled to trial within a reasonable time, etc.'. In Article 8, on the right to a fair trial, the text submitted to the conference provided for 'a fair hearing' without further definition. The conference agreed to a proposal to strengthen this very important provision by adding the words 'by a competent, independent and impartial tribunal established by law' (taken from the U.N. Covenant) and also the words 'within a reasonable time' (taken from the European Convention).[5]

The question was discussed whether the American Convention should also include economic, social and cultural rights. Now the Charter of the Organization of American States, as amended by the Protocol of Buenos Aires, contains separate chapters on economic standards, on social standards and on educational, scientific and cultural standards; it also set up an Inter-American Economic and Social Council and an Inter-American Council for Education, Science and Culture. These councils have the task of promoting the achievement of the standards set out in the Charter and may make recommendations to the governments for the purpose; moreover, the governments will send in to them annual reports. Consequently, it was decided not to set out in detail a number of economic, social and cultural rights (as in the first U.N. Covenant and in the European Social Charter), but to include in the American Convention (Article 26) a general undertaking by States to take appropriate measures, by legislation and otherwise, to secure the rights resulting from the standards set out in the Charter; also (Article 42) a requirement that the governments would send to the Inter-American Commission on Human Rights copies of their annual reports on these matters, in order that the Commission should consider whether they are effectively promoting the rights resulting from their obligations under the Charter.

3. The system of international control

The American Convention on Human Rights provides, like the European Convention, for two organs of control: a Commission and a Court. But there are important differences in the composition, functions and powers of the organs established under the two regional systems, to which we will revert in the last section of this chapter.

One problem which faced those who drafted the American Convention was that when they came to define the composition, functions and powers of the Inter-American Commission on Human Rights, they were not creating a new organ but conferring new functions and powers on an existing body. As we have seen in the first section of this chapter, the Inter-American Commission had been created ten years earlier by Resolution VIII of the meeting of consultation of the Ministers for Foreign Affairs at Santiago in 1959 – mainly as a promotional organ; it was granted limited powers to consider individual petitions or complaints at the Rio conference in 1965; and in 1967 the conference in Buenos Aires on the revision of the Charter had transformed it into one of the statutory organs of the Organisation of American States, indicating that its structure and competence would be determined by the new Convention, which was already projected.

One result of this evolution was that the Convention drafted in 1969 was able to confer new functions and powers on the existing Inter-American Commission, but these new provisions would apply only in relation to States which ratified the new Convention. It was therefore necessary to provide in addition that the existing functions and powers of the Commission would remain and continue to be exercised in relation to States which did not ratify the new Convention. In other words, the Inter-American Commission would have a double mandate: that resulting from the Convention in relation to States parties to the Convention; and that resulting from the earlier decisions of 1959, 1965 and 1967 in relation to all members of the Organisation of American States, whether or not they ratified the Convention.

This was in fact what happened. And since the American Convention on Human Rights entered into force only on 18 July 1978, and it was necessary for some time to elapse before its new functions provided for in the Convention could be effectively exercised, almost all the work of the Commission during the first twenty years of its existence was in the discharge of its 'old functions'. It is therefore appropriate to indicate briefly what have been the activities of the Commission independently of the Convention.[6]

(a) The 'old functions' of the Inter-American Commission

After its creation in 1959 the Inter-American Commission elaborated a Statute which was approved by the O.A.S. Council in 1960. Under this Statute the Commission had power to examine the situation of human rights in the O.A.S. member States where flagrant and repeated violations were occurring; to request

s concerned and, if

it their territory; to

was obtained; to make

ble and to prepare

to take decisions on

ights, but it could take

rmation on the state of

nplaints of violation of

s conferred on the

io conference in 1965,

ngly. The new text

munications submitted

, to request pertinent

make appropriate

activities to the Inter-

at the result of these

nd reports, but not to

the Inter-American

of human rights in a

republics, sometimes

and evidence obtained

es its examination has

of witnesses, who may

ives and individual

estigations have been

.

ries of reports on the

d in 1962, 1963, 1967,

1970, 1970 and 1979. The Cuban government did not co-operate with the Commission when it was preparing these studies. A particularly striking case of visits on the spot, on the other hand, concerned the Dominican Republic, during the civil war in that country in 1965. Members of the Commission spent several months there and were able to intervene successfully on behalf of detained persons, and secure the release of prisoners on both sides and the observance of other humanitarian measures.[9] Another sort of humanitarian mission was undertaken by the Commission in 1980, when about twenty diplomats attending a reception at the Dominican embassy in Bogotá were held as hostages by a group of terrorists; as the result of an agreement negotiated with the government of Colombia, the Inter-American Commission supervised the release of the hostages and the evacuation of the terrorists and also undertook to monitor the trials of certain political prisoners.

Other 'country reports' produced by the Inter-American Commission in recent years concern the situation of human rights in Haiti (1980 – after a visit in 1978); Uruguay (1977); Chile (there were annual reports or special chapters in the annual report of the Commission dealing with the situation of human rights in Chile from 1974 to 1980, one resulting from a visit *in loco* in 1974); Panama (1978, after a visit during the previous year); Nicaragua (visit and report in 1978); El Salvador (visit in 1978, report in 1979); and Argentina (visit in 1979 followed by a report in 1980). In all these countries serious violations were established.[10]

A major crisis developed in the Organisation of American States over the Commission's report on Argentina. It was considered by the General Assembly of the O.A.S., meeting in Washington from 19 to 27 November 1980. The report was highly critical of the Argentine government and the United States proposed a resolution condemning the violations of human rights in that country. Argentina threatened to leave the Organisation if this was adopted, being supported by Bolivia, Chile, Paraguay and Uruguay. There was on the agenda of the conference not only the special report on Argentina, but also the annual report of the Commission, which recounted serious violations of human rights in Chile, El Salvador, Paraguay and Uruguay. Finally the conference adopted a resolution in which it took note of the reports and made a general condemnation of countries which violated human rights but without naming any of them specifically.[11] At the same time, several countries, including Mexico, Venezuela, Colombia, Ecuador and Peru, expressed their support for the Inter-American Commission and the conference requested it to undertake an investigation on the situation of human rights in Bolivia.

As regards the complaints which it receives from individuals and groups of individuals, the Commission is evidently struggling with an uphill – some would say an impossible – task. This is partly due to the number of complaints received; for example, it opened more than a thousand case files in 1978.[12] And the Commission holds only two regular sessions a year, totalling not more than eight weeks, though there is usually one additional or extraordinary session. Moreover it has only seven members, all with other professional occupations, to cope with the volume of work. An even greater obstacle is the lack of effective co-operation from the governments concerned; in the great majority of cases they reply to the Commission's enquiries with a minimum of information and are evidently seeking to cover up rather than investigate the violations brought to their attention.

In these circumstances the Commission has adopted a rule the effect of which is that, once a communication has been declared admissible, the facts alleged will be presumed to be confirmed if the government concerned has not adduced satisfactory evidence in rebuttal.[13] It is on the basis of this presumption, which is eminently reasonable in the circumstances, that the majority of the decisions of the Commission are reached on individual complaints.

The results of this work can be seen in the annual reports of the Commission to the General Assembly of the Organisation of American States. As one example, about half the annual report for 1978 was devoted to the consideration of individual complaints. Out of more than a thousand complaints received, the Commission reported in detail on thirty-seven cases: five concerning Argentina, ten concerning Bolivia, twenty concerning Chile and one each concerning Panama and Uruguay. They give a depressing account of arbitrary arrest, detention without trial, interrogation accompanied by torture, exile without judicial process and similar violations. Co-operation of governments in investigating the complaints was minimal. In all cases except one, serious violations were established.[14]

From this brief summary two conclusions may be drawn. First, that almost all the work of the Commission in the past – and, no doubt, a considerable part of its work in the future – results from its 'old functions' which antedate the entry into force of the American Convention on Human Rights in 1978. The Permanent Council of the Organisation recognised this in a resolution of 20 September 1978, which decided that the Commission should continue to apply its existing Statute and Regulations without change to those member States which are not parties to the Convention, and should apply any new Statute and Regulations that might be approved only to States that have ratified the Convention.[15] Matters were taken a stage further at the ninth regular session of the General Assembly of the Organisation of American States in October 1979, when a new Statute of the Commission was approved. This contained three separate articles on the functions and powers of the Commision. Article 18 deals with its powers with respect to all members of the O.A.S., which are mainly promotional, while Article 19 deals with its powers in relation to States which have ratified the Convention; these concern principally its action on petitions and communications under the terms of the Convention and its relations with the Inter-American Court of Human Rights. Article 20 then sets out its powers in relation to States which have not yet ratified the Convention and authorises the Commission to continue to act in accordance with the old procedures.[16]

The second conclusion one must draw arises from a comparison of the work of the Inter-American Commission on Human Rights with that of the European Commission of Human Rights described in the previous chapter. One cannot help being struck by the fact that they are immeasurably different. The two Commissions operate in quite different circumstances, one might almost say at quite different levels. The European Commission has – with very rare exceptions, such as the Greek case – been concerned with what might be called the finer points of human rights law – such questions as what is a reasonable time in detention pending trial, what is the precise content of the right to a fair trial (when the fundamental principle is not in doubt), what limitations may be placed in the public interest on freedom of expression, what are the implications of the right of freedom of association, and so on. And in dealing with such problems the European Commission had had (with very rare exceptions) the full co-operation of the governments concerned and the full support of the organisation of which it forms a part. The Inter-American Commission, on the other hand, has had to deal with problems of a different order: arbitrary arrests on a massive scale, systematic use of torture, scores or hundreds of 'disappeared persons', total absence of judicial remedies, and other flagrant violations. And in dealing with such cases it has found the governments concerned more in the role of antagonists than willing partners, while at the General Assembly of the O.A.S. the lip service paid to its work, and the genuine support of some governments, have not prevented others from criticising it violently.

When, therefore, we are studying the development of international techniques for the protection of human rights, we must remember that the problems confronting the Inter-American Commission are far graver than those in Western Europe and we must pay tribute to the efforts of the Commission to expose the serious violations which occur and seek to find a remedy for the victims.

(b) The 'new functions' of the Inter-American Commission

First, a few words about the organisation of the Commission (Articles 34 to 40 of the American Convention on Human Rights).

It was decided to keep the number of members at seven, as in the original decision of 1959. They must be persons of high moral character and recognised competence in the field of human rights (Article 34). A proposal was made at the San José conference that the General Assembly of the O.A.S. should have the power to enlarge the membership of the Commission should this prove desirable (e.g. on account of the volume of work, particularly if the members of the Commission have other professional occupations). The proposal was rejected, however, apparently through a fear that the possibility of such action by a political body might affect the independence of the Commission. The fact remains, however, that the burden of work falling on the seven members of the Commission is excessive.

The Commission represents all the member countries of the Organisation of American States (Article 35). The members of the Commission sit in a personal capacity (Article 36); this is an important provision which protects their independence.

There was a long discussion during the drafting of the Convention as to whether all member States of the Organisation or only contracting parties should have the right (a) to propose candidates, (b) to elect members, (c) to have their nationals sit as members of the Commission. On the one hand, it was argued that if only a limited number of member States ratify the Convention, then it is only they who should decide on the membership of the organ whose full jurisdiction only they accept. On the other hand, it was pointed out that the Commission is an organ of the O.A.S. as a whole (as a result of the Protocol of Buenos Aires) and that, consequently, all member States should participate in the election and be able to have their nationals sit as members. It was the second argument which prevailed. As a result, all member States may propose candidates and vote in the election by the General Assembly of the O.A.S. They may propose up to three candidates; an unusual provision is that, in that event, at least one must be of another nationality.

The term of office of members of the Commission is for four years; they may be re-elected, but only once (Article 37). The necessary secretariat services are to be furnished by a specialised unit in the General Secretariat of the O.A.S. (Article 40).

The first election under the terms of the Convention took place at the ninth regular session of the General Assembly of the O.A.S. in October 1979.[17]

Articles 41–3 of the Convention relate to the functions of the Commission. They repeat the 'old functions' of a promotional character conferred on the original Commission in 1959, which include the making of recommendations to member governments and requesting information from member governments on human rights matters, and the submission of an annual report to the General Assembly (Article 41). There is provision for the examination by the Commission of governments' reports on compliance with the economic, social and cultural standards established by the O.A.S. Charter (Article 42) and an undertaking by States parties to provide the Commission with information which it may request as to the manner in which their domestic law complies with the Convention (Article 43).

The new functions of the Commission are set out in Articles 44–7. It will have competence (comparable to that in Article 25 of the European Convention) to consider petitions from individuals, groups of individuals or non-governmental organisations alleging violation of the Convention by States parties (Article 44). But – by contrast with Article 25 of the European Convention – acceptance of this competence is not optional but obligatory. This difference represents problably the most important advance enshrined in the American Convention.

This was not achieved without much discussion. When the article was under examination in Commission II of the San José conference, Argentina proposed that the right of individual petition should be made optional and was supported by the delegate from Panama (who quoted the European Convention) and those from Nicaragua and the Dominican Republic. Chile, supported by Uruguay, the United States and others, and followed by Mexico, argued in favour of an obligatory provision on the right of individual petition. This view was accepted in the Commission by ten votes to none, with five abstentions, and subsequently in the plenary meeting.

Article 45 then deals with inter-State complaints. The working party of Commission II recommended, by a majority, that this should also be made an obligatory procedure. But in the plenary Commission Argentina and Mexico opposed it, supported by Nicaragua, while Brazil, Panama, Paraguay and the Dominican Republic abstained, with the result that the proposal was not carried. As a result, the procedure for inter-State complaints is optional. A declaration accepting this competence of the Commission may be made at any time and may be for a limited or unlimited period of time. A suggestion was made that it should also be possible for a State to make such a declaration accepting the competence of the Commission *ad hoc* for a particular case; this was accepted.

It will thus appear that the American Convention is, as regards the competence of the Commission, just the opposite of the European Convention. Acceptance of the right of individual petition follows automatically from ratification, whereas the procedure for inter-State complaints is optional. This is undoubtedly a major advance in establishing an effective system of international control, once it is recognised that a compulsory system of inter-State complaints would be politically dangerous in the Latin American context.

The rules on admissibility (Articles 46 and 47) are generally similar to those contained in the European Convention. They include the requirement of exhaustion of domestic remedies and require that the petition should be filed within six months of the notification of the final domestic decision. In order to take account of the problem whether an applicant may bring his case successively before the U.N. Committee and the regional commission, the suggestion was made that a petition should be declared inadmissible if it had at an earlier stage been submitted to another procedure of international settlement. This was accepted and incorporated into Article 47(d) of the final text.

The Commission has as its first task (once it has declared a case admissible) to establish the facts. It may undertake an investigation, for the effective conduct of which the States concerned will furnish all necessary facilities (Article 48 (1)(d). An urgent procedure for emergency cases is set out in Article 48 (2).

The Commission then has the task of trying to bring about a friendly settlement. The procedure (Article 48 (1) (f) and 49) is broadly similar to that under the European Convention. If no friendly settlement is achieved, the Commission is required to draw up a report setting out the facts and stating its conclusions; it may make such proposals and recommendations as it thinks fit (Article 50).

There was much discussion as to what should happen at the next stage. The draft submitted to the conference proposed that, if the case was not submitted to the Court within a period of three months, the Commission should take a final decision on the question of violation. This, however, did not meet with general agreement, on the ground that many States were not willing to confer on the Commission such extensive powers. Consequently the article was redrafted so as to provide that if, within a period of three months, the matter is not settled or submitted to the Court, then the Commission may, by an absolute majority of its members, 'set forth its opinion and conclusions concerning the question submitted for its consideration'. It may also 'make pertinent recommendations' and fix a period of time within which the State concerned is to take the measures incumbent on it to remedy the situation. At the expiry of that period the Commission will decide whether the State has taken adequate measures, and whether to publish its report (Article 51).

This was, no doubt – politically speaking – a wise compromise. Legally speaking, however, it must be noted that the American Convention does not provide for a definite *decision* on the question of violation if a case does not go to the Court; nevertheless, it does go a good deal further than the U.N. Covenant in this respect. Indeed, if the Commission gives as its opinion that a State has violated the Convention and sets a period of time within which remedial measures should be taken, and subsequently decides that adequate measures have not been taken and publishes its report giving the reasons for its action, this is practically tantamount to a formal decision of violation.

(c) The Inter-American Court of Human Rights The draft Convention submitted to the San José conference included provision for the creation of an Inter-American Court of Human Rights, which would have power to take a final decision on an alleged violation of the Convention if the contracting party concerned should decide to refer the case to the Court after the Commission has examined the matter and expressed its opinion. The jurisdiction of the Court, however, would be optional.

During the conference there was first of all a general discussion of the question whether it was desirable to set up a Court of Human Rights in the American framework. The representative of Mexico considered that it would be premature, and stated that his government could not agree that such a body should be in a position to pass judgement on the legality of the acts of a State; he would therefore prefer that the Court should be omitted from the Convention altogether. A number of delegations, however, thought that it was indispensable to include provision for the Court (Costa Rica, Colombia, Ecuador, Guatemala, Salvador, Honduras, Venezuela and Uruguay), the representative of Chile pointing out that this would be the logical culmination in 1969 of the process which had begun in 1948 with the proclamation of the American Declaration of the Rights and Duties of Man, and continued with the establishment of the Inter-American Commission on Human Rights in 1959. The United States also favoured the creation of the Court and pointed out that, if its jurisdiction was optional, this would create no problems for States which were unwilling to accept it. At the conclusion of the general discussion, it was agreed to establish an Inter-American Court of Human Rights with optional jurisdiction.

The Court consists of seven judges, elected in an individual capacity from among jurists of the highest moral authority and recognised competence, possessing the qualifications required for the highest judicial office (Article 52). By contrast with the procedure for the election of the members of the Commission, only the contracting parties to the Convention may propose candidates and take part in the election; but candidates may be of the nationality of any member State of the O.A.S., and the lists of three candidates to be proposed by the parties must include at least one candidate who is not of the nationality of the proposing State (Article 53).

The right to participate in the election of the judges is not limited to States which have accepted the compulsory jurisdiction of the Court. Moreover, there is no provision (as in the European Convention) requiring a stated number of acceptances of the jurisdiction of the Court before the first election of the judges can take place. As a result, it was possible to set in motion the procedure for the constitution of the Court shortly after the entry into force of the Convention in 1978. In fact the election took place in the course of the meeting of the General Assembly of the O.A.S. on 22 May 1979.[18]

The judges are elected for a term of six years, and may be re-elected, but only once (Article 54). Article 58 left the choice of the seat of the Court to be determined by the General Assembly of the O.A.S. In July 1978, when it was known that the entry into force of the Convention was imminent, the General Assembly recommended that the seat should be established in Costa Rica.[19] This was subsequently confirmed by the States parties in November 1978 and was a tribute to the fact that that country had acted as host to the conference which had drafted the Convention in 1969, was the first State to ratify the Convention (on 8 April 1970) and the first to accept the compulsory jurisdiction of the Court. It also recalled that Costa Rica was the seat of the Central American Court of Justice established in 1907.

Article 55 deals with the question of the 'national judge', i.e. whether a judge who is a national of a State party to a case which comes before the Court should have the right to sit and act as judge in a case in which his own country is involved; this question involves as a corollary that, if there is no 'national judge', then the State in question may appoint an *ad hoc* judge. This is the system adopted by the International Court of Justice and the European Court of Human Rights. The Inter-American Commission on Human Rights had proposed in its draft Convention that a judge who is the national of a State party to a dispute should stand down and not participate in the proceedings; the representative of Brazil argued that this was a more liberal system than that of national judges and *ad hoc* judges, and that it was more likely to secure impartiality in the composition of the Court. This view, however, did not prevail. The final text therefore follows the traditional system of national judges and *ad hoc* judges (Article 55).

After explanations had been given by the 'special advisers' about the role of the European Commission in the proceedings of the European Court of Human Rights, an article was included in the American Convention providing that 'the Commission shall appear in all cases before the Court' (Article 57).

The Court appoints its own secretary (Article 58). Article 59 provides that the Court shall establish its own secretariat, which shall function under the direction of the Secretary of the Court, but in accordance with the administrative regulations of the General Secretariat of the O.A.S. to the extent that they are not incompatible with the independence of the Court. The care taken to ensure such independence is manifest.

(d) The competence of the Court Only States parties and the Commission may submit cases to the Court (Article 61). Consideration was given to the idea of allowing an individual applicant to refer his case to the Court if he was dissatisfied with the opinion of the Commission, and the precedent of the Central American Court of 1907 was cited. But the system established by the European Convention was adduced in the contrary sense, and several delegates stated that their governments would be unwilling to accept the right of individuals to seize the Court. A proposal to that effect was then rejected by a majority vote.

Under Article 62 of the Convention, contracting parties may declare that they accept the jurisdiction of the Court unconditionally or on condition of reciprocity, for an indefinite or for a limited period of time.[20] The suggestion was made, and accepted, that this should also be possible *ad hoc*; the words 'or for specific cases' were then added.

The delegate of Costa Rica proposed the insertion of an article authorising the Court to order interim measures 'in cases of extreme seriousness and urgency, and when it is necessary to avoid irreparable damage . . .'. This was accepted as paragraph 1 of Article 63.

The Inter-American Court of Human Rights possesses very wide powers, which are considerably greater than those of the European Court. If it finds that there has been a violation, it may order that the injured party be reinstated in his rights, and it may also, if appropriate, order that the consequences of a violation should be remedied and that damages should be paid (Article 63). Moreover, the contracting parties undertake to abide by the judgment of the Court, and an order for damages will be directly enforceable in the State concerned (Article 68). This last provision recalls Articles 187 and 192 of the Treaty of Rome, 1957, establishing the European Economic Community.

One may ask, is there any ultimate sanction if a State refuses to comply with a judgment of the Court? Though there is not, and perhaps cannot be, any really compelling sanction, there is provision whereby the Inter-American Court is required to submit an annual report to the General Assembly of the O.A.S., indicating, in particular, cases in which a State has not complied with its judgments and making 'the pertinent recommendations' (Article 65). Though the making of an annual report is an unusual procedure for a judicial body, and though it may not always be easy for the Court to know whether a State has effectively complied with the judgment, Article 65 of the Convention was introduced in order to provide some form of sanction; the reporting of a State for non-compliance to the General Assembly, which will be attended by several hundred delegates and widely publicised, is undoubtedly a procedure which most governments would prefer to avoid.

Article 64 of the Convention confers on the Inter-American Court of Human Rights wide powers to give advisory opinions. Requests for advisory opinions may relate not only to the American Convention on Human Rights, but also to other treaties concerning the protection of human rights in the American States. All the organs of the O.A.S. listed in Chapter X of the Charter (as amended by the Protocol of Buenos Aires) may consult the Court on matters within their competence.[21] In addition, any member State of the O.A.S. may request and receive an opinion on the compatibility of any of its domestic laws with the American Convention on Human Rights or any other treaty relating to human rights in the American States. It is significant, moreover, that the right to request advisory opinions is not limited to contracting parties to the American Convention. The suggestion was made, and accepted, that this right should be given to all member States of the Organisation; it was thought that this procedure would be useful, *inter alia*, in permitting a State which is thinking of ratifying the Convention, but uncertain of the compatibility therewith of one of its domestic laws, to obtain an authoritative opinion in advance and then, if necessary, amend the law in question.

4. Other provisions of the Convention

Article 70 provides for the privileges and immunities of members of the Commission and the Court. Throughout their term of office they enjoy the immunities extended to diplomatic agents. In the first draft their immunities were limited to the period during which they hold office; however, if it was pointed out that the immunity accorded to judges and members of the Commission as regards the contents of their judgments and opinions should be absolute, if they are to be able to act with the necessary independence. This view was generally accepted, and a second sentence was added to Article 70 to this effect.

Article 72 of the Convention deals with the budget of the Commission and the Court. It provides that the conditions under which the emoluments and expenses of the members are to be paid are to be set forth in the respective Statutes of the two organs. The Statute of the Commission (Article 13) provides for expenses and fees; that of the Court (Article 17) for salaries and expenses. The actual amounts – as well as the general expenses of the Court and of the Commission – are to be fixed each year in the budget of the Organisation. The draft budget of the Court is to be drawn up by the Court itself and submitted to the General Assembly of the O.A.S. by the Secretary-General, but the latter has no power to amend it; this is in order to protect the independence of the Court *vis-à-vis* the Secretariat of the O.A.S. – a concern that was also manifested, as we have seen, when the provisions about the Secretary of the Court (Article 58) and about its Secretariat (Article 59) were drafted.

Article 73 of the Convention is a provision of a very unusual nature. It relates to 'sanctions to be applied to the members of the Commission and the Court'. A provision was introduced by the representative of Argentina to the effect that the General Assembly of the O.A.S. could pronounce sanctions against members of those bodies for reasons which would be set out in their respective Statutes. This proposal caused some concern, because it could seriously prejudice the principle of independence of the judiciary. A revised version was subsequently adopted which admits the possibility of sanctions, but only on the proposal of the Commission or the Court themselves.

Article 74 relates to ratification. The draft submitted to the conference provided that the Convention would enter into force when ratified by seven States. There was a general feeling that this number was too low, and finally the number was fixed at eleven. As stated in the first section of this chapter (where the names of the ratifying states are given) this number was achieved on 18 July 1978.

The question of reservations is dealt with by Article 75. During the negotiations some delegations argued that reservations should be permitted only in respect of constitutional provisions which are in conflict with the provisions of the Convention, because if a State were permitted to make a reservation whenever a provision of its domestic law was inconsistent with the Convention, the number of reservations would be excessive; it would be preferable that a State should amend its law before ratifying. On the other hand, it was argued that too rigid an attitude in this respect would make ratifications at least more difficult, and probably slower, and might even prevent the entry into force of the Convention. The former point of view gained majority support in Commission II, but was not accepted by the plenary conference; agreement was finally reached on a proposal of Uruguay which permits reservations 'in conformity with the provisions of the Vienna Convention on the Law of Treaties signed on 23 May 1969'. In fact it seems that the fears of some delegations were rather exaggerated. Of the fifteen States which had ratified the Convention by 1980, only three had made reservations (El Salvador, Guatemala and Venezuela).

5. Comparison with the U.N. Covenant and the European Convention

In Section 2 of this chapter we indicated the similarities and differences in the rights protected in the American Convention, the U.N. Covenant on Civil and Political Rights and the European Convention. We may therefore conclude with a brief comparison of the different systems of international control.

In the first place, this concerns the U.N. Human Rights Committee and the two regional Commissions. Attention has already been drawn to some of the differences between them. We may perhaps summarise the position as follows.

(a) Membership and election; sessions The Inter-American Commission has only seven members (Article 34). It is an organ of, and represents all the member countries of, the O.A.S. (Article 35; cf. Articles 112 and 150 of the Charter of the O.A.S. as amended at Buenos Aires in 1967). It is elected by the General Assembly of the O.A.S. (Article 36).

The U.N. Committee consists of eighteen members (Article 28 of the Covenant). It is elected by the States parties (Article 30) and has competence only in relation to the States parties. It is not an organ of the United Nations.

The European Commission has a number of members equal to

the number of the High Contracting Parties (Article 20 of the European Convention). This means that at present there are twenty members. They are elected by the Committee of Ministers of the Council of Europe (Article 21). The functions of the Commission extend only to the contracting parties.

In all three cases the members serve in a personal capacity (Articles 36, 28 and 23 respectively).

In the case of the Inter-American Commission, one may wonder whether a Commission of only seven members is big enough to fulfil the functions imposed on it by the Convention, particularly as the number of individual applications increases, as it probably will.

All three bodies meet intermittently: the U.N. Committee usually holds three sessions a year, the Inter-American Commission two regular and often one additional session, the European Commission usually five plenary sessions a year. It may well be that in all three cases the need will be felt for more frequent sessions, in order to cope with the volume of work.

But then another problem arises. The great majority of the members of these bodies have other professional occupations and may not be able to devote more time to serve on the international organs. Is there a case for full-time membership on a salaried basis? Are the organisations concerned prepared to accept the consequential budgetary implications? These questions pose real problems, but it will be necessary to face them before long.

(b) Competence of the three organs

(i) *Reporting procedures* This is the principal function of the U.N. Committee (Article 40). States parties to the American Convention report to the Inter-American Commission only in reply to a specific request for information (Article 41(d) and Article 43) except as regards economic, social and cultural rights, with regard to which there is an obligation to send to the Commission copies of the annual reports sent to the Inter-American Economic and Social Council and the Inter-American Council for Education, Science and Culture (Article 42).

Under the European Convention there is no automatic requirement of submitting reports to the Commission, but only, on request, to the Secretary-General of the Council of Europe (Article 57).

(ii) *Inter-State communications* This is an optional procedure in both the Inter-American and the U.N. systems (Article 45 of the American Convention; Article 41 of the U.N. Covenant). It contrasts with the procedure under the European Convention, according to which all contracting parties accept the jurisdiction of the European Commission to consider any breach of the Convention alleged by another contracting party (Article 24 of the European Convention).

The Inter-American Commission (Article 48), the U.N. Committee (Article 41) and the European Commission (Article 28) all have the task of trying to achieve a friendly settlement. If this fails, the Inter-American Commission draws up a report stating the facts and its conclusions, proposals and recommendations (Article 50). The European procedure is broadly similar (Article 31). The U.N. Committee must confine itself to a brief statement of the facts (Article 41, paragraph h).

The European procedure leads to a binding decision by the Committee of Ministers or the European Court of Human Rights, on the basis of the report of the Commission.

One should also note the procedure under the U.N. Covenant (Article 42) for the appointment of an *ad hoc* Conciliation Commission for inter-State disputes, if both parties agree. This has no counterpart in the two regional Conventions.

(iii) Individual communications The biggest advance made by the American Convention on Human Rights is that acceptance of the procedure for individual petitions to the Inter-American Commission follows automatically from ratification of the Convention (Article 44). In other words, acceptance of this procedure is not optional but obligatory.

This contrasts with the procedure under the European Convention, whereby acceptance of the right of individual petition is optional (Article 25). By 1 November 1981 sixteen out of twenty contracting parties had accepted this optional provision.

The U.N. Covenant on Civil and Political Rights contains no provision authorising the U.N. Committee to consider individual communications. Instead, this procedure is enshrined in an Optional Protocol. By 1 January 1981 twenty-five States had ratified the Optional Protocol, out of sixty-five which had ratified the Covenant.

All three instruments contain detailed rules about exhaustion of domestic remedies and other conditions of admissibility (American

Convention, Articles 46 and 47; U.N. Optional Protocol, Articles 3 and 5; European Convention, Articles 26 and 27).

The Inter-American Commission has power to carry out an investigation on the spot, for the purpose of which 'it shall request, and the States concerned shall furnish to it, all necessary facilities' (Articles 48, paragraph 2(d)). The U.N. Committee has no such power. The European Commission can carry out, if necessary, an investigation 'for the effective conduct of which the States concerned shall furnish all necessary facilities, after an exchange of views with the Commission' (Article 28(a)).

The conclusions of the three bodies after they have examined individual communications or petitions take the same form as when they have dealt with inter-State communications, as explained above.

When one comes to consider the judicial organs invested with responsibility in human rights matters the possibility of comparison is limited to the two regional Courts, because the U.N. Covenant on Civil and Political Rights does not include provision for any judicial organ.

We may summarise the points which arise in the comparison of the two Courts in the following propositions:

1. As regards the size of the Courts, i.e. the number of judges, there is a big difference: seven judges on the Inter-American Court (Article 52) and twenty-one on the European Court (Article 38), though the European Court often hears cases in a chamber of seven judges.

2. The European Court was only established six years after the entry into force of the European Convention, i.e. after eight States had accepted its jurisdiction as compulsory (Article 56). Since there is no comparable provision in the American Convention, the Inter-American Court was set up shortly after the Convention entered into force.

3. The jurisdiction of both courts is optional and extends only to States which have expressly declared that they accept it (Articles 62 and 46). They may do so for a limited or unlimited period of time, on condition of reciprocity, or on an *ad hoc* basis.

4. In both cases, only States and the Commission may refer a case to the court – not individual applicants (Articles 61 and 48).

5. As regards the effect of their judgment the Inter-American Court (Article 63) has considerably wider powers than the European Court (Article 50), but the procedure of supervision of

the judgements of the European Court by the Committee of Ministers (Article 54) is valuable and likely to be more effective than that of annual reports by the Inter-American Court to the O.A.S. General Assembly (Article 65).

6. The power of the Inter-American Court to order 'provisional measures' (Article 63, paragraph 2) is valuable and has no counterpart in the European Convention.

7. The powers of the Inter-American Court to give advisory opinions (Article 64) are much wider than those conferred on the European Court by the Second Protocol to the European Convention.

NOTES

1   The development of the Organisation of American States is described more fully in the first edition of this book at pp. 111–21.
2   They are summarised in A. H. Robertson, 'Revision of the Charter of the O.A.S.', *I.C.L.Q.* (1968), pp. 346–62.
3   The three 'special advisers' were M. René Cassin, President of the European Court of Human Rights, Professor Balladore-Pallieri, judge on the European Court and subsequently its President, and the author of this book.
4   The text of the American Convention on Human Rights may be found in many collections and publications, including the following: *O.A.S. Handbook of existing Rules pertaining to Human Rights*, 1979, pp. 48–74; *United Nations Yearbook on Human Rights*, 1969, p. 390; *Council of Europe: Human Rights in International Law – Basic Texts*, 1979, pp. 65–91; the first edition of this book, pp. 249–73.
5   An unfortunate change was made, on the proposal of the U.S. delegation, in para. 2 of Article 8. This was to limit the presumption of innocence in criminal proceedings so that it applies only to persons 'accused of a serious crime'. This, however, is less serious than might at first appear, because the Spanish text (which will be used by the great majority of the contracting parties) uses the same words as Article 14 (2) of the U.N. Covenant: 'toda persona inculpada de delito . . .'. For a comparison of the rights protected by the two regional instruments see: J. Frowein, 'The European and American Conventions – a comparison' *Human Rights Law Journal*, 1980, pp. 44–65.
6   See also D. V. Sandifer, 'Human rights in the inter-American system', *Harvard Law Journal* (spring 1965), pp. 508–26; L. Ronald Scheman, 'The Inter-American Commission on Human Rights', 59 *A.J.I.L.* (1965), pp. 335–44; P. Pablo Camargo, 'The protection of human rights in America', *Proceedings of the Washington Conference*

on World Peace through Law, 1965; José A. Cabranes, 'Human rights and non-intervention in the inter-American system', *Michigan Law Review* 1967, pp. 1147–82; K. Vasak, *La Commission Interaméricaine des Droits de l'Homme*, Paris, 1968; Carlos Garcia-Bauer, 'Protection of human rights in America' in *Mélanges Cassin*, 1970, I, p. 75; Anna Schreiber, *The Inter-American Commission on Human Rights*, Leyden, 1970; L. J. Leblanc, *The O.A.S. and the Promotion and Protection of Human Rights*, The Hague, 1977. On the American Convention in general see P. P. Camargo, 'The American Convention on Human Rights', *Human Rights Journal*, III 1970, pp. 333–56.

7 *O.A.S.: Handbook of Existing Rules pertaining to Human Rights*, Washington, D.C., 1979, pp. 11–12.

8 *Ibid.*, pp. 13–15.

9 Carlos Dunshee de Abranches, 'A special protection of human rights in the Dominican Republic', *Proceedings of the Washington Conference, op. cit.* n. 6; Manuel Bianchi, *Mision cumplida – La Comision de Derechos Humanos en la Republica Dominicana*, Santiago de Chile, 1967; K. Vasak, *op. cit.* n. 6, chapter VIII.

10 The conclusions of the Inter-American Commission were also communicated to the Commission on Human Rights of the United Nations under the procedure established by ECOSOC Resolution 1159 (XLI) of 1967 – see, for example, doc. E/CN.4/1333/Add. 1 of 15 February 1979. On the practice of the Inter-American Commission see Robert E. Norris 'Observations *in loco*: practice and procedure of the I.A.C.H.R.', 15 *Texas International Law Journal*, 1980, pp. 46–95.

11 General Assembly of the O.A.S., Tenth Regular Session, AG/doc. 1348/80 of 27 November 1980.

12 At its forty-sixth session (March 1979) the Commission was seized of 425 new cases, involving 643 victims from sixteen countries. At its forty-eighth session (December 1979), 171 new cases, in addition to 4,153 new complaints which it had received during its 'on-site observation' in Argentina in September that year.

13 *Regulations of the Inter-American Commission*, Article 51, in *Handbook of Existing Rules* (cited *supra*, n. 7), p. 37.

14 *Annual Report of the I.A.C.H.R. for 1978*, Washington, D.C., 1979, pp. 28–109. The one exception concerned Panama. The report of the Commission for 1979–1980 recounts the proceedings in eleven cases in which the Commission found violations, nine concerning Argentina and two concerning Panama.

15 Resolution of 20 September 1978 (OEA/Ser.G/CP/Res. 253/78).

16 OEA/Ser.P/AG/doc. 1180 of 31 October 1979.

17 The following were elected members of the Commission: Andrés Aguilar (Venezuela), Luis Tinoco Castro (Costa Rica), Marco Gerardo Monroy (Colombia), Carlos Dunshee de Abranches (Brazil), Tom J. Farer (U.S.A.), Francisco Bertrand Galindo (El Salvador) and César Sepúlveda (Mexico). In December 1979 Dr Tinoco Castro was elected President and Professor Tom Farrer Vice-

President. In 1980 Professor Tom Farrer was elected President.

18   The following were elected members of the Court: Rodolfo Piza Escalante (Costa Rica) President 1979–1981; Máximo Cisneros Sánchez (Peru) Vice-president 1979–1981; M. Rafael Urquía (El Salvador); Huntley Eugene Munroe (Jamaica); César Ordóñez Quintero (Colombia); Carlos Roberto Reina (Honduras) elected President in 1981; Thomas Buergenthal (United States). Pedro A. Nikken (Venezuela) was elected to the Court at the Ninth Regular Session of the General Assembly to replace Dr Urquía who had not accepted the judgeship. Dr Nikken was elected Vice-President in 1981.

19   Resolution AG/Res. 372 (VIII–0/78) of 1 July 1978.

20   By April 1981 the jurisdiction of the Court had been accepted by Costa Rica, Peru and Honduras.

21   That is to say, the General Assembly, the meeting of consultation of Ministers of Foreign Affaires, the councils, the Juridical Committee, the Commission on Human Rights, the General Secretariat, the specialised conferences and the specialised organisations.

Chapter five

OTHER REGIONAL COMMISSIONS ON HUMAN RIGHTS

I. THE PERMANENT ARAB COMMISSION ON HUMAN RIGHTS

The League of Arab States was founded on 22 March 1945, shortly before the end of the Second World War, by the signature by seven countries – Egypt, Iraq, Jordan, Lebanon, Saudi Arabia, Syria and Yemen – of the *Pact of the League of Arab States*. The Pact described the purpose of the League as:

the strengthening of the relations between the Member States; the co-ordination of their policies in order to achieve their independence and sovereignty; and a general concern with the affairs and interests of the Arab countries.

Article 2 of the Pact continued by providing for co-operation in the following matters: economic and financial affairs, including commerce, agriculture and industry; communications of all sorts; cultural affairs; various legal matters; social affairs; and health problems. The treaty deliberately established only loose ties between the members, believing that this would facilitate the accession of other Arab States; at the same time, Article 9 of the Pact authorised 'Member States which desire to establish closer co-operation and stronger bonds than are provided for by this Pact . . . to conclude agreements for that purpose'.

The next major step was the conclusion of a Treaty for Joint Defence and Economic Co-operation, which was signed by Egypt, Lebanon, Syria, Saudi Arabia and Yemen in June 1950, by Iraq in February 1951, by Jordan a year later and by the remaining Arab countries at a 'summit conference' in Alexandria in September 1964. Thus were laid the foundations for a new international regional organisation, whose membership was to extend within a few years from the Atlantic Ocean to the Arabian Gulf.[1] The Joint Defence Treaty of 1950 specifically recognises the status of the Arab League as a regional organisation within the meaning of the

United Nations Charter, and the General Assembly for its part has equally recognised this status and granted the League observer status at U.N. meetings.[2] In addition, the Arab League has concluded agreements for co-operation with UNESCO (1957), the I.L.O. (1958), F.A.O. (1960) and W.H.O. (1961).

Three separate developments have led the Arab League to interest itself in human rights matters. The first of these arose out of its practice of co-operation with the United Nations. In August 1966 the Economic and Social Council invited the four regional organisations — the Council of Europe, the Organisation of American States, the Organisation of African Unity and the League of Arab States — to attend sessions of the Commission on Human Rights of the United Nations and to exchange information with the Commission on their respective human rights activities.[3] At about the same time, the same four regional organisations were invited to take action to support the initiative of the United Nations in celebrating 1968 as International Human Rights Year and were also invited to attend the International Conference on Human Rights in Tehran, the principal event of International Human Rights Year.[4] While the Council of Europe and the Organisation of American States already had their own organs and programmes for the protection and promotion of human rights, the Arab League had not — but was now led to consider the desirability of establishing one. In September 1966 the Council of the Arab League decided to accept the invitation of the United Nations to participate in International Human Rights Year and appointed an *ad hoc* committee in the Secretariat General to make proposals for the implementation of this decision.[5] A steering committee of governmental representatives was appointed a few months later to consider how the League should participate in the celebrations.[6]

The second development leading to the same result was that about the same time (that is to say, March 1967) the U.N. Commission on Human Rights decided to study the possibility of setting up regional Commissions in areas where they did not already exist.[7] Later that year the Arab League, like other regional organisations, was asked for its views on this proposal. Its statement in reply included the following paragraphs:

1. The field of human rights is a vital one for strengthening links among countries which belong to a regional area.
2. As for the procedure of establishing regional commissions on human rights and specifying their functions, the League of Arab States

believes that the proper foundations for setting up such regional commissions are the foundations on which a regional inter-governmental organisation is based. Thus the *regional commissions should be established within the framework of international or regional inter-governmental organisations* [emphasis added].

After having gone on record in this sense in an official statement to the United Nations, it was inevitable that the Arab League should give further consideration to the idea of establishing its own regional Commission on Human Rights.

The third development occurred at the International Conference on Human Rights at Tehran in April–May 1968. A number of Arab countries sought to include on the agenda of the conference the question of 'respect and implementation of human rights in occupied territories', meaning the territories occupied by Israel during the war of June 1967. Now, whatever view one takes about the merits of, or justification for, that war, there is no doubt that one result was that many thousands of people found themselves living in occupied territory with some of their basic rights restricted, if not violated. Consideration of this problem was included on the agenda of the Tehran conference, with the support of the majority of delegations. The concerted action of the Arab States at the conference, assisted by the Secretariat of the Arab League, showed that it was possible for them to use human rights as a platform from which to challenge Israel about the treatment accorded to the inhabitants of the occupied territories.

These three separate developments led the Arab League to the conclusion that the time was ripe to set up its own Commission on Human Rights. The Council of the League decided to organise an Arab regional Conference on Human Rights in Beirut in December 1968, as part of its contribution to International Human Rights Year; this conference was the occasion to make known to the world the decision of the Council in the previous September to set up a *Permanent Arab regional Commission on Human Rights*.[8]

The rules of procedure of the Commission[9] in fact deal not only with the procedure of the Commission but also with its composition and other matters. Each member State of the League is represented on the Commission, which means that its members are representatives of governments (as is the case with the U.N. Commission) and not independent persons serving in a personal capacity (as with the European and Inter-American Commissions). Other Arab States may be invited to attend, and representatives of the Gulf Emirates are invited as observers. The Council of the League appoints the chairman of the Commission for a term of office of two years, which is renewable; the Secretary-General of the League appoints the Secretary of the Commission.

The functions of the Commission – like those of other Commissions of the League – are essentially to prepare draft agreements or other proposals for the Council; but it has a right of initiative and may submit its own recommendations and suggestions to the Council.

In accordance with this right, the Commission, at its second session in April 1969, prepared a plan of action or programme which was approved by the Council of the League at its session in September 1969. This programme is based on the principle that all matters relating to human rights in the Arab world fall within the competence of the Commission, particularly the co-ordination of joint action by the Arab countries, the protection of the rights of the individual Arab and promoting respect for human rights in Arab countries in general. The Commission has given priority to the question of the rights of Arabs living in the occupied territories.

The programme is in two parts, relating respectively to action at the national level and to action at the international level. In the former case it includes the establishment of national Commissions on human rights in the member States and linking them to the Permanent Commission of the League; receiving reports from member States on their activities for the promotion of human rights and making recommendations thereon; and undertaking preparatory work for the proclamation of an Arab Charter of Human Rights. At the international level the Commission has concentrated on organising the participation of the Arab League in, and assisting the delegations of member States at, various international conferences, including sessions of the U.N. Commission on Human Rights and of its *ad hoc* Working Group of Experts appointed by Resolution 6 (XXV) to investigate Israel's alleged violations of human rights in the occupied territories. The Commission also sends an annual communication about its activities to the United Nations Commission, and its representatives played an active part in the U.N. seminar on the establishment of regional Commissions on Human Rights with special reference to Africa, held in Cairo in September 1969.

Rather sparse information is available about the results achieved by the Permanent Commission on Human Rights of the Arab

League. Perhaps inevitably, its initial activities have been principally concerned with a political situation which we may hope is temporary. Its functions resulting from the terms of reference given to it by the Council of the League are essentially those of the promotion of human rights (as with the U.N. Commission) rather than their protection (as is the task of the European Commission). Some work has been done on the proposed Arab Charter of Human Rights, but it has not been brought to a successful conclusion at the intergovernmental level. More recently the idea has been taken up by the Union of Arab Lawyers, which at a conference in Bagdad in May 1979 proposed the conclusion of an Arab Convention on Human Rights which would guarantee fundamental rights as they are understood in a specifically Islamic context. The symposium recommended *inter alia* the establishment of a non-governmental 'Permanent Committee for the Defence of Human Rights and Fundamental Freedoms in the Arab Homeland', with competence to receive complaints from individuals and to send missions of enquiry. It also appealed to the Arab League 'to activate the Permanent Committee on Human Rights', stating that, in spite of the fact that that Committee had been formed, and its chairman elected every two years by the Council of the League, 'the Committee has not assumed its duties, nor convened any session for years'.

It is evident therefore that much remains to be done. We may hope that the Arab Commission, inspired by this appeal of the Union of Arab Lawyers, will make a more positive contribution in the future in an area of the world where resolute action is necessary to protect the fundamental rights of the great majority of the population.

II. THE PROPOSED AFRICAN COMMISSION ON HUMAN RIGHTS

The evolution leading to the establishment of regional organisations which we have observed in other parts of the world has also produced results in Africa. A series of conferences of independent African States were held from 1958 to 1962. The conference in Lagos in January 1962 approved a proposal for permanent machinery for economic and technical co-operation; Liberia suggested additional machinery of a political character, including annual meetings of the Foreign Ministers and the appointment of a permanent secretariat. The following year a 'summit conference' of heads of state and of government held in Addis Ababa in May 1963 adopted the *Charter of the Organisation of African Unity*. Article II of the Charter sets out among the aims of the O.A.U. 'to promote the unity and solidarity of the African States', 'to eradicate all forms of colonialism from Africa' and 'to promote international co-operation, having due regard to the Charter of the United Nations and the Universal Declaration of Human Rights'. While many national constitutions refer to – and sometimes incorporate by reference – the provisions of the Universal Declaration, this was the first time that the constituent instrument of a new international organisation has done so. Article III of the Charter proclaims a number of principles which all member States accept; these include the sovereign equality of all member States and non-interference in their internal affairs (as with the Organisation of American States) and also 'absolute dedication to the total emancipation of the African territories which are still dependent' and 'a policy of non-alignment with regard to all blocs'.

'Each independent, sovereign African State' is entitled to become a member of the O.A.U. (Article IV), but no doubt the white regime in South Africa would not be held to comply with this description.

The organs of the O.A.U. are the Assembly of Heads of State and Government, which is the supreme organ and meets at least once a year; the Council of Foreign Ministers, which meets at least twice a year and whose principal function is to prepare or execute decisions of the Assembly; the General Secretariat; and the Commission of Mediation, Conciliation and Arbitration. Article XIX of the Charter contains a specific undertaking about peaceful settlement of disputes and provides for the creation of the Commission by a separate Protocol; such an instrument was concluded in 1964 and is considered an integral part of the Charter. The establishment of this specifically African machinery for the settlement of disputes no doubt represents an attempt to settle them on a regional basis without referring them to the Security Council; this is, of course, quite consistent with Articles 52 and 53 of the U.N. Charter.[10]

The headquarters of the O.A.U. are at Addis Ababa, which is also the seat of the Economic Commission for Africa of the United Nations – a fact which, of course, facilitates contacts between them.

The creation of an African Commission on Human Rights was

first proposed at the African Conference on the Rule of Law, organised by the International Commission of Jurists in Lagos in 1961. The conference adopted the 'Law of Lagos', in which it declared, *inter alia*:

that in order to give full effect to the Universal Declaration of Human Rights, this Conference invites the African Governments to study the possibility of adopting an African Convention on Human Rights . . .

This launched an idea which developed slowly over the next twenty years, and led to the adoption of an *African Charter of Human and People's Rights* in 1981. It may be interesting for those concerned with human rights in Africa to know something of the history of the matter.

At the twenty-third session of the Commission on Human Rights of the United Nations, held in March 1967, a proposal was tabled aimed at encouraging the establishment of regional Commissions on Human Rights in those parts of the world where they did not already exist.[11] The most interesting thing about this proposal was that it was signed by the representatives of five African States (Congo, Dahomey, Nigeria, Senegal and Tanzania) and clearly envisaged the creation of a Human Rights Commission in Africa.

The U.N. Commission, by its Resolution 6 (XXIII), decided to set up an *ad hoc* study group to consider this proposal. The group met in New York in January 1968. Its members were sharply divided on the question whether it was desirable to create regional Commissions, the East European members expressing their traditional view that such bodies were likely to interfere with matters which fall within the domestic jurisdiction of States, which would be contrary to the principle of national sovereignty and in violation of Article 2 (7) of the Charter. The contrary view, of course, was that once States have assumed international obligations to promote and respect human rights – as they have done in the Charter and were to do much more explicitly in the Covenants – then these matters are no longer exclusively within their domestic jurisdiction.

The report of the *ad hoc* study group was largely a record of dissenting views, but there was agreement on one point: that if further regional Commissions were to be created, this should be done on the initiative of the States in the region and not be imposed by the world Organisation.[12] The report was considered by the U.N. Commission at its twenty-fourth session in March 1968; the

Commission, in its Resolution 7 (XXIV), requested the comments on the report of the member governments and of the regional organisations. In the reply which he sent to this request, the Secretary-General of the Council of Europe stated that, while it was not for him to say what advantages would be gained from the establishment of regional Commissions in other parts of the world, the European experience had shown that it was possible for a group of States in one region 'which have a common heritage of political traditions, ideals, freedom and the rule of law' to set up a more effective system for the protection of human rights than appeared to be possible on a world-wide basis.

By the time that the U.N. Commission came back to the matter at its twenty-fifth session, in March 1969, two things had happened which had changed the situation and improved the prospects. The League of Arab States had set up the Permanent Arab Commission on Human Rights, which showed that the idea of regional Commissions was gaining ground and had met with the support of a number of governments in Asia and North Africa; secondly, the government of the United Arab Republic had invited the United Nations to hold a seminar in Cairo in September 1969 – in the framework of the programme of advisory services – to discuss the question of the establishment of regional Commissions, with particular reference to Africa.

This seminar took place from 2 to 15 September 1969.[13] It was attended by participants from twenty African countries and representatives of the Council of Europe and the Arab League.

There was a surprising degree of unanimity on the desirability of establishing a regional Commission on Human Rights for Africa. The lead was taken by the delegation of the United Arab Republic and was generally supported. This was evidently due in part to the desire to achieve a greater respect for human rights throughout the African continent; and also, no doubt, to the fact that human rights has now become an accepted basis in the U.N. for attacking one's political opponents, whether as regards the Israeli-occupied territories, the practice of apartheid, the situation in Namibia, or elsewhere. Whatever the reasons, there was soon general agreement that an African Commission should be created.

The type of Commission which most of the participants had in mind was not one comparable to the European Commission, with its quasi-judicial functions, but rather a Commission for the promotion of human rights, more on the lines of the U.N.

Commission, or the Inter-American Commission as originally established in 1959. The agenda drawn up by the U.N. Secretariat listed the following possible functions:

(a) Education and information activities.
(b) Undertaking research and studies.
(c) Performance of advisory services.
(d) Holding seminars and awarding fellowships.
(e) Fact-finding and conciliation.
(f) Consideration of communications from States, individuals and groups of individuals and the kind of action to be taken thereon.

In conclusion of the discussion of the competence of the African Commission, it was agreed to include the functions set out under points (a) – (d) above without reservation, and points (e) and (f) as optional provisions.

The second item for consideration was the method of establishing a regional Commission for Africa, and its geographical extent. On the latter point, it was agreed that it should include all African countries sharing the same political ideas, i.e. cover the whole of Africa except those countries practising policies of apartheid and colonialism. It was also agreed to propose that the African Commission should be created by resolution of the Organisation of African Unity – rather than by the conclusion of a Convention – and, for this purpose, to invite the Secretary-General of the U.N. to send the report of the seminar to the Secretary-General of the O.A.U. with the request that he should communicate it to his member governments and should place the question on the agenda of a forthcoming meeting of the O.A.U. At the same time the hope was expressed that the U.N., interested Specialised Agencies and regional organisations would lend their advice and assistance to the O.A.U. if it decided to proceed with the project.

The report on the Cairo seminar[14] was duly communicated to the U.N. Commission on Human Rights at its twenty-sixth session in March 1970 and, as the participants had requested, to the Secretary-General of the Organisation of African Unity. The latter body, however, took no action at this stage.

The next step was a conference held in Addis Ababa in April 1971 under the auspices of the Economic Commission for Africa of the United Nations and with the participation of the O.A.U. The matters discussed – African legal process and the individual –

related more to the protection of human rights in African countries
than to the creation of new institutions for this purpose; but the
conference was deliberately conceived as a 'follow-up' to the Cairo
seminar, and repeated the recommendation for the establishment of
a regional Commission on Human Rights for Africa.

Though this conference also was not followed by any practical
action, the idea was kept alive at various subsequent meetings. One
of these was the UN Seminar on the Study of New Ways and Means
for Promoting Human Rights with Special Attention to the
Problems and Needs of Africa, held in Dar-es-Salaam (Tanzania) in
October and November 1973.[15] Two unofficial meetings which
discussed the question were the Third Biennal Conference of the
African Bar Association in Freetown (Sierra Leone) in August
1978, and a Seminar on Development and Human Rights organised
by the International Commission of Jurists in Dakar in the
following month, in association with the Association Sénégalaise
d'Etudes et de Recherches Juridiques.

In 1979 an important step forward appeared to be taken within
the framework of the Organisation of African Unity by the
Assembly of Heads of State and Government with the adoption of a
'Decision on Human Rights and Peoples' Rights in Africa', at the
Assembly's sixteenth Ordinary Session, which was held in
Monrovia (Liberia) from 17 to 20 July 1979. In that decision[16] the
Assembly called on the Secretary-General of the O.A.U. to
'organise as soon as possible in an African capital a restricted
meeting of highly qualified experts to prepare a preliminary draft of
an *African Charter on Human Rights* providing, *inter alia*, for the
establishment of bodies to promote and protect human rights'.

The decision stated that human rights 'are not confined to civil
and political rights but cover economic, social and cultural
problems', that special attention must be given to the latter, and
that 'economic and social development is a human right'. The
decision also called on the O.A.U. Secretary-General to draw the
attention of member States to 'certain international conventions
whose ratification would help to strengthen Africa's struggle
against certain scourges, especially against *apartheid* and racial
discrimination, trade imbalance and mercenarism'.

Two months later the United Nations organised a further
seminar on 'The Establishment of Regional Commissions on
Human Rights, with particular reference to Africa', which was held
in Monrovia (Liberia) in September 1979. It was attended by

participants from thirty African countries, as well as observers from specialised agencies, regional organisations (particularly the O.A.U.) and non-governmental organisations.[17] It was, of course, encouraged by the O.A.U. decision taken the previous July about the preparation of an African Charter on Human Rights.

Widespread support was expressed for the idea of establishing an African Commission on Human Rights, but it was also observed that the member States of O.A.U. did not show the political homogeneity which characterised the members of certain other regional organisations; that they were primarily concerned with improving the living conditions and basic education of their peoples; and that recommendations would only be made within the framework of the O.A.U. decision adopted by the heads of state in July 1979.

It was stated that the principle of non-interference in the internal affairs of a sovereign State should not exclude international action when human rights were violated in a particular State, but it was also considered that the functions of an African Commission on Human Rights should, in the beginning, be primarily promotional. As regards functions of protection, some participants stated that the Commission could be charged to investigate alleged gross violations of human rights and to act as a mediator, but the majority found that it would be premature to admit individual petitions. It was necessary, in the first stage, to inform people and make them aware of their individual human rights and, in this respect, a useful role could be played by national and local institutions as well as non-governmental organisations. It was also necessary to take account of the size of the African continent, the great number of African States (there were then forty-nine members of O.A.U.), their cultural diversity and the poor state of communications in many parts of Africa.

The seminar worked out a 'Monrovia proposal' for establishing an African Commission on Human Rights of sixteen members, to be elected by the Assembly of Heads of State and Government of the O.A.U. and to serve in their personal capacity. Its functions would be 'to promote and protect human rights in Africa'. It would apply 'the international law of human rights', including any specific African instruments on human rights that may be concluded, the charters of the U.N. and the O.A.U., the Universal Declaration, the U.N. Covenants and other relevant texts of the U.N., the O.A.U. and the Specialised Agencies. While the functions of the

Commission would be mainly promotional, it could also study alleged violations, their causes and manifestations, propose its good offices and make reports and recommendations to the O.A.U.

The seminar requested its chairman, the Minister of Justice of Liberia, to submit the Monrovia proposal to the Chairman of the O.A.U., President Tolbert of Liberia. The intention was obviously that the proposal should be considered by the meeting of experts which the O.A.U. had already decided to convene with the task of preparing an African Charter on Human Rights.

Matters were not facilitated by the fact that President Tolbert and his government were overthrown a few months later by a military *coup d'état*. Nevertheless the O.A.U. meeting did take place in the form of a Ministerial conference held in Bangui (Gambia) in June 1980. It was presented with a draft *African Charter of Human and Peoples' Rights* which had been prepared by a meeting of experts held in Dakar in November 1979. This was really a draft for an international Convention containing in sixty articles both normative provisions about the rights to be protected and procedural provisions establishing an *African Commission on Human and Peoples' Rights* with both promotional and investigatory functions – the latter in the examination of communications from States and, subject to certain conditions, from individuals. However, the Ministerial conference in 1980 was able to examine only the first seven articles, with the result that a further meeting was held in January 1981. This completed work on the draft Charter, which was then submitted to the 18th summit meeting of the Organisation of African Unity, held in Nairobi in June 1981.

The summit meeting approved the Charter and submitted it for ratification by the member States of the O.A.U., now fifty in number. As regards its substantive provisions the Charter has three special characteristics: first, that it relates to both categories of human rights (civil and political – economic, social and cultural); secondly, that it relates also to 'People's Rights', by which is meant the rights of self-determination and of sovereignty over natural resources (recognised by the U.N. Covenants) and the rights to peace, to security, to the environment and to development (the so-called 'Third Generation'). The third special characteristic is that the African Charter reflects the idea that man can only realise his personality fully as a member of a group; consequently he has duties as well as rights, to the family, to the group and to the whole community (including military service).

The implementation of the Charter is confided to a Commission of eleven members to be appointed by the Conference of Heads of State of the O.A.U. They are to sit in a personal and independent capacity. The Commission will have functions of a promotional character, will receive and examine reports from States on their compliance with the Charter and can receive both inter-State communications and individual petitions. It will endeavour to arrange a friendly settlement of any disputes and will report to the Conference of Heads of State, with which the final decisions will lie.

This is an important and ambitious project for a continent which suffers widely from underdevelopment and authoritarian régimes; it will be interesting and instructive to see how many African States are willing to ratify the Charter.

III. REGIONALISM AND UNIVERSALISM

The existence of three regional systems or Commissions for the protection or promotion of human rights – the European, the American and the Arab – and the proposal for a fourth regional Commission in Africa inevitably lead one to ask the question whether these regional arrangements are compatible with the universal system of the United Nations or whether they are likely at least to diminish the value of the human rights work of the U.N. and perhaps even undermine its effectiveness.

This question formed the subject of a lively debate at the second International Colloquy about the European Convention organised by the University of Vienna and the Council of Europe in 1965.[18] The report on this subject presented by M. Jean-Flavien Lalive of Geneva argued in favour of the establishment of regional arrangements and regional Commissions,[19] while the statement made by Mr Egon Schwelb, in the light of his long experience of the work of the United Nations Commission, took the contrary view.[20]

There is, of course, a good deal to be said on both sides of the question. On the one hand, experience has shown that it was possible in Europe to conclude a Convention containing binding obligations and setting up new international machinery at a time when this was not possible in the world-wide framework; and though the U.N. Covenants have now been widely ratified, the number of States which have accepted their optional provisions is strictly limited, so that it is likely to be the case for a considerable period of time that the European system will contain far more effective procedures than the universal system. If a regional system can be justified in this way in one part of the world, logic requires that one should take the same view as regards regional systems in other parts of the world.

On the other hand, it can be argued that human rights appertain to human beings by virtue of their humanity and should be guaranteed to all human beings on a basis of equality, without distinction, wherever they may live. Discrimination on grounds of race, sex, religion or nationality is forbidden both in the United Nations texts and in the regional Conventions. Equally there should be no distinction based on regionalism. The African and the Asian should have the same human rights as the European or the American.

This last argument is incontrovertible. How then can one choose between, or reconcile, the two points of view?

The answer would seem to be on the following lines. Human rights should be the same for all persons, everywhere, at all times. In other words, the normative content of different international instruments should be, in principle, the same. There may, of course, be minor differences in formulation, due to differences in drafting techniques or in legal traditions, but the basic rights and fundamental freedoms should be the same for all. Here the touchstone, or the yardstick, is the Universal Declaration, which sets out, in the words of its Preamble, 'a common standard of achievement for all peoples and all nations'. No regional system should be allowed to exist which is not consistent with the norms and principles set out in the Universal Declaration.

When we come to measures of implementation, however, the position is different. While it is desirable that the most effective system possible should be established everywhere, it is a fact that the same system is not at present acceptable in all parts of the world. Even inside Europe this is the case, because not all members of the Council of Europe have accepted the optional provisions of the European Convention. If this is the case inside one regional organisation, how much more is it true of different regions of the world, two of which – Eastern Europe and Asia – have so far shown no signs of willingness to accept any form of international control at all.

It is therefore reasonable, as a practical matter, to set up regional arrangements for the protection of human rights which may differ *inter se*, provided that the rights to be protected are essentially the same and are substantially those established in the Universal Declaration. It will be noted at this stage that (as explained in Chapter III) this is the approach adopted by the European Convention, in which the contracting parties expressed their determination '. . . to take the first steps for the collective enforcement of certain of the rights stated in the Universal Declaration'. Other regional systems are therefore equally legitimate if they also seek to enforce, by means of regional procedures which can be accepted by a group of States in a particular area, some or all of the rights proclaimed in the Universal Declaration.

This reasoning is supported by two other arguments. First, that it is in the nature of things that regional systems of enforcement should be more readily accepted than the universal. A State cannot be forced to submit itself to a system of international control; it will do so only if it has confidence in that system. It is much more likely to have such confidence if the international machinery has been set up by a group of like-minded countries, which are already its partners in a regional organisation, than if this is not the case. Moreover, it will be willing to give greater powers to a regional organ of restricted membership, of which the other members are its friends and neighbours, than to a world-wide organ in which it (and its allies) play a proportionally smaller part.

The second supporting argument is the purely practical one of distance. To take Europe as an example, it is obviously much easier and more convenient for all concerned that a complaint by one European State against another European State, and *a fortiori* an individual application against a European State – either of which may involve hearing witnesses[21] – should be heard in Strasbourg rather than New York. The same will apply *mutatis mutandis* to other regions of the world, in so far as their regional commissions will have the competence to consider inter-State complaints or individual applications.

A third point to be made in this context is that the principle of regional settlement is quite consistent with the Charter of the United Nations. Articles 33 and 52 of the Charter expressly recognise the principle of regional settlement of disputes threatening international peace and security; the same principle can properly be extended to disputes about the violation of human rights. This indeed is specifically recognised in Article 44 of the U.N. Covenant on Civil and Political Rights.

To sum up, then, we may say that regional systems for the protection and promotion of human rights are not in contradiction with, or opposition to, the world-wide system of the United Nations, provided that they consitute local arrangements to secure greater respect for the norms established by the United Nations in the Universal Declaration and other relevant texts. If this condition is complied with, then regional arrangements should be welcomed as complementary to – and sometimes more effective than – the universal system of the world Organisation.

NOTES

1   Further information on the history and structure of the Arab League was given in the first edition of this book at pp. 140–3.
2   General Assembly Resolution 477 (V) of 1 November 1950.
3   ECOSOC Resolution 1159 (XLI) of 5 August 1966.
4   General Assembly Resolution 2081 (XX) of 20 December 1965.
5   Arab League Council Resolution 2259 (XLVI) of 12 September 1966.
6   Arab League Council Resolution 2304 (XLVII) of 18 March 1967.
7   Recommendation 6 (XXIII) of 23 March 1967. The progress of this study will be recounted in the following section of this chapter.
8   Arab League Council Resolution 2443 of 3 September 1968. The creation of the Commission and the decisions of the conference were reported to the U.N. Commission on Human Rights at its twenty-fifth session (doc. E/CN.4/L.1042 of 18 February 1969). Cf. Stephen P. Marks, 'La Commission Permanente Arabe des Droits de l'Homme', *Human Rights Review*, III, 1970, p. 101.
9   They were reproduced in the first edition of this book at Appendix 6.
10   Cf. T. O. Elias, 'The Commission of Mediation, Conciliation and Arbitration of the O.A.U.', *B.Y.I.L.* 1964, p. 336; D. W. Bowett, *The Law of International Institutions*, second edition, London, 1970, pp. 280–3. On the O.A.U. in general see Bowett, *op. cit.*, pp. 217–20; T. O. Elias, 'The Charter of the O.A.U.', *A.J.I.L.* 1965, p. 243; C. Hoskyers, 'Trends and developments in the O.A.U.', in *Yearbook of World Affairs*, 1967, p. 164.
11   Document E/CN.4/L.940, draft Recommendation II, *Report of the Twenty-third Session* (E/4322), pp. 109–25.
12   Document E/CN.4/966 and addendum 1 (*Report of the UN ad hoc Study Group established under Resolution 6 (XXIII) of the Commission on Human Rights*). See also L. O. Adegbite, 'African attitudes to the international protection of human rights', in *Nobel Symposium* 7, pp. 69–80.
13   The official report of the session is contained in U.N. doc.

ST/TAO/HR/38 1969. Part of this account was published in *Human Rights Journal*, II, 1969, pp. 696–702. A fuller account of the Cairo seminar was given in the first edition of this book at pp. 151–7.

14 U.N. doc. ST/TAO/HR/38 (1969).
15 Report in U.N. doc. ST/TAO/HR/48.
16 O.A.U. doc. AHG/115 (XVI).
17 U.N. *Bulletin of Human Rights*, No. 25 (July–September 1979), pp. 23–5. I am indebted for information about this seminar to Mr K. Rogge, who attended as the representative of the Council of Europe.
18 *Human Rights in National and International Law*, Manchester University Press, 1967.
19 *Ibid.*, pp. 330–42. See also R. Pinto, 'Régionalisme et universalisme dans la protection des droits de l'homme', in *Nobel Symposium 7*, pp. 177–92; K. Vasak, 'Vers la création de Commissions régionales des droits de l'homme', in *Mélanges Cassin*, p. 467.
20 *Human Rights in National and International Law*, pp. 355–6.
21 In the case brought by the governments of Denmark, Norway, Sweden and the Netherlands against the government of Greece (1967–69) the European Commission of Human Rights heard more than eighty witnesses (*Yearbook of the Convention*, XII *bis*, 1969).

Chapter six

ECONOMIC, SOCIAL AND CULTURAL RIGHTS

I. THE INTERNATIONAL COVENANT ON ECONOMIC, SOCIAL AND CULTURAL RIGHTS

In 1950 the General Assembly of the United Nations decided, as recounted in Chapter II, that economic, social and cultural rights should be included in the single international Covenant which was then projected, but two years later changed its position and decided that there should be two separate Covenants dealing with the two categories of rights, that they should be prepared simultaneously and that they should contain as many similar provisions as possible. The Commission on Human Rights drafted accordingly, with the result that the General Assembly approved the *International Covenant on Economic, Social and Cultural Rights* on 16 December 1966, at the same time as the International Covenant on Civil and Political Rights (Resolution 2200 (XXI)).

In fact it did not prove possible to respect to any significant extent the wish that the two Covenants should contain as many similar provisions as possible. Of course the rights protected are different – with the exception of the right of all peoples to self-determination, which forms Article 1 of both Covenants. But also the obligations assumed by the States parties and the two systems of international control are also, as we shall see, very different in character.

Articles 2–5 of both Covenants set out the general provisions on the obligations of the States parties. But whereas the obligation in the Covenant on Civil and Political Rights is intended, in general, to be of immediate application, the general obligation assumed by contracting parties in the Covenant on Economic, Social and Cultural Rights (as explained in Chapter II) is different in character – which is the natural result of the difference in the nature of the rights secured. Paragraph 1 of Article 2 reads as follows:

Each State Party to the present Covenant undertakes to take steps, individually and through international assistance and co-operation, especially economic and technical, to the maximum of its available resources, with a view to achieving progressively the full realization of the rights recognized in the present Covenant by all appropriate means, including particularly the adoption of legislative measures.

It is thus quite clear that this is what has come to be called a *promotional convention* — that is to say that it does not set out obligations which contracting parties are required necessarily to accept immediately, but rather standards which they intend to promote and which they pledge themselves to secure progressively, to the maximum extent possible having regard to their available resources. As already indicated, this difference in the obligation results from the very nature of the rights recognised in this Covenant.

Of the remaining general provisions in the Covenant on Economic, Social and Cultural Rights, the 'non-discrimination clause' (Article 2 (2)) is similar to that in the other Covenant, as are also the text on the equal rights of men and women (Article 3) and the provisions in Article 5 designed to prevent abuse of the rights secured and containing the general saving clause. Article 4 relates to limitations on the rights protected; they are permissible only 'as determined by law . . . and solely for the purpose of promoting the general welfare in a democratic society'. But there is no provision for derogations in a state of emergency, as in the other Covenant. Finally, paragraph 3 of Article 2 contains an unusual provision designed to protect developing countries from economic exploitation by their more powerful neighbours:

Developing countries, with due regard to human rights and their national economy, may determine to what extent they would guarantee the economic rights recognized in the present Covenant to non-nationals.

It will be observed that this paragraph reintroduces the principle of discrimination. It would permit developing countries to discriminate against foreigners as regards the enjoyment of certain economic rights. It was perhaps intended to establish the principle that the Covenant could not be invoked in order to protect foreign investments in developing countries; however, neither Covenant protects the right of property, so that this provision would have little relevance to that problem.

When we come to the rights protected in the Covenant on Economic, Social and Cultural Rights, we find a longer list and more detailed definitions than those contained in the Universal Declaration. The latter included only six articles relating to these rights in 1948; by the time the Covenants were concluded in 1966 the number had increased to ten. This illustrates the tendency in the United Nations over the last thirty years – due largely to the admission of so many developing countries as new members – to give more attention to economic and social rights, a tendency which has been accompanied by a diminished interest in many quarters in the classic rights of a civil and political character. It is perhaps significant – though evidently one should not attach too much importance to this point – that in *Resolution 2200* the Covenant on Economic, Social and Cultural Rights was placed before the Covenant on Civil and Political Rights.

The economic, social and cultural rights protected by the relevant Covenant are the following:

Article   6. The right to work.
        7. The right to just and favourable conditions of work, including, *inter alia* fair wages, equal pay for equal work and holidays with pay.
        8. The right to form and join trade unions, including the right to strike.
        9. The right to social security.
      10. Protection of the family, including special assistance for mothers and children.
      11. The right to an adequate standard of living, including adequate food, clothing and housing and the continuous improvement of living conditions.
      12. The right to the highest attainable standard of physical and mental health.
      13. The right to education, primary education being compulsory and free for all, and secondary and higher education generally accessible to all. (Article 14 permits the progressive implementation of this right.)
      15. The right to participate in cultural life and enjoy the benefits of scientific progress.

There is, in effect, a great measure of common ground between this list and that contained in the European Social Charter of 18 October 1961. As we shall see in section V of this chapter, the latter proclaims nineteen economic and social rights, but often sets out as two or three separate rights provisions which are grouped together in one article of the Covenant.

There is a major difference to be noted in the formulation of the economic, social and cultural rights as compared with the civil and political rights. The latter are stated in the classic form 'Everyone has the right to . . .' or 'No one shall be subjected to . . .'. In the Economic and Social Covenant, on the other hand, the normative articles adopt a different formulation, usually 'The States Parties to the present Covenant recognise the right . . .' (as in Articles 6, 7, 9, 10, 11, 12, 13 and 15) or 'The States Parties to the present Covenant undertake to ensure . . .' (as in Article 8). In other words, we find an undertaking or a recognition by States rather than the affirmation of a right inherent in the individual as such. When we recall that the undertaking of the contracting parties in Article 2 of the Covenant is (as explained above) '. . . to take steps . . . with a view to achieving progressively the full realisation of the rights recognised in the present Covenant . . .' the 'promotional character' of the instrument is clearly apparent.

For the implementation of the Covenant on Economic, Social and Cultural Rights, Articles 16–25 provide for a system of periodic reports by States parties concerning the measures adopted and the progress made in achieving the observance of the rights recognised therein. These reports are to be considered by the Economic and Social Council. The reports are to be furnished in accordance with a programme to be established by ECOSOC (Article 17); the Secretary-General is to send copies of all reports to that body (Article 16); ECOSOC may make arrangements with the Specialised Agencies in order to obtain from them reports on the progress made in achieving the observance of the provisions of the Covenant falling within the scope of their activities (Article 18); it may transmit the reports of States to the Commission on Human Rights for study and general recommendation (Article 19); the States may then submit to the Council their comments on such general recommendations (Article 20); finally, the Council may submit a summary of the information it has received, together with its reports and recommendations of a general nature, to the General Assembly (Article 21) and draw appropriate matters to the attention of other organs of the United Nations and of the specialised agencies concerned (Article 22).[1]

It is thus clear that the Economic and Social Council is the keystone in the system of implementation of this Covenant. No surprise need be expressed at this fact, since it is a question of implementation of economic and social rights. Two comments may nevertheless be made. The principle of independence of the organ responsible for supervision of implementation (which is respected in the Covenant on Civil and Political Rights) has been jettisoned in the other Covenant, since ECOSOC consists of representatives of governments and not of persons acting in an independent capacity. Secondly, the tasks conferred on ECOSOC by Articles 16–22 of the Covenant on Economic, Social and Cultural Rights are very extensive, and the amount of paperwork involved in obtaining, receiving and analysing reports from more than sixty governments, consulting the Commission on Human Rights and appropriate Specialised Agencies, making and transmitting general recommendations to governments and obtaining their comments thereon, and finally reporting on all this to the General Assembly, will be formidable. When one considers the length and complexity of the agenda of ECOSOC at present, and the difficulty which the Council experiences in coping with its existing tasks, one may wonder whether, as a practical matter, it is the most appropriate body to serve as the organ of implementation of the Covenant on Economic, Social and Cultural Rights.

Be that as it may, the obligation exists and ECOSOC will have to do its best to comply with it. In 1976 it considered the matter and adopted its *Resolution 1988 (LX)*, entitled 'Procedures for the Implementation of the International Covenant on Economic, Social and Cultural Rights'. It decided *inter alia* to establish a Sessional Working Group to assist it in the discharge of its functions in the implementation of the Covenant, and set up the group in 1978 (Resolution 1978/10 of the Council). It also established a programme for the periodic reports, requiring their presentation in biennial stages.

The *Sessional Working Group* consists of fifteen members of the Council which are also States parties to the Covenant. It will be noted that the members of the group are States, which delegate their representatives, and not individual experts. The principle of equitable geographical distribution is secured by the fact that there are three members from each of the five regional groups: African, Asian, East European, Latin American, Western and other States. Various others are invited as observers, including other parties to the Covenant; also representatives of the specialised agencies concerned when matters within their competence are discussed.

The first session of the Working Group was held in April–May 1979. It was devoted to organisational matters, especially the formulation of its methods of work, as had been requested by the Economic and Social Council. In so doing it took account not only of the relevant basic texts (the Covenant and ECOSOC decisions) but also the practice of the Committee on the Elimination of Racial Discrimination and of the Human Rights Committee. While the task of the Working Group is to 'assist the Economic and Social Council in the consideration of the reports submitted by the States parties . . .', it is clear from the rules adopted[2] that it will in fact discharge this function on behalf of the Council.

The rules provide, following the practice of C.E.R.D. and the Human Rights Committee, that representatives of the reporting States are entitled (which presumably means that they are expected) to be present when their reports are examined, to make statements and to answer questions. The group will also consider reports submitted by the specialised agencies under Article 18 of the Covenant. It will, of course, report to the full Economic and Social Council and may make proposals for the 'recommendations of a general nature' which the Council may submit to the General Assembly under Article 21 of the Covenant.

Many members of the Working Group considered that it could not discharge its functions effectively unless it was allotted more time for its work. Others emphasised that it was a 'sessional' body, i.e. intended to meet only during sessions of the Council. The latter view prevailed, and the rules provide that it will meet annually during the first regular session of ECOSOC.[3] Moreover, it 'will endeavour to work on the basis of the principle of consensus'.[4]

It will be apparent from this brief summary that the system does not at all comply with three of the four conditions indicated in Chapter II as necessary for an effective reporting system: examination of the reports by independent persons who are not government officials; the availability of further (and perhaps critical) information from other responsible sources; and the right to make recommendations about any necessary improvements in the law or practice of the country concerned. Indeed, the reports presented under the Covenant on Economic, Social and Cultural Rights will be considered by a working group of government officials who clearly will not have the time during one annual session to do their work thoroughly; there is no provision for obtaining information from other sources (except to a limited extent from the specialised agencies); as the conclusion of its work, the Working Group may (but is not required) to make proposals – in principle, by consensus – to ECOSOC; and the latter body has no right to address itself to governments which may have defaulted on their obligations, it can only make 'recommendations of a general nature' to the General Assembly.

One cannot therefore expect that the measures of implementation established by the Covenant on Economic, Social and Cultural Rights will have an important effect in securing the observance by States parties of the obligations they have assumed in that Covenant.

II. ECONOMIC AND SOCIAL RIGHTS: THE I.L.O.[5]

The Constitution of the I.L.O. was set out in Part XIII of the Treaty of Versailles in 1919. Though it did not speak of human rights as such, it conferred on the Organisation important functions in the field of what we now call economic and social rights, notably in such matters as the regulation of the hours of work, the prevention of unemployment, the provision of adequate wages, social security, equal pay for equal work and freedom of association.

The *Declaration of Philadelphia* of 1944, which was incorporated in the Constitution of the I.L.O. two years later, made more specific references to freedom of expression and of association and continued: 'All human beings, irrespective of race, creed or sex, have the right to pursue both their material well-being and their spiritual development in conditions of freedom and dignity, of economic security and equal opportunity'. Here we are coming closer to the conception of human rights as generally understood today.

As a result, the I.L.O. has been a pioneer in the international protection of economic and social rights and has an unequalled record of achievement in this field. As with other international organisations, there are two principal aspects of this work; standard-setting and measures of implementation or of international control. Though these two aspects are intimately and necessarily linked, it is convenient – at least at a first stage – to consider them separately.

The principal method used by the I.L.O. in standard-setting is twofold: the conclusion of international Conventions and the adoption of recommendations. The Conventions, of course, are binding only on the States which ratify them, but under Article 19 of the I.L.O. Constitution the member States are required to submit Conventions to the competent authority (normally the Parliament) with a view to their ratification within a period of twelve or eighteen months. This provision is designed to avoid the situation which so often occurs elsewhere, that is to say that a text is approved in the framework of an international organisation but no action is taken subsequently at the national level. Recommendations of the I.L.O., on the other hand, do not create legal obligations of States; their purpose is rather to set standards which are intended to provide guidance for governments in their national legislation or administrative practice.

Over a period of sixty years more than 150 international Conventions have been adopted by the I.L.O., which constitutes an unequalled record of 'international legislation'. The number of ratifications approaches 5,000. Forty States have ratified more than forty Conventions and fifteen States more than sixty.[6] The number of recommendations addressed to governments is slightly larger than the number of Conventions.

It is clearly impossible in this section to enumerate all the Conventions adopted, but one may mention among the most important from the point of view of human rights: the Convention on Freedom of Association and Protection of the Right to Organise (1948), the Convention on the Right to Organise and Collective Bargaining (1949), the Equal Remuneration Convention of 1951, the Abolition of Forced Labour Convention (1957) and the Discrimination (Employment and Occupation) Convention of 1958.[7] Another instrument of particular importance is the Convention on Minimum Standards of Social Security of 1952. Other matters dealt with in I.L.O. Conventions and Recommendations are various aspects of the right to work (employment agencies, vocational training, etc.), conditions of work (minimum wages, reduction of hours of work, a weekly rest period, holidays with pay), the protection of children and young workers, and the protection of women as regards confinement, night work and so on.

Of particular interest to those concerned with the international protection of human rights are the measures of implementation or of international control established in the framework of the International Labour Organisation. As will be seen, they are considerably more effective than those provided for in the United Nations Covenants.

In the first place, there is the I.L.O. reporting system. This system is not the result of some particular Convention, which would therefore apply only to States which have ratified that Convention; it is provided for in the I.L.O. Constitution itself, and therefore applies to all members of the Organisation. Under Articles 19 and 22 of the Constitution member States are required to report to the I.L.O. on the measures they have taken to bring Conventions and Recommendations to the attention of the competent national authorities with a view to ratification or other suitable action; as regards Conventions which they have ratified, they report on their implementation; as regards Conventions which they have not ratified, they report on their intentions for giving effect to them and on any difficulties which impede ratification. About three thousand reports a year are sent to the I.L.O. in accordance with these provisions.

A particularly important aspect is that governments must send copies of their reports to national organisations of employers and workers, who thus have the opportunity of commenting on them if they wish. Their observations must be communicated by the governments to the I.L.O. We see, therefore, that one of the elements necessary in an effective reporting system – the availability of critical information from other responsible sources – which is lacking in the International Covenant on Economic, Social and Cultural Rights, is provided for in the procedures of the I.L.O.

Another important element, also lacking in that Covenant, is the examination of the governments' reports by an independent organ consisting of persons who are not government officials. This is secured in the I.L.O. system at two stages. First, there is the *Committee of Experts on the Application of Conventions and Recommendations*. It consists of eighteen members, appointed by the Governing Body of the I.L.O. on the recommendation of the Director-General, and thus not appointed by their own governments. They are persons who are experts in legal and social matters, such as judges and university professors, whose task is to examine in complete independence and objectivity whether the situation revealed in the national reports (and in the comments of the professional organisations) corresponds to the obligations which have been assumed. The Committee of Experts makes 'observations' on any situation which it considers not in conformity with those obligations; the observations are included in its published reports to the annual sessions of the International Labour Conference. The committee also makes 'requests' direct to governments, which permit the latter to explain or rectify certain discrepancies without the matter becoming public. Several hundred observations and requests are made each year.

The second stage is at the International Labour Conference, which appoints each year a *Committee on the Application of Conventions and Recommendations*. This body, being a committee of the conference, has the same tripartite structure which is the distinctive feature of the I.L.O., consisting of representatives of governments, employers and workers, totalling over a hundred members. It examines the reports of the Committee of Experts, particularly the observations showing discrepancies between the obligations assumed and the national practice in the various countries, and asks the governments concerned for explanations. The presence of representatives of the professional organisations means that the discussions are well informed; they may – and often do – lead to lively criticism of governments whose record is not above reproach. In due course the committee reports to the plenary conference.

We thus see the operation of a system of international control which, by reason of the scrutiny of independent experts and the participation of responsible organisations with their own sources of information, is far more effective than one operated exclusively by representatives of governments. It has been ascertained that over one period of fourteen years more than a thousand improvements in national practice resulted from the use of these procedures, while in the particular sphere of freedom of association there were fifty-five cases in which discrepancies were eliminated.[8]

In addition to these reporting procedures, the I.L.O. Constitution also provides (Articles 26–34) for a complaints procedure, whereby one State may bring a complaint against another if it considers that the latter is not complying with the obligations set out in a Convention which both of them have ratified. In such a case the Governing Body of the I.L.O. sets up a *Commission of Enquiry* of three members which will hear the evidence, including witnesses, in proceedings of a judicial character and may decide to undertake an investigation *in situ*. The use of this formal procedure, however, is comparatively rare and has occurred mainly in cases with political overtones: *Ghana* v. *Portugal*, concerning allegations of forced labour in the Portuguese colonies (1961); *Portugal* v. *Liberia*, raising similar issues (1961); complaints about freedom of association under the military regime in Greece (1968); and about working conditions in Chile (1974). The respective Commissions of Enquiry established the facts in each case and made various recommendations which the governments concerned accepted.

One of the economic and social rights to which the I.L.O. rightly attaches particular importance is freedom of association, because this right is the basis of all trade union activities. Those who followed the events in Poland in the summer of 1980, leading up to the recognition of the independent union 'Solidarity', will readily appreciate this point. Quite apart from the two Conventions on Freedom of Association (1948) and the Right to Organise and Collective Bargaining (1949), the I.L.O. has set up special procedures to protect freedom of association which apply not only to the parties to those Conventions but also, by virtue of the Constitution, to all members of the Organisation.

These procedures were established in 1950 and formally recognised by the Economic and Social Council of the United Nations (*Resolution 277 (X)*), which accepted the I.L.O.'s services in this matter.

First, there is the *Committee on Freedom of Association*, consisting of nine members of the Governing Body, three from each of the three groups (governments, employers, workers). The committee may be seized of a complaint either by a government or by one of the professional organisations; naturally it is the workers' organisations which most frequently start proceedings. The examination of a complaint is generally conducted on the basis of documents, but an investigation *in situ* is sometimes undertaken on the committee's behalf. Detailed reports containing proposed recommendations to the governments concerned are then submitted to the Governing Body, which has almost invariably approved them.

More than 900 cases have been handled in this way over a period of thirty years, concerning many aspects of freedom of association, including the dissolution of trade unions, the arrest of trade union leaders and interference by governments in trade union affairs. An assessment of the results indicates that in a number of cases governments have acted on the committee's recommendations, though regrettably this is not always so; but a substantial body of case law has developed, and the principle of accountability is being progressively asserted and other organs of the I.L.O. are being brought into play when appropriate.[9]

A second organ concerned with freedom of association is the *Fact-finding and Conciliation Commission*, which consists of independent persons appointed by the Governing Body of the I.L.O. on the proposal of the Director-General. As its name implies, it has a primary task of ascertaining the facts concerning a particular situation and attempting to achieve a solution by agreement. But it can examine a problem only with the consent of the government concerned. As a result it has dealt with many fewer cases than the Committee on Freedom of Association, but has done important work in several cases, including those concerning Japan (1964), Greece (1965) and Chile (1974).[10]

We may therefore conclude by recognising that in the particular field of economic and social rights the International Labour Organisation has established a number of different methods – some based on reporting by governments, others on complaints procedures – which constitute a highly developed system of international control over the compliance by governments with their international obligations. This system is unfortunately too little known outside a limited group of specialists. It is regrettable that more account was not taken of the I.L.O. system when the measures of implementation of the Covenant on Economic, Social and Cultural Rights were worked out. It may be that a number of governments were unwilling to see included in that Covenant measures as effective as the I.L.O. system precisely because they would have involved a greater measure of international control. But we may hope that ECOSOC, acting in accordance with Article 18 of the Covenant, will make arrangements to profit to the maximum extent from the experience of the I.L.O. and thus render more effective the protection of the economic and social rights enshrined in the Covenant.

III. CULTURAL RIGHTS: UNESCO[11]

Several of the Specialised Agencies of the United Nations are concerned with the promotion, in the broadest sense of the word, of various economic and social rights. For example, the Food and Agriculture Organisation (F.A.O.) does important work in helping governments to improve and increase food supplies, thus helping to combat undernourishment and starvation, particularly through its 'Freedom from Hunger' campaign; these activities were carried on long before – and quite independently of – the adoption of the U.N. Covenants in 1966, but nevertheless are directly relevant to the obligations assumed by States in Article 11 of the Covenant on Economic, Social and Cultural Rights, in which they recognise the right of everyone to an adequate standard of living for himself and his family, including adequate food, clothing and housing, and the fundamental right of everyone to be free from hunger.

Similarly, the work of the World Health Organisation is directly relevant to the right of everyone to the enjoyment of the highest attainable standard of physical and mental health recognised in Article 12 of the same Covenant. Equally, the World Bank is concerned, though perhaps less directly, with the right of all peoples freely to pursue their economic development, which is recognised in Article 1 on the right of self-determination, common to both Covenants. However, the F.A.O., W.H.O. and the World Bank have not – and doubtless could not – establish international systems for the protection of these rights, which is the subject matter of this book, so that it is sufficient for our purpose to note in passing that their work is relevant to – and designed to promote – the rights we have mentioned, without going into details of their respective programmes. This relevance is indeed recognised in Article 18 of the Covenant on Economic, Social and Cultural Rights, which – as already explained – provides that ECOSOC may make arrangements with the Specialised Agencies for their reporting to it on the progress made in achieving the observance of the provisions of the Covenant falling within the scope of their activities.

Of more direct concern to us is the work of UNESCO in the promotion and protection of cultural rights.

Article 1 of the Constitution of UNESCO, which was drafted at a conference held in London in the autumn of 1945, states that the purpose of the Organisation is:

to contribute to peace and security by promoting collaboration among the nations through education, science and culture in order to further universal respect for justice, for the rule of law and for the human rights and fundamental freedoms which are affirmed for the peoples of the world, without distinction of race, sex, language or religion, by the Charter of the United Nations.

The promotion of human rights and fundamental freedoms is thus consciously conceived as one of the aims to be pursued by UNESCO when undertaking activities in the fields of education, science and culture.

As in the case of F.A.O. and W.H.O., these activities started and were developed over a period of twenty years before the U.N. General Assembly approved the two Covenants in 1966, but the fact that the first Covenant is concerned with economic, social *and cultural* rights establishes a field of common interest. Article 13 of this Covenant, it will be recalled, relates to the right of everyone to education, and continues by providing that primary education shall be compulsory and free for all, while secondary education (including technical and vocational training) and higher education shall be made generally accessible, in particular by the progressive introduction of free education. Article 15, moreover, relates to the right to take part in cultural life and to enjoy the benefits of scientific progress and its applications. It is evident, therefore, that UNESCO should be able, in accordance with Article 18 of this Covenant, to make a significant contribution to the work of ECOSOC in supervising its implementation.

Quite independently of this, however, UNESCO produced the *Convention against Discrimination in Education*, adopted by the General Conference on 14 December 1960.[12] This Convention, which is comparatively short and simple, contains undertakings to eliminate and prevent discrimination in education based on race, colour, sex, language, religion and other grounds. It provides that primary education shall be free and compulsory and secondary and higher education generally available and accessible; these provisions correspond closely to Article 13 of the Covenant on Economic, Social and Cultural Rights, which already existed in draft form. The Convention itself does not provide for measures of implementation in the generally accepted sense, apart from a provision for information to be communicated to UNESCO in periodic reports and for disputes about its interpretation or application to be referred to the International Court of Justice. A *Special Committee to examine the Reports of Member States*, consisting of twelve members, was established in 1965.

Two years after the conclusion of the Convention, a Protocol was approved and opened for signature on 10 December 1962, providing for a *Conciliation and Good Offices Commission*, to which any State party can refer a dispute if it considers that another State party is not respecting its obligations under the Convention.

The Commission of eleven members, serving in their personal capacity, has the task of ascertaining the facts, offering its good offices and seeking a friendly settlement of the matter. It may make recommendations but has no judicial function. The Commission has been set up but has not yet been called on to deal with a dispute.

Another aspect of the matter is that UNESCO, like the United Nations but on a much smaller scale, receives complaints about the violation of human rights in the educational and cultural fields. Initially – again like the United Nations – it considered that it had no competence to deal with such communications. However, as U.N. practice changed and after the Optional Protocol had been approved by the General Assembly in 1966, UNESCO's policy changed too. After various preliminary decisions of the Executive Board and after consideration of a detailed study by the UNESCO Secretariat,[13] the Executive Board in April 1978 took a decision on the *Procedures which should be followed in the examination of cases and questions which might be submitted to UNESCO concerning the exercise of human rights in the spheres of its competence.*[14] This decision recognised that UNESCO is called upon to examine two types of communications: those concerning individual and specific cases and those concerning massive, systematic or flagrant violations forming a consistent pattern. The essence of the new procedure is that communications of both types should be referred to the committee which had been originally established in 1965 to consider the reports of States on the implementation of the Convention and Recommendation against Discrimination in Education. The name of this body had been changed in 1971 to 'Committee on Conventions and Recommendations in Education' and its membership increased to fourteen; in 1978 it was given the revised title of *Committee on Conventions and Recommendations*, and in the following year the number of members was increased to twenty.

The resolution of the Executive Board requires that communications should, provided the author agrees, be transmitted to the government concerned and to the Committee and examined by the latter in private sessions, which the representatives of the government concerned may attend. The Committee must first decide whether the communication is admissible, as regards which various rules apply, e.g. that the matter is within the competence of UNESCO, that the applicant has exhausted domestic remedies, and so on. The task of the Committee is then to try to bring about a friendly solution of the matter. It is required to submit confidential reports to the Executive Board on these activities, and the latter will consider the reports in private session and then decide what further action is necessary. But questions of massive, systematic or flagrant violations will be considered by the Executive Board and the General Conference in public meetings.

It is too soon to say what will be the result of the instauration of these new procedures; and it may be difficult to judge for some time, since most of the work will be confidential. One may hope that they will make a positive contribution to the protection of human rights in the limited sphere of UNESCO's competence. But a note of caution should perhaps be sounded. The resolution of the Executive Board refers explicitly to the provision in the Constitution stating that UNESCO is prohibited from intervening in matters which are essentially within the domestic jurisdiction of States and adds that UNESCO should not play the role of an international judicial body. The representative of the Soviet Union drew particular attention to these provisions when the new procedures were approved. The competence of the organisation in these matters is therefore likely to be interpreted restrictively.

IV. SOME OTHER PROPOSALS: 'NEW HUMAN RIGHTS'

There has been talk in recent years of extending the scope of human rights so as to embrace a number of concepts which are not included in the Universal Declaration of 1948 or in the two international Covenants of 1966. Perhaps the first tendency of this sort was the affirmation of a 'right to development', to which we have already referred in Chapter I.[15] The idea is that the economic development of underdeveloped countries is necessary for their social well-being and political stability, without which they cannot ensure effectively the civil, political, economic, social and cultural rights announced in the major international texts and that therefore the 'right to development' is a human right.[16]

The general concern felt in many countries and international organisations about the need for the protection of the environment – particularly against the pollution generated by modern industrial societies – has led some people to the conclusion that there is a human right to a clean and healthy environment.[17]

Some experts go further and consider that there is a human right to peace and a human right to share in the 'common heritage of mankind' constituted by the unexplored natural resources under the oceans, which belong to no one country and are therefore held to be the property of all mankind. One specialist in this field considers that the so-called 'new human rights' – including the four just mentioned – constitute the 'third generation of human rights' which should receive international recognition after the two first 'generations' or categories protected by the two U.N. Covenants of 1966.[18]

A distinct but related question much discussed in the United Nations in recent years is the establishment of a *new international economic order*. The developing countries constitute 70 per cent of the world's population but possess only 30 per cent of the world's income. However, since so many of them have become independent in recent years and, on attaining independence, have become members of the United Nations, their political influence in international organisations has increased correspondingly. The group of non-aligned developing countries established at Bandung in 1955 with seventy-seven members now comprises more than 110, and thus constitutes two-thirds of the total membership of the General Assembly. It has been pressing vigorously for concerted new measures to redress the existing inequalities between the richer and poorer nations; for this purpose it has adopted as its slogan the notion of a 'new international economic order'.

Everyone agrees on the desirability of helping the less developed countries to develop their economies in an attempt to achieve an adequate standard of living and, among other things, implement the right to work, as proclaimed in the Universal Declaration and the Covenant on Economic, Social and Cultural Rights. The problem is how to achieve this objective – particularly at a time when the developed countries whose aid is required for this purpose are themselves suffering from inflation, unemployment and other effects of the current economic crisis.

The United Nations has held in recent years a series of special sessions devoted largely to these problems and announced successive 'development decades'. The Sixth Special Session of the General Assembly on 1 May 1974 adopted a *Declaration and Programme of Action on the Establishment of a New International Economic Order* (NIEO),[19] which was followed on 12 December that year by the *Charter of Economic Rights and Duties of States*.[20] It is beyond the scope of this book to examine these important texts in detail,[21] but we mention them here for their relevance to human rights. They proclaim *inter alia* twenty principles on which the new economic order should be founded, including the broadest co-operation of all States in fighting inequality, better prices for raw materials and primary commodities, active assistance to developing countries by the whole international community, free of political conditions, the use of a reformed international monetary system for the better promotion of development, and so on. Clearly, if this ambitious programme can be carried out, it will make an important contribution to the realisation of economic and social rights in the Third World. Some go further and assert that the establishment of the new economic order is a pre-condition of respect for human rights in many countries. The General Assembly of the United Nations has gone further still, because its important Resolution of 1977 on the future work of the United Nations with respect to human rights states that the realisation of the new economic order is 'an essential element for the effective promotion of human rights and fundamental freedoms'.[22] This last affirmation is evidently an exaggeration, because there are many countries which respect human rights without waiting for a new international economic order, but it reflects the thinking of the majority in the General Assembly and illustrates clearly the tendency to link human rights and economic development.

This tendency contains some truth but also much danger. It is evident that many economic and social rights, including freedom from hunger, the right to an adequate standard of living and to the enjoyment of physical and mental health (Articles 11 and 12 of the first Covenant) cannot be secured in countries where the majority of the population are living on or below the poverty line; and it is right that the developed countries should be frequently reminded of this. The danger, however, is that the fact may be used as an alibi for the non-observance of other rights of a different character which have little or nothing to do with underdevelopment. Economic circumstances are never a justification for arbitrary arrest, ill-treatment of prisoners or detention without trial. Without waiting for the achievement of the Utopian goal of a new international economic order as proposed by the General Assembly in 1974, we should recognise, on the one hand, that better economic conditions are essential in many countries for the effective realisation of economic and social rights but, on the other, that their absence is no justification for the abuse of civil and political rights.

This brings us back to consideration of the so-called 'new rights': the right to development, the right to the environment, the right to share in the common heritage of mankind, the right to peace. Are these concepts human rights in any meaningful sense of that term? In trying to answer this question, there are several considerations to be borne in mind.

In the first place, the word 'human' in the expression 'human rights' has a specific meaning. It indicates that the rights we are talking about are rights pertaining to human beings by virtue of their humanity. As stated in both the U.N. Covenants, 'these rights derive from the inherent dignity of the human person'. This means clearly, in our view, that the rights which can properly be called 'human rights' are rights of individual human beings, resulting from their nature as human beings, and not rights of groups, associations or other collectivities. This is born out by the wording repeatedly used in the Universal Declaration and in the Covenant on Civil and Political Rights, '*Everyone* has the right . . .'; while the Covenant on Economic, Social and Cultural Rights repeatedly stipulates that 'the States Parties . . . recognise the right of *everyone* to . . .' the different rights protected. It is quite clear from the drafting that what the Universal Declaration and the Covenants are talking about is the rights of individual human beings. (There is one clear exception in Article 1 of both Covenants, which states, '*All peoples* have the right of self-determination'. But this is clearly seen as an exception,[23] and its exceptional character is shown by the fact that it is placed in a distinct chapter of each Covenant, and separated from the articles relating to individual human rights.)

This being so, is it accurate or appropriate to designate as '*human* rights' so-called rights which pertain not to individuals but to groups or collectivities? Opinions may differ on this point, but in our view both our language and our thinking will be clearer — and clarity should be an objective of lawyers — if we use the expression 'human rights' to designate individual rights and 'collective rights' to designate the rights of groups and collectivities. This distinction, moreover, will have the advantage of being consistent with the generally accepted practice over many years.

The second consideration relates to the use of the word 'rights' in the expression 'new human rights'. Economic development, the protection of the environment, the common heritage of mankind and peace: are these concepts *rights* in any meaningful sense? As Professor C. E. M. Joad, the philosopher, would have replied, 'It all depends what you mean by "rights" '. Now, the generally accepted meaning of the word 'right' is 'a legally enforceable claim'.[24] It is clear that the 'new human rights' are not rights in this sense. They may – and should – be objectives of social policy; they may be items in a political programme; but they are certainly not legally enforceable claims. We all (or nearly all) want peace. But if one's country is at war, it is certain that there is no legally enforceable 'right to peace'.[25] Conceivably, one could define 'rights' in such a way as to include all desirable objectives of social policy; in that event, the 'new human rights' would become 'rights' by virtue of the new definition. But this would be to distort the ordinary meaning given to the term 'human rights'[26] and would not be conducive to clear thinking.

The trouble arises because the advocates of the 'new human rights' are confusing objectives of social policy with rights. If one wishes to see some objective achieved (e.g. a clean and healthy environment) it is tempting to say that this is a right to which we are all entitled. But it is not a counsel of wisdom to take our wishes for reality.

The last consideration to be borne in mind in this context is that it is necessary to distinguish between *legal* rights and *moral* rights. We may consider that we have a moral right to something, when we have no legal right to it at all; many examples could be given. If the advocates of the 'new human rights' assert that we have a moral right to peace, to the environment, and so on, then one cannot disagree; but the notion is so vague that it has no legal meaning, and it has no place in the technique of drafting international treaties, which are the tools with which we have to work.

V. THE EUROPEAN SOCIAL CHARTER

As explained in section 2 of Chapter III, the Council of Europe made a deliberate choice, when drafting the European Convention on Human Rights, to concentrate in the first place on the protection of civil and political rights and to leave for later consideration the action to be taken as regards economic and social rights. Once the Convention on Human Rights had entered into force in 1953, and its First Protocol in 1954, the Council turned its attention to the second category of rights.

The task proved far more difficult. There were two principal reasons. The first was the wide difference in the economic and social development of the member States. It is sufficient to compare the economy and social services of Britain and the Scandinavian countries, on the one hand, with those of Greece and Turkey, on the other, in order to understand the problem of securing agreement on common standards. The second difficulty arose from the very nature of the rights to be protected. The civil and political rights of the citizen can be enforced by a court of law: if a man is wrongfully imprisoned, he can apply for a writ of *habeas corpus*; if he is not given a fair trial, he can appeal to a superior court; and so on. With economic and social rights, however, it is different. The realisation of the right to work depends on economic circumstances, and if the labour exchange is unable to find a man employment the writ of a court of law will be of no avail. A reasonable standard of living for everyone is an objective of social policy, but it depends much more on a flourishing export trade than on legislation. This does not mean that there cannot be legally enforceable measures designed to give effect to economic and social rights (as we shall see shortly), but it did mean that the whole approach to the protection of those rights had to be different from that of the European Convention dealing with civil and political rights – as was also the case with the two United Nations Covenants.

The first step required was a political decision that a new legal instrument should be prepared. During the winter of 1953–54 the Committee of Ministers was engaged on preparing 'a well-defined programme of work for the Council of Europe';[27] in transmitting this programme to the Assembly in May 1954, the Committee recorded the following decision as part of the social programme:[28]

Our Committee will endeavour to elaborate a European Social Charter which would define the social objectives aimed at by Members and would guide the policy of the Council in the social field, in which it would be complementary to the European Convention on Human Rights and Fundamental Freedoms.

The task of preparing this Social Charter was to be confided to the new Social Committee, whose constitution was decided at the same time, as a permanent organ of co-operation between the member States in social matters, under the authority of the Committee of Ministers.[29]

The Assembly welcomed this new development[30] and instructed its Committee on Social Questions to prepare a draft setting out its views; by October 1955 the Committee had done so and submitted a complete draft Charter, containing far-reaching provisions for the protection of various economic and social rights;[31] this also proposed the creation of a European Economic and Social Council as an organ for its implementation. But the Assembly was far from unanimous in accepting the proposals, and a further draft was produced in the following April. It provided for rather less extensive rights for the workers than the earlier one – and was therefore considered retrograde by some and more realistic by others; it also proposed the convocation of an Economic and Social Conference on an *ad hoc* basis (i.e. as and when required) instead of as a permanent institution established by treaty.[32] This draft was acceptable to the Economic Committee and the majority of the Social Committee, but the dissident minority then arranged to have the whole matter referred to the Political Committee for further study. This resulted in the preparation of a third draft, which was discussed by the Assembly in the following October.[33] It was clear, however, that there were irreconcilable differences of opinion on many points; the Assembly refrained from endorsing the latest draft that had been submitted to it, but recommended that the Committee of Ministers should 'establish a European Convention on Social and Economic Rights, taking into consideration the present draft and the observations and suggestions during the debates in public session . . .'.[34]

It was now the turn of the governmental Social Committee to see what provisions were acceptable to the member governments. In December 1958 the Committee of Ministers published a draft Charter which its experts had produced;[35] taking advantage of a provision in the agreement concluded between the Council of Europe and the I.L.O. in 1951, it invited the latter to convene a tripartite conference (with delegations representing governments, employers and workers) to examine this text. The conference was held in Strasbourg from 1 to 12 December 1958; it did not produce any formal conclusions, but published a report which contained the record of its proceedings, including the views of the participants or of the various groups on the provisions contained in the draft Social Charter.[36]

After receiving a further opinion from the Assembly in January 1960,[37] the experts then worked out, in the light of all these discussions, the final draft of the Charter, which was duly signed at a ceremony held in Turin on 18 October 1961, in connection with the celebration of the centenary of the independence of Italy. These long negotiations, extending over seven years, have been summarised in order to show how the different organs of the Council of Europe, parliamentary and governmental, each played their part, and how – as a happy illustration of co-operation between international organisations – the I.L.O. also made its contribution to a successful outcome. In its final form the Charter has a character which is intended to correspond to the needs of contemporary free Europe and which might well be unacceptable both to Societ planners and American liberals. Its ideal is security in freedom; by proposing a system of guarantees for what have been called 'the bread-and-butter rights of the working man', it is intended to bring him the practical benefits of the European idea.[38]

There are three basic characteristics of the Social Charter which it is necessary to observe *in limine*. The first is its approach to the problem that a number of the 'rights' which it seeks to assert are really objects of social policy rather than rights which are legally enforceable. The difficulty here was that if these 'rights' were merely proclaimed as objectives, the Charter would have little value as an effective guarantee of economic and social standards; on the other hand, if its provisions were limited to the legal obligations which member governments could reasonably be expected to assume, its scope would be rather restricted and the results of so much work disappointing. The solution adopted was to divide the Charter into several distinct parts. In the first part are set out nineteen separate rights, the realisation of which the contracting parties accept as the aim of their policy; this permits general affirmations of a far-reaching character, as statements of policy without precise legal commitments. Part II then contains the legal obligations which the parties undertake with a view to ensuring the effective exercise of the rights proclaimed in Part I. With this double formulation it is thus possible to combine the general statement of long-term objectives with particular, more limited commitments of immediate application.[39]

The second basic characteristic of the Charter is its approach to the problem raised by the varying states of economic and social development in the different member States. It was clearly unrealistic to expect that the less developed countries could assume the same obligations as their more fortunate partners; equally it would have been contrary to the general policy of the Council of Europe to draft an instrument to which only the more developed countries could subscribe. It was therefore provided that a member

State would not be obliged to accept all the provisions of the Charter before ratifying it, but that it could – at least initially – be bound only by a stated minimum, in the hope and expectation that it could accept additional obligations with the passage of time. In this way it was hoped to achieve the progressive implementation of a Charter which, when fully applied, would guarantee a high standard of economic and social rights.

The third basic feature of the Charter is the attention given to the question of supervision of its implementation. As we have seen, the Assembly had suggested an Economic and Social Council or Chamber, with representatives of employers, workers and consumers; the governments did not favour this formula, but agreed to an elaborate system of control based on the sending of reports by governments on the way in which they were implementing the Charter and the examination of these reports by the various committees and organs of the Council of Europe. This system will be described later in this chapter.

1. The rights protected

Part I of the Charter starts off by providing that 'the Contracting Parties accept as the aim of their policy, to be pursued by all appropriate means, both national and international in character, the attainment of conditions in which the following rights and principles may be effectively realised ...'. These 'rights and principles' are then listed:

1. The right to work, which is thus formulated: 'Everyone shall have the opportunity to earn his living in an occupation freely entered upon'.
2. The right to just conditions of work.
3. The right to safe and healthy working conditions.
4. The right to a fair remuneration.
5. The right to organise.
6. The right to collective bargaining.
7. The right of children and young persons to protection.
8. The right of employed women to special protection, in case of maternity, when nursing their infants and so on.
9. The right to vocational guidance.
10. The right to vocational training.
11. The right to protection of health.

12. The right to social security.
13. The right to social and medical assistance.
14. The right to social welfare services.
15. The right of the disabled to special facilities.
16. The right of the family to social, legal and economic protection.
17. The right of mothers and children to social and economic protection.
18. The right to earn one's living in another country.
19. The right of migrant workers and their families to protection and assistance.

Part II of the Charter, as explained above, then contains more precise commitments which the contracting parties assume with a view to ensuring the effective exercise of these rights. The provisions vary considerably, according to the nature of the right to be protected. The right to just conditions or work, for example, involves *inter alia* limitation of working hours, public holidays with pay, two weeks' annual holiday with pay and a weekly rest period; similarly, the right to a fair remuneration includes additional pay for overtime, equal pay for men and women, and so on. The right of children and young persons to protection includes ten separate provisions for their benefit. The undertakings designed to secure the right to protection of the family and of mothers and children, on the other hand, are more general and imprecise.

A number of the rights dealt with in the Social Charter also form the subject of other conventions and agreements previously concluded by the member States of the Council of Europe. Though cross-references are, quite naturally, not given in the Charter, it is clear that its authors had these other instruments in mind. The right to organise, for example, is already guaranteed by Article 11 of the Convention on Human Rights. The right to social security in its international aspects forms the subject of the two Interim Agreements on Social Security signed in Paris on 11 December 1953,[40] while standards of social security are dealt with in the European Code of Social Security signed on 16 April 1964;[41] moreover, the right to social and medical assistance, also in its international aspects, forms the subject of the European Convention on Social and Medical Assistance of 11 December 1953.[42] Furthermore, the right to earn one's living in another country is one of the matters covered in the European Convention on Establishment of 13 December 1955.[43]

Part III of the Charter contains the provisions which permit progressive implementation. They are rather complicated, but their essence is as follows. Seven rights were regarded as of particular importance:

The right to work.
The right to organise.
The right to collective bargaining.
The right to social security.
The right to social and medical assistance.
The right of the family to special protection.
The right of migrant workers and their families to protection and assistance.

Under the provisions of Article 20, any contracting party must agree to be bound by the Articles in Part II of the Charter relating to at least five of these rights. In addition, it must agree to be bound by the provisions relating to at least five other rights as set out in Part II. It is possible, however, instead of accepting ten articles *in toto*, to accept a larger number in part.[44].

2. Measures of implementation

Part IV of the Charter contains the provisions relating to the control of its implementation. The Committee of Ministers, while rejecting the idea of a new European Economic and Social Council – as proposed at one stage by the Assembly – did agree to the appointment of an independent Committee of Experts 'of the highest integrity and of recognised competence in international social questions', who would be joined by a representative of the International Labour Organisation, participating in a consultative capacity.[45] This Committee of Experts receives and examines every two years reports by the contracting parties on the way in which they are applying the Charter. Moreover, copies of the reports are sent to national organisations of employers and trade unions, whose comments the governments are obliged to transmit to the Council of Europe. This ensures the possibility of obtaining information from independent sources, which we have insisted to be necessary in an effective reporting system. The governments' reports, and the comments thereon of the Committee of Experts, are then to be examined by a Governmental Committee on the Social Charter, representing the contracting parties and assisted by selected organisations of employers and trade unions. The conclusions of the experts are also sent to the Consultative Assembly, which communicates its views to the Committee of Ministers. Finally, the latter body examines the results of these consultations and may, by a two-thirds majority, make any necessary recommendations to each contracting party.[46]

This machinery is admittedly complicated, but it has instituted a system of supervision whereby watch is kept at regular intervals to ensure that the Charter is effectively applied and that any undue reticence by a particular government is exposed to the light of publicity and brought to the attention of both the governmental and the parliamentary organs of the Council of Europe.

Other points of interest in the final clauses (Part V) of the Charter are the inclusion of an article permitting derogations 'in time of war or other public emergency threatening the life of the nation' similar to Article 15 of the Convention on Human Rights; Article 32 of the Charter (similar to Article 60 of the Convention), which preserves any more favourable treatment that may already be provided for under domestic law or other international treaties; and Article 33, which preserves the principle of collective bargaining between the two sides of industry in relation to social rights for which it is appropriate.

The Charter was signed on 18 October 1961 on behalf of the following members of the Council of Europe: Belgium, Denmark, France, Germany, Greece, Ireland, Italy, Luxembourg, the Netherlands, Norway, Sweden, Turkey and the United Kingdom. Article 35 provides for its entry into force after the deposit of the fifth instrument of ratification; this occurred on 26 February 1965. By 31 December 1980 it had been ratified by Austria, Cyprus, Denmark, France, the Federal Republic of Germany, Iceland, Ireland, Italy, the Netherlands, Norway, Spain, Sweden and the United Kingdom.

3. The application of the Charter[47]

Article 20 of the Charter, as we have seen, requires that a contracting party should agree to be bound by at least ten out of the nineteen articles in Part II setting out the measures to be taken to secure economic and social rights (including at least five out of the seven more important articles); as an alternative, it may agree to be bound by at least forty-five out of the seventy-two separate paragraphs in those nineteen articles.

In fact, nearly all States which have ratified the Charter have accepted considerably more than the minimum number of obligations. Italy and Spain have accepted the total of seventy-two; France and the Netherlands have accepted all but two of them; the Federal Republic, all but five; Ireland, all but nine; Austria, Sweden and the United Kingdom, all but ten; Norway, all but twelve.[48] It is satisfactory that ten countries out of thirteen are now bound by more than 80 per cent of the provisions of the Charter.

The reporting system has been in operation for more than ten years. Each 'supervision cycle' covers a period of two years, and the governments of the contracting parties, in accordance with Article 21 of the Charter, send in regularly to the Council of Europe reports on the application of those provisions of the Charter which they have accepted. As might be expected, the independent experts have been more critical of the governments' reports than the governmental Committee on the Social Charter; equally the Parliamentary Assembly has been more diligent in detecting shortcomings than the Committee of Ministers. The professional organisations of employers and workers have been less active than one might have expected. On the whole the system has functioned reasonably well, and a certain number of discrepancies between obligations and performance have been detected. In the course of the first five 'supervision cycles', covering the first ten years of application of the Charter, the Committee of Ministers of the Council of Europe has preferred to transmit the reports of the various organs of control to the governments concerned, drawing their attention to the contents of the reports, rather than make any formal 'recommendations' in the sense of Article 29 of the Charter. This is no doubt more diplomatic, and was perhaps natural in the early years, but the Committee of Ministers should assume the responsibility of acting in accordance with Article 29 if the system instituted by the Charter is to be fully effective.

What practical results have been achieved? A number of discrepancies have been remedied as a result of the control system and – perhaps more important – a number of changes have been made in national legislation and practice in accordance with the spirit of the Charter, sometimes as a prerequisite to ratification. Cyprus, for example, introduced a new scheme of social security in

1973 in accordance with the requirements of Article 12 of the Charter. Some other examples of its effects may be grouped together under four headings:[49]

(a) The right to work and related rights Austria has amended two laws which were incompatible with the guarantee of freedom of choice of occupation (Article 1 of the Charter). The Federal Republic has granted additional holidays with pay to miners working underground (Article 2) and limited the working hours of young persons of school age (Article 7). Ireland has taken similar measures concerning the working hours of young persons under sixteen (Article 7) and introduced legislation requiring adequate notice in the event of dismissal (Article 4). The United Kingdom has also limited the working hours of young persons (Article 7), while Sweden has forbidden the employment in agriculture of children of school age (Article 7).

(b) Special provisions concerning women Both Ireland and Italy have increased substantially the amount of maternity benefits (Article 8). Ireland has also abolished the prohibition of the employment of married women in the public service (Article 1), while Sweden is extending the duration of maternity leave (Article 8).

(c) Migrant workers Article 19 of the Charter contains ten separate provisions for the protection of migrant workers. In order to comply with these obligations, Cyprus and Italy have changed their law as regards the expulsion of foreigners, Denmark and Sweden have done so as regards residence permits for foreign workers, while France now grants maternity benefits for the children of foreign workers on the same basis as for French children. She has also changed the age limit for the children of foreign workers seeking to rejoin their families and has abolished the *cautio judicatum solvi* (a financial deposit previously required of foreigners before they could bring an action at law).

(e) Seamen The law of many countries until recently made it illegal for a seaman to leave his ship during the period for which he had accepted an engagement. Though the reason for this rule can be understood, it violated the principle of freedom of choice of one's occupation (Article 1 of the Charter). Consequently Cyprus,

Denmark, the Federal Republic, Norway, Sweden and the United Kingdom have all amended their law in this respect.

The results of the application of the European Social Charter have perhaps not been spectacular — certainly less so than those of the European Convention of Human Rights — but they have been useful and constitute an apt illustration of the different measures of implementation which are appropriate for rights of an economic and social character.[50] Its effect will, of course, be greater if more of the contracting parties agree to be bound by the totality of its provisions, and if the eight member States of the Council of Europe which have not yet ratified it can be persuaded to do so. It is in that direction that more intensive efforts are required if the Charter is to guarantee effectively, as its drafters intended, 'the bread-and-butter rights of the working man'.

NOTES

1 Cf. Egon Schwelb, 'Some aspects of the measures of implementation of the Covenant on Economic, Social and Cultural Rights', *Human Rights Journal*, I, 1968, pp. 363–77; Kamleshwar Das, in *UNESCO Manual* (see Chapter II, n. 15), Part II, Chapter 11; B. G. Ramcharan, 'Implementing the International Covenants', in *Human Rights: Thirty Years after the Universal Declaration*, The Hague, 1979, pp. 159–74; V. Kartashkin, 'Economic, social and cultural rights', in *UNESCO Manual, chapter 6*.

2 *U.N. Bulletin of Human Rights*, No. 24, April–June 1979, pp. 24, 31.

3 *Ibid.*, Rule 2.

4 *Ibid.*, Rule 4.

5 In compiling this section I have been much assisted by — and express my thanks for — the contributions by Nicolas Valticos, Assistant Director-General of the I.L.O. to the *UNESCO Manual*, Part II, chapter 12, and to the Ramcharan book (*supra*, n. 1), chapter 10. There is much literature about the work of the I.L.O. in protecting the social rights with which it is especially concerned. I have found the following particularly useful: C. W. Jenks, *The International Protection of Trade Union Freedom*, London, 1957; idem, *Human Rights and International Labour Standards*, London and New York, 1960; idem, *Social Justice in the Law of Nations — the ILO Impact after Fifty Years*, Oxford, 1970; N. Valticos, 'Un système de contrôle international: la mise en oeuvre des conventions internationales du travail', *A.D.I. Recueil des Cours*, 1968, I, pp. 311–407; idem, *International Labour Law*, Deventer, 1979; *The I.L.O. and Human Rights*, report presented to the International Conference on Human Rights, Tehran, 1968. Further references may be found in Valticos's chapter in the *UNESCO Manual* (cited above).

6   N. Valticos, in *UNESCO Manual*, p. 448 (French edition).
7   The texts of these Conventions may be found in *Human Rights – a Compilation of International Instruments*, U.N. publication ST/HR/1/Rev. 1, New York, 1978.
8   N. Valticos, in *UNESCO Manual*, p. 457 (French edition).
9   *Ibid.*, p. 466.
10   For further information on these cases see *ibid.*, pp. 467–9.
11   On the activities of UNESCO in this field see Hanna Saba, 'UNESCO and human rights', in *UNESCO Manual* (*supra*, n. 1), Part II, chapter 13. He explains *inter alia* the functioning of the *UNESCO Convention for the Protection of Cultural Property in the Event of Armed Conflict* of 14 May 1954 and its measures of implementation. See also the present author's article 'The right to culture' in the UNESCO review *Cultures*, V, No. 1, 1978. For the UNESCO publication *The Birthright of Man*, produced as a contribution to International Human Rights Year, 1968, see above, Chapter I, section II(2). See also the Ramcharan book (*supra*, n. 1), chapter 9.
12   The text may be found in the U.N. publication *Human Rights: a Compilation of International Instruments* (ST/HR/1/Rev. 1), 1978, pp. 35–7. See also H. Saba, 'La Convention et la Recommendation concernant la lutte contre la discrimination dans le domaine de l'enseignement', *Annuaire français de Droit International*, 1960, pp. 646–52.
13   The history of the matter is recounted in H. Saba's contribution to the *UNESCO Manual* cited in n. 11.
14   Decision of the Executive Board 104 Ex/Decision 3.3 of 28 April 1978.
15   *Supra*, Chapter I, Section II (4).
16   See references given in Chapter I, n. 10; also Stephen Marks, 'Development and human rights', *Bulletin of Peace Proposals*, VIII, 1977, p. 236; Osita C. Eze, 'Les Droits de l'Homme et le sous-developpement', *Human Rights Journal*, 1979, pp. 5–18; Philip Alston, 'Human rights and basic needs: a critical assessment', *ibid.*, pp. 19–67; Report of the Secretary-General, *The International Dimension of the Right to Development as a Human Right*, U.N. doc. E/CN.4/1334 (1979). The U.N. Division of Human Rights organised a seminar on the subject in Geneva in July 1980, and the U.N. Commission on Human Rights at its thirty-seventh session in March 1981 appointed a group of experts entrusted with the task of defining the right to development as a human right.
17   Paul W. Gormley, *Human Rights and Environment: the need for international co-operation*, Leiden, 1976. S. Erçman, *European Environmental Law, Legal and Economic Appraisal*, Berne, 1977. The International Institute of Human Rights and the Institute for European Environment Policy organised a conference in Strasbourg in January 1979, at which a number of participants favoured the consecration of the 'right to the environment' in a European Declaration on the Environment. Such a declaration was in fact

drafted at a further conference held in Salzburg in December 1980; it starts off by proclaiming 'Everyone has the right to a healthy environment which is favourable to the development of his personality and ecologically balanced'.

18 Karel Vasak, in his inaugural lecture entitled 'Pour une "troisième génération" des droits de l'homme: les droits de solidarité' at the Tenth Study Session of the International Institute of Human Rights, Strasbourg, July 1979. M. Vasak considers that, in addition to the 'rights' mentioned in the text, there is a 'right to communication' which should be the basis of a 'new international information order'. UNESCO organised a colloquy about the 'new human rights' in Mexico City in August 1980.

19 Resolutions 3201 (S–VI) and 3202 (S–VI). See also Resolution 3362 (S–VII) of the Seventh Special Session.

20 Resolution 3281 (XXIX).

21 There is much literature on the subject. UNESCO produced in 1976 a booklet *Moving towards change – some thoughts on the new international economic order*. A useful article is A. A. Evans 'The new world economic order', *Transnational Perspectives*, Geneva, IV, No. 3, pp. 12–23 (1978).

22 Resolution 32/130, para. 1 (f). In 1979 the sub-commission on Prevention of Discrimination and Protection of Minorities undertook a study of the relationship between human rights and the N.I.E.O.

23 This is evident from the *travaux préparatoires*; see U.N. doc. A/2929 of 1 July 1955, chapter IV, paras. 2–7.

24 Jowitt's *Dictionary of English Law* (London, 1959) defines a right as 'the liberty of doing or possessing something for the infringement of which there is a legal sanction'.

25 The argument may be made against the thesis exposed in the text that many undoubted human rights (e.g. the right to liberty and freedom from arbitrary arrest) cannot be enforced in a court of law in certain circumstances (e.g. under a repressive dictatorship); but this fact does not invalidate the assertion that there is a right to liberty. Therefore, it may be said, the fact that the right to peace cannot be enforced by a court of law does not deprive it of the quality of a right. The answer is that the right to liberty exists as a right in many countries, even though it is violated in others, and that it is *capable* of enforcement by a court of law, even if sometimes it is not enforced in practice. The so-called 'new human rights', on the other hand, are not 'rights' in the proper sense, because they are quite incapable of legal enforcement. Consider the example already given of the 'right to peace'.

26 The Vienna Convention on the Law of Treaties of 23 May 1969 provides in its Article 31: 'A treaty shall be interpreted in good faith in accordance with the ordinary meaning to be given to the terms of the treaty in their context and in the light of its object and purpose'.

27 Special Message of the Committee of Ministers transmitting to the Consultative Assembly the Programme of Work of the Council of Europe, *Documents of the Assembly*, 1954, doc. 238, para. 1.

28 *Ibid.*, para. 45.

29   *Ibid.*, paras. 42–4.
30   Opinion No. 9, *Texts adopted by the Assembly*, May 1954.
31   *Documents of the Assembly*, 1955, doc. 403. The discussions in the Assembly and its various committees are recounted more fully in A. H. Robertson, *Human Rights in Europe*, first edition, 1963, chapter VIII.
32   *Documents*, 1956, doc. 488.
33   *Ibid.*, doc. 536.
34   Recommendation 104, *Texts adopted*, October 1956.
35   *Documents*, 1959, doc. 927.
36   I.L.O., *Record of Proceedings of the Tripartite Conference convened by the I.L.O. at the request of the Council of Europe*, Geneva, 1959.
37   Opinion No. 32, *Texts adopted*, January 1960.
38   The text of the Charter may be found in various publications, including the Council of Europe's *Human Rights in International Law: Basic Texts*, Strasbourg, 1979, pp. 41–64; *European Yearbook*, IX, 1961, pp. 247–77; and *European Conventions and Agreements*, I, 1949–61, pp. 338–65.
39   See F. Tennfjord, 'The European Social Charter – an instrument of social collaboration in Europe', *European Yearbook*, IX, 1961, pp. 71–83.
40   *European Treaty Series*, Nos. 12 and 13.
41   *Ibid.*, No. 48.
42   *Ibid.*, No. 14.
43   *Ibid.*, No. 19. These five Conventions and Agreements may be found in the collection published by the Council of Europe, *European Conventions and Agreements*, I (1949–61) and II (1961–70).
44   The nineteen articles in Part II of the Charter contain seventy-two numbered paragraphs. A State may ratify the Charter if it agrees to be bound by no fewer than forty-five numbered paragraphs, provided that it accepts no fewer than five of Articles 1, 5, 6, 12, 13, 16 and 19.
45   Articles 25 and 26 of the Charter.
46   Articles 27–9 of the Charter.
47   On this subject see F. Sur, 'La Charte Social Européenne: dix années d'application', *European Yearbook*, XXII, 1974, p. 88; H. Wiebringhaus, 'La Charte Sociale Européenne et la Convention Européenne des Droits de l'Homme', *Human Rights Journal*, VIII, 1975, p. 527; *idem*, 'Les Effets de la Charte Sociale Européenne en droit interne', *Essays in memoriam Sir Otto Kahn-Freund*, Munich, 1980, p. 755; Council of Europe document *The European Social Charter* (doc. (80)3), Strasbourg, 1980.
48   The details are given in the Council of Europe document cited in n. 47, appendix I.
49   Further details are given in the articles and document cited in n. 47.
50   The Committee of Ministers of the Council decided in their *Declaration on Human Rights* of 27 April 1978 to give priority to the work of 'exploring the possibility of extending the lists of rights of the individual, notably rights in the social, economic and cultural fields, which should be protected by European conventions or any other

appropriate means'. As a result, studies have been undertaken of the possibility of including some economic and social rights in a further Protocol to the European Convention on Human Rights. Work on this matter had not been completed by the end of 1980.

Chapter seven

HUMANITARIAN LAW[1]

I. INTRODUCTION

The origins of humanitarian law were briefly recounted in Chapter I, which mentioned various developments during the nineteenth century relating to the first three matters of concern to the Red Cross: the condition of the sick and wounded in the field, the condition of the sick and wounded and shipwrecked at sea, and the care (and exchange) of prisoners of war. These developments culminated in the international recognition accorded to the Red Cross in 1919 by Article 25 of the Covenant of the League of Nations. During the decade which followed, various steps were taken to establish the constitutional structure of the Red Cross. The League of Red Cross Societies was founded in 1919, as the 'parent body' of the various national societies; while the eighteenth international conference of the Red Cross at The Hague in 1928 approved statutes which established the following structure: the International Committee of the Red Cross (I.C.R.C.) in Geneva, the League of Red Cross Societies (originally in Paris, but transferred to Geneva during the Second World War) and the national societies themselves. The latter took the title of the Red Crescent in Moslem countries, and the Red Lion in Iran.

The fourth main trend in the development of humanitarian law concerns the rules which regulate the weapons which may be used in warfare. At the Hague Peace Conference in 1899, a Declaration concerning Asphyxiating Gases was adopted which contained an undertaking not to use projectiles for the diffusion of such substances. The Hague Convention of 1907 went further and contained a general prohibition of the use of poison or poisonous weapons in land warfare. This, however, did not prevent the extensive use of poisonous gases on the western front during the war of 1914–1918. Matters were taken a stage further by the *Geneva Protocol of 1925*, which prohibited the use in war of asphyxiating, poisonous or other gases and also extended the prohibition to the use of bacteriological methods of warfare – prohibitions which, happily, were respected during the Second World War.

How far it is possible to limit by humanitarian law the use of weapons in a situation which is itself in flat contradiction of the basic concepts of humanity? Or, as Professor Draper has put it,[2] how is an essentially inhumane activity to be conducted, even in part, in a humane manner? The problem which arose earlier this century over poisonous gases and bacteria became much more acute in 1940 with mass bombardments, in 1945 with the atomic bomb and, in the second half of the century, with the threat of thermonuclear weapons. This is a question to which we will revert later. But it shows at this stage that the horizons of humanitarian law have widened immensely during the course of this century. One hundred years ago humanitarian law was concerned with combatants who, through sickness or injury, could no longer take part in the combat. It was extended to prisoners of war – combatants who, on account of their capture, can no longer fight. It is now concerned with whole sectors of the population consisting of persons – including women, children and the aged – who have never been and never intended to be combatants, but whose very existence is imperilled by the methods of warfare now utilised by belligerents.

This leads us to the fifth main concern of humanitarian law; the protection of the civilian population. Until recent times a clear distinction could be, and usually was, made between the armed forces and the civilian population – not but what the latter was often the victim of appalling atrocities, as in the religious wars of the sixteenth and seventeenth centuries. But the distinction was easy to make, even if the necessary conclusion was not always drawn; and in the eighteenth century it was not unknown for civilians to travel without difficulty in countries with which their own State was at war because, being civilians, they were not concerned with the hostilities and their status as non-combatants was respected.

In the twentieth century things have changed for the worse. Quite apart from the question of weapons of mass destruction, the concept of total war involves the fate of the civilian population as never before. This applies with particular force, of course, in occupied territories. The taking of hostages, reprisals on the civilian population, the treatment of resistance groups (considered on the one side as patriots and on the other as terrorists), the conscription of labour, and many other problems arise. These matters practically fell outside the provisions of conventional law until recent years, but formed the subject of one of the Geneva Conventions in 1949.

The cataclysm of the Second World War led to a stocktaking and rethinking of humanitarian law. It had produced inhumanities on a scale never before even imagined. It is estimated that the First World War was responsible for 10 million deaths, but the Second for 50 million; this included 26 million combatants and 24 million civilians, of whom $1\frac{1}{2}$ million were civilians killed in air raids.[3] The League of Red Cross Societies, the International Committee and the national governments agreed to undertake the revision of humanitarian law. The result was the four *Geneva Conventions* of 1949, which amount to a codification of existing law plus a marked development thereof in the light of what was then recent history.

The Geneva Conventions of 1949 related to:

1. The amelioration of the condition of the sick and wounded in the field.
2. The amelioration of the condition of the wounded, sick and shipwrecked members of armed forces at sea.
3. The treatment of prisoners of war.
4. The protection of the civilian population in time of war.

The first three Conventions dealt with what might be called the classic functions of the Red Cross; the fourth was quite new and represented the first attempt to find solutions on a conventional basis for the problems mentioned in the preceding paragraph; the question of chemical and bacteriological warfare remains regulated by the Geneva Protocol of 1925.

By 31 December 1980 the Geneva Conventions of 1949 had been ratified by 146 States.[4] It is beyond the scope of this chapter to analyse them in detail;[5] certain matters which arise will be discussed in the following section. The following general observations, however, should be made at this stage. Article 1, common to all four Conventions, provides that the parties 'undertake to respect and to ensure respect for the present Convention in all circumstances'. In other words, the obligation is general and absolute and does not depend upon reciprocal respect for its obligations by the other party or parties to the conflict. Article 1, in addition, requires States to use their best endeavours to secure respect for the Conventions by non-governmental organisations under their control and also – a matter to which we shall return – by other contracting States.

Article 2 of all four Conventions states that they shall apply to 'all cases of declared war or of any other armed conflict . . .' so that a legal state of war is no longer a necessary prerequisite for the application of humanitarian rules.

Article 7 of the first three Conventions, and Article 8 of the fourth, provide that a beneficiary of their provisions may in no circumstances renounce the rights thus conferred on him. In other words, the rules established by the humanitarian conventions are rules of *ordre public*. Offenders who violate their provisions incur obligations under international law, though those obligations must be enforced by the national courts to whose jurisdiction the offenders are subject. Should there be an international organ before which they are responsible? Should the individual beneficiary have an international remedy if his rights are violated? These are some of the issues which are coming to be discussed and which may indicate an area of international law where humanitarian law could profit by following the example of human rights law.

II. CURRENT PROBLEMS AND RECENT DEVELOPMENTS: THE PROTOCOLS OF 1977

The two major problems under discussion in recent years concern the situation which arises in cases of undeclared war or civil strife and the problem of the use of weapons of mass destruction.

1. Undeclared war or civil strife

The typical situation which gave rise to the application of the rules of humanitarian law in the past was a war as generally understood, i.e. an international conflict between two or more States. Traditionally this occurred after a declaration of war, but international conflicts can and do take place without such a declaration; usually, however, there is no difficulty in ascertaining the existence of a conflict of an international character. Article 2 of the Conventions of 1949, as we have seen, makes it clear that they apply to 'all cases of declared war or of any other armed conflict'.

In the twentieth century there have been an increasing number of conflicts of a different nature. Do the rules of humanitarian law then apply? How is such a situation to be defined? There are marked differences between a full-scale civil war, such as those in Spain (1936–39), in the Congo in the early 1960s, in the Yemen (1965), or in Nigeria (1968–69), on the one hand, and various situations of rebellion or civil strife in which the established government maintains that it is simply suppressing a local insurrection but other States may lend it clandestine support on the ground that it is a national liberation movement. Such situations, moreover, lead to particularly passionate feelings and thus sometimes to appalling atrocities. While most soldiers will respect the integrity – and therefore the human rights – of a member of the armed forces of an enemy State, they may feel – and behave – very differently to one whom they consider a traitor to their own country. Thus the application of humanitarian law becomes particularly difficult in situations of civil strife; even more so when the insurgents receive assistance (usually of a clandestine nature) from a foreign power which shares their political ideology, with the result that the conflict is in some respects international, even though the armed forces of two countries are not, as such, involved.

Article 3 of the four Conventions of 1949 attempted for the first time to deal with this problem.[6] It sets out rules which shall apply to 'armed conflict not of an international character occurring in the territory of one of the High Contracting Parties'. In such cases 'persons taking no part in the hostilities, including members of armed forces who have laid down their arms and those placed *hors de combat* by sickness, wounds or any other means . . . are, in all circumstances, to be treated humanely, without any distinction founded on race, colour, religion or faith, sex, birth or wealth, or any other similar criteria . . .'. Article 3 also prohibits specifically:

(a) Violence to life and person, in particular, murder of all kinds, mutilation, cruel treatment and torture.
(b) The taking of hostages.
(c) Outrages upon personal dignity, in particular, humiliating and degrading treatment.
(d) The passing of sentences and the carrying out of executions without previous judgment pronounced by a regularly constituted court, affording all the judicial guarantees which are recognised as indispensible by civilised peoples.

This provision marked an important advance in international

humanitarian law and is a cause for real satisfaction. It has been described by M. Jean Pictet as 'an audacious and paradoxical provision which aims at applying international law to a national phenomenon'.[7] Nevertheless, there has been considerable difficulty in securing its application. This is principally because States are reluctant to admit the existence of 'an armed conflict not of an international character', perhaps through fear of the interpretation that may be given internationally to such an admission, even though the same article states that 'the application of the preceding provisions shall not affect the legal status of the parties to the conflict'.

As one example, during the Algerian war, in which France had about 400,000 troops engaged and the F.L.N. had a well developed organisation of its own, it was only at a late stage in the fighting that the French government admitted that Article 3 was applicable. It has been estimated that the applicability of Article 3 has been recognised in only a modest proportion of the cases in which internal conflicts have in fact occurred during the last thirty years. The need for further international action on this subject was thus apparent.

2. Weapons of mass destruction

The problem raised by modern methods of mass destruction – whether bombing with conventional weapons, as in the Second World War, or by the utilisation of atomic and thermo-nuclear devices – is obvious. Whereas humanitarian law as it has developed over the last hundred years has sought to distinguish between combatants and non-combatants, such methods of warfare by their very nature do not, and cannot, make such a distinction.

The twentieth Red Cross Conference in Vienna in 1965 attempted to tackle this problem, and adopted its Resolution XXVIII, which declared in part as follows:

The Conference,
... solemnly declares that all Governments and other authorities responsible for action in armed conflicts should conform at least to the following principles:
  that the right of the parties to a conflict to adopt means of injuring the enemy is not unlimited;
  that it is prohibited to launch attacks against the civilian populations as such;
  that distinction must be made at all times between persons taking part in

the hostilities and members of the civilian population to the effect that
the latter be spared as much as possible;
that the general principles of the law of war apply to nuclear and similar
weapons.

The same matter was discussed (together with other aspects of
humanitarian law) by the *International Conference on Human
Rights at Tehran* in 1968. In its Resolution XXIII the conference
noted that the provisions of the Geneva Protocol of 1925 had not
been universally accepted or applied and might need revision in the
light of modern developments. In the operative part of the
Resolution the conference requested the General Assembly of the
United Nations to invite the Secretary-General to study:

(a) Steps which could be taken to secure the better application of
existing humanitarian international conventions and rules in
all armed conflicts.

(b) The need for additional humanitarian international
Conventions or for possible revision of existing Conventions
to ensure the better protection of civilians, prisoners and
combatants in all armed conflicts and the prohibition and
limitation of the use of certain methods and means of warfare.

The conference also requested the Secretary-General, in
consultation with the International Committee of the Red Cross, to
make certain démarches on the subject to all States members of the
United Nations.

There was much discussion of these problems during the next few
years, both in the General Assembly of the United Nations[8] and at
the *twenty-first International Conference of the Red Cross* held in
Istanbul in September 1969. Resolution XIV of the Istambul
conference related to weapons of mass destruction, and read in part
as follows:

The twenty-first International Conference of the Red Cross, Considering
that the first and basic aim of the Red Cross is to protect mankind from the
terrible suffering caused by armed conflicts,
Taking into account the danger threatening mankind in the form of new
techniques of warfare, particularly weapons of mass destruction,
. . .
Requests the United Nations to pursue its efforts in this field, Requests the
International Committee of the Red Cross to continue to devote great
attention to this question, consistent with its work for the reaffirmation
and development of humanitarian law and to take every step it deems

possible,
Renews its appeal to the Governments of States which have not yet done so
to accede to the 1925 Geneva Protocol and to comply strictly with its
provisions,
Urges Governments to conclude as rapidly as possible an agreement
banning the production and stock-piling of chemical and bacteriological
weapons.

In addition, the conference, in its Resolution XIII, encouraged the
I.C.R.C. to maintain and develop its co-operation with the United
Nations and to pursue its efforts with a view to proposing new rules
to supplement the existing rules of humanitarian law, and
recommending the convocation of a diplomatic conference for the
purpose.

As the result of these and other developments the Swiss
government convened the *Diplomatic Conference on the
Reaffirmation and Development of International Humanitarian
Law applicable in Armed Conflicts*, which held four sessions in
Geneva from 1974 to 1977, attended by the representatives of more
than a hundred governments, and produced two Protocols to the
Geneva Conventions of 1949. This conference was in fact prepared
by two sessions of a Conference of Government Experts which met
in 1971 and 1972, so that the Protocols were the result of seven
years' work by some of the principal specialists in the world on the
subject of humanitarian law.

3. The Protocols of 1977[9]

The First Protocol relates to the protection of victims of
international armed conflicts and is concerned to bring up to date
the provisions of the Conventions of 1949 on this subject,
principally as regards the use of weapons of mass destruction and
the protection of the civilian population. The Second Protocol
relates to the protection of victims of *non-international* armed
conflicts and develops further the rules previously enshrined in
Article 3 common to the four Conventions of 1949 and quoted
above.

Before agreement was reached on the Protocols there was a sharp
difference of opinion on the question whether international treaties
can properly equate what is essentially an internal, national conflict
with an international conflict. As recounted above, there have been
since 1945 an increasing number of conflicts which involve national

liberation movements but which are not wars in the traditional sense. Many Third World countries – both in the United Nations and at the Diplomatic Conference – tend to support the international recognition of what they consider struggles against colonial and alien domination and against racist regimes in pursuit of the right to self-determination and independence. On the eve of the Diplomatic Conference the General Assembly adopted on 12 December 1973 its *Resolution 3103 (XXVIII)* in which it declared that such conflicts should be regarded as international armed conflicts in the sense of the Geneva Conventions of 1949 and that the participants in such conflicts should be accorded the same legal status as that accorded to participants in international conflicts by the Conventions of 1949.[10] Whether the Protocols should accept this idea was hotly debated by the Diplomatic Conference in 1974. There, as in the U.N. General Assembly, there was a majority in favour of it, and as a result paragraph 4 of Article 1 of the First Protocol states explicitly that it applies to 'armed conflicts in which peoples are fighting against colonial domination and alien occupation and against racist régimes in the exercise of their right to self-determination . . .'. The notion is thus clearly enshrined in the text, but it raises many problems,[11] and it remains to be seen how many governments will accept it by ratifying this Protocol.

The more interesting provisions of the First Protocol are contained in Part III, section 1 (Articles 35–42), concerning 'Methods and Means of Warfare', and Part IV (Articles 48–79), relating to the civilian population. Both of them concern the problems raised by modern weapons of mass destruction. Article 35 sets out three basic rules:

1. In any armed conflict, the right of the parties to the conflict to choose methods or means of warfare is not unlimited.
2. It is prohibited to employ weapons, projectiles and material and methods of warfare of a nature to cause superfluous injury or unnecessary suffering.
3. It is prohibited to employ methods or means of warfare which are intended, or may be expected, to cause widespread, long-term and severe damage to the natural environment.[12]

The following article relates to the development of new weapons and provides that in developing or acquiring them contracting parties are under an obligation to determine whether their use would violate the Protocol or any other rule of international law. The remaining articles of this section deal with other rules of general application, including the prohibition of killing, injuring or capturing an adversary by resort to perfidy; the prohibition of the improper use of special emblems (those of the Red Cross and of the United Nations); the prohibition of giving no quarter; and the prohibition of attacking a person *hors de combat*. Section 2 of Part III sets out a number of rules on combatant and prisoner-of-war status.

Part IV of the First Protocol, then, contains more than thirty articles on the *protection of the civilian population during hostilities*, designed to develop and bring up to date the principles established in the Fourth Convention of 1949. Article 48 sets out the basic rule requiring that the parties to a conflict 'shall at all times distinguish between the civilian population and combatants and between civilian objects and military objectives and accordingly shall direct their operations only against military objectives'. Article 51 develops this further by providing that 'the civilian population as such, as well as individual civilians, shall not be the object of attack' and that indiscriminate attacks are prohibited – including indiscriminate attacks by bombardment on a city, town or village, even if they contain some military objectives. Many other prohibitions are set out in the following articles, including that of attacks on civilian objects, on historic monuments and works of art; the prohibition of the starvation of civilians or destruction of their food supplies and of attacks on the natural environment; reprisals against the civilian population are also prohibited. There are also separate and detailed provisions (Articles 61–7) about respect for civil defence organisations and services and about humanitarian relief measures (Articles 68–71). It is evident that these provisions are based on humane considerations and that, if they can be observed in practice, they would do much to mitigate the effect of hostilities on the non-combatant population.

The Second Protocol of 1977 relates to *the protection of victims of non-international armed conflicts*. It must be remembered, however, that wars of national liberation and against racist regimes have, as already explained, been 'promoted' by Protocol I to the status of international conflicts. Protocol II is therefore concerned with other forms of internal conflict, that is to say, with civil wars as generally understood.

The main object of the Protocol is to secure the humane treatment of those threatened by but not directly involved in such conflicts. This is stated in the following words in Article 4,

'Fundamental Guarantees', of Part II, which is devoted to 'Humane Treatment':

1. All persons who do not take a direct part or who have ceased to take part in hostilities, whether or not their liberty has been restricted, are entitled to respect for their person, honour and convictions and religious practices. They shall in all circumstances be treated humanely, without any adverse distinction. It is prohibited to order that there shall be no survivors.

2. Without prejudice to the generality of the foregoing, the following acts against the persons referred to in paragraph 1 are and shall remain prohibited at any time and in any place whatsoever:
   (a) violence to the life, health and physical or mental well-being of persons, in particular murder as well as cruel treatment such as torture, mutilation or any form of corporal punishment;
   (b) collective punishments;
   (c) taking of hostages;
   (d) acts of terrorism;
   (e) outrages upon personal dignity, in particular humiliating and degrading treatment, rape, enforced prostitution and any form of indecent assault;
   (f) slavery and the slave trade in all their forms;
   (g) pillage;
   (h) threats to commit any of the foregoing acts.

Protocol II, with twenty-eight articles, is much shorter than Protocol I (102 articles). Part III contains five articles on the treatment of the wounded, sick and shipwrecked, recalling the first two Conventions of 1949. Part IV then sets out in Articles 13–18 provisions concerning the protection of the civilian population. These rules are broadly similar to, though less detailed than, the corresponding provisions of the First Protocol, containing prohibitions of attacks on the civilian population, of starvation and destruction of food stocks, of attacks on historic monuments and works of art, of the displacement of the civilian population and rules protecting the personnel of relief organisations. The last ten articles are the Final Provisions of a technical nature.

To summarise, we may say that the two Protocols of 1977 represent the culmination of many years' work by the representatives of more than a hundred governments.[13] It was a positive factor that many States from the Third World which had not obtained their independence at the time when the Conventions of 1949 were drafted were able to play their part in the development of humanitarian law nearly thirty years later. There is no doubt that the substantive provisions of the Protocols were conceived in a liberal and humanitarian spirit which we can only commend. The danger is that the attempt to equate struggles against 'colonial domination and alien occupation and racist régimes' with international conflicts as recognised by international law in the past may create unnecessary difficulties in the way of their ratification by the States which have the major responsibility for the maintenance of international peace and security.[14]

4. The protecting power

Another matter much under discussion in recent years is the institution of the 'protecting power'.[15]

The utilisation of protecting powers is traced back to the Franco-Prussian War of 1870; the system was widely adopted during the First World War. It was first established on a conventional basis in the Geneva Convention on the Treatment of Prisoners of War of 1929. It involves a 'triangular arrangement' between the two belligerents and a third, neutral power; each of the belligerents accepts that a third power should be charged with the protection of its interests in the other belligerent State. During the Second World War the number of neutral States which could act as protecting powers was very small; Switzerland represented thirty-five belligerents, while Switzerland and Sweden together represented practically all of them.

All four Geneva Conventions of 1949 recognised the system of the protecting power. They also provided that 'the High Contracting Parties may at any time agree to entrust to an organisation which offers all guarantees of impartiality and efficacy, the duties incumbent upon the protecting powers by virtue of the present Convention'. When there is no agreed protecting power or organisation so appointed, then humanitarian organisations, such as the International Committee of the Red Cross, may request or be requested to assume the humanitarian functions provided for in the Convention.

Thus, in the words of the U.N. report, the system of the Geneva Conventions may be summed up by stating that while the primary responsibility for the application of the Conventions rests with the parties themselves, a protecting power or a substitute humanitarian organisation should be available in all cases to co-operate with the parties and to supervise the application of the Convention.[16]

In practice, it appears that this system has not functioned as intended in the armed conflicts which have broken out since the Second World War. Over the last thirty years advantage has practically never been taken of the institution of protecting powers. It is estimated that the offers of services of the International Committee of the Red Cross have been accepted in approximately half the armed conflicts which have occurred during this period. Another element is that the functions of the protecting power or agency should not be, as in the classic conception, to look after the interests of the belligerent State; what is required, in the context of humanitarian law, is a system to look after the interest of – and secure the humane treatment of – the sick, the wounded, prisoners and other victims of armed conflict.

These considerations led the U.N. Secretary-General to conclude that:[17]

While the International Committee of the Red Cross and certain organisations play a most useful role, there would be pressing need for measures to improve and strengthen the present system of international supervision and assistance to parties to armed conflicts in their observance of humanitarian norms of international law. These measures, based on what already exists, should be regarded as complementary rather than competitive.

The need for strengthening and improving the existing system led him to put forward the suggestion that an international agency of an independent character, possibly within the framework of the United Nations system, should be set up in order to exercise the necessary functions.[18] Reference was made to a proposal by the French delegation at the Geneva conference of 1949 for the constitution of a 'High International Committee' consisting of thirty members, who would be eminent personalities known for their independence and the services they have rendered to humanity, such as religious leaders, eminent scientists and Nobel Prizewinners. This proposal was not adopted in 1949, but the report suggested that it might be revived in a modified form. The usefulness of a U.N. organ to discharge humanitarian functions is illustrated by the record of service of the International Refugee Organisation, UNRWA, UNICEF and the Office of the High Commissioner for Refugees.

This suggestion was clearly not meant to be in any way to the detriment of the International Committee of the Red Cross, but was put forward in the belief that an intergovernmental organisation, financed by governments, would probably have possibilities of action and financial resources greater than those of the I.C.R.C. A possible variant of the idea would be to entrust the proposed functions to the I.C.R.C., if this would be acceptable to that body, while enlarging its competence and increasing its budget by international agreement, in order to enable it to carry out the additional tasks involved.

Ideas of this sort, however, did not find favour with the diplomatic conference. Instead, the First Protocol, in its Article 5, retains and strengthens the existing system of the protecting power. Paragraph 3 of this article provides that if a protecting power is not appointed the I.C.R.C. 'shall offer its good offices to the Parties to the conflict' with a view to the designation of a protecting power; while, if this attempt is unsuccessful, 'the Parties to the conflict shall accept without delay an offer which may be made by the I.C.R.C. . . .'. There is thus a definite obligation on them to admit the good offices of the I.C.R.C. and, if necessary, to accept it as a substitute. There is, however, no corresponding provision in the Second Protocol relating to internal conflicts.[19]

III. HUMAN RIGHTS AND HUMANITARIAN LAW

This brief survey of the recent evolution of humanitarian law and of some of its current problems permits us to come to what is for the human rights lawyer the heart of the matter: the relationship between human rights and humanitarian law.[20]

M. Jean Pictet has written: 'Humanitarian law comprises two branches: the law of war and the law of human rights.[21] With all respect for this eminent authority, who has made such an important contribution to the development of humanitarian law, the submission of this chapter is quite different from, if not opposed to, his thesis. Our contention is that humanitarian law is one branch of the law of human rights, and that human rights afford the basis for humanitarian law.

It is not difficult to see why the opposite view is held. The evolution of humanitarian law antedates that of human rights law; the former has developed over the last hundred years, while the latter has been the concern of international law for only a third of a century. The United Nations Charter in 1945 contained brief, if numerous, references to human rights; it was only in 1948 that the Universal Declaration was adopted in Paris, just a year before humanitarian law, already developed, was codified in the Geneva Conventions of 1949.

But when we look at the substance of the two disciplines, it is apparent that human rights law is the genus of which humanitarian law is a species. Human rights law relates to the basic rights of all human beings everywhere, at all times; humanitarian law relates to the rights of particular categories of human beings – principally, the sick, the wounded, prisoners of war – in particular circumstances, i.e. during periods of armed conflict.

When seen in this perspective, we can realise that the basic texts relating to human rights – and we think here principally of the Universal Declaration and the United Nations Covenants – lay down standards of general application to all human beings, by reason of their humanity. Those standards, ideally should apply at all times and in all circumstances. Unfortunately, some of them are suspended in time of war, which is itself the very negation of human rights. But even in time of war certain rights must be respected by combatants towards their enemies and, precisely because war is a circumstance when many rights are suspended, it becomes all the more necessary to define and protect those rights which must still be respected in these exceptional circumstances. They constitute what might be called the 'sacrosanct rights', to which no derogation is permitted even in times of armed conflict.

The United Nations Covenant on Civil and Political Rights, as explained in Chapter II, recognises this principle in its Article 4. This permits derogations from the obligations resulting from the Covenant 'in time of public emergency which threatens the life of the nation and the existence of which is officially proclaimed'; but paragraph 2 of Article 4 lists seven 'sacrosanct' rights with regard to which no derogation may be made. These are:

1. The right to life.
2. The prohibition of torture or inhuman treatment.
3. The prohibition of slavery and servitude.
4. The prohibition of imprisonment for debt.
5. The prohibition of retroactivity of the criminal law.
6. The right to recognition as a person before the law.
7. The right to freedom of thought, conscience and religion.

A similar system is followed in Article 15 of the European Convention on Human Rights, which permits derogation 'in time of

war or other public emergency threatening the life of the nation'
but permits no derogation as regards four rights: the right to life
(except in respect of deaths resulting from lawful acts of war), the
prohibition of torture and inhuman treatment, the prohibition of
slavery or servitude, and the prohibition of retroactivity of the
criminal law.

There are similar provisions in the American Convention on
Human Rights, signed in Costa Rica on 22 November 1969.[22]

It is thus clear that modern conventional texts are based on the
principle that a number of basic human rights are so fundamental
that they must be respected at all times, even in periods of armed
conflict. This constitutes one of the bases of humanitarian law. But
it is not sufficient. The effective protection of the victims of armed
conflict requires not only that they should enjoy certain of the basic
rights which appertain to everyone, but also that they should
benefit from certain supplementary rights which are necessary for
them precisely because they are victims of armed conflict, such as
medical care, the right of prisoners to correspond with their
families, the right of repatriation in certain circumstances, etc.
These are the matters with regard to which the provisions of
humanitarian law in the particular situation of armed conflict go
beyond the requirements of human rights law, which are of general
application.

It thus appears that a certain number of the rights which
humanitarian law attempts to ensure to the victims of armed
conflict have been enshrined in recent international texts as rights
which should be guaranteed to everyone. In order to understand
this interrelationship more clearly, it is necessary to look at these
texts more closely. Which humanitarian rights are secured by the
U.N. Covenant on Civil and Political Rights even in times of war?

The first of the rights from which no derogation may be made is
the right to life (Article 6). The text permitting derogations (Article
4) does not indicate that they are permissible in time of war, no
doubt on account of the reluctance of the General Assembly to
admit that war can ever be lawful, but the phrase 'in time of public
emergency which threatens the life of the nation' is clearly wide
enough to include a time of war. It should be observed, however,
that in order for a derogation to be lawful, the public emergency
must be 'officially proclaimed'. This means that in situations of
undeclared war or civil strife no derogation is permissible in the
absence of an official proclamation of a state of emergency, so that

all the rights proclaimed in the Covenant must then continue to be respected.

The sacrosanct character of the right to life means that even in time of armed conflict such acts as the killing of prisoners and the execution of hostages are unlawful. The clause of the European Convention permitting derogations (Article 15) also treats the right to life as sacrosanct, but adds the limitation 'except in respect of deaths resulting from lawful acts of war'. However, such acts as the killing of prisoners and the execution of hostages are never 'lawful acts of war', so the result is the same. Does not this article also prohibit the killing of civilians by weapons of mass destruction? It would seem difficult to maintain the contrary.

The second sacrosanct article in the U.N. Covenant is of capital importance. 'No one shall be subjected to torture or to cruel, inhuman or degrading treatment or punishment. In particular, no one shall be subjected without his free consent to medical or scientific experimentation' (Article 7). This prohibition of inhuman treatment is far-reaching and covers many of the rights protected by humanitarian law. Admittedly, one would prefer to see a positive formulation, such as 'all persons shall be treated with humanity and with respect for the inherent dignity of the human person'. Such a positive formulation is to be found in Article 10 of the Covenant, where it relates to 'all persons deprived of their liberty' – which would, of course, include prisoners of war. But this is a less effective guarantee, because Article 10 is not one of the sacrosanct articles from which no derogation may be made.

Article 8 is also important in the present context. Its first two paragraphs prohibit slavery and servitude and are not subject to derogation. Unfortunately, paragraph 3, containing the prohibition of forced or compulsory labour, is subject to derogation, so that this guarantee does not necessarily apply at a time of public emergency which is officially proclaimed. Nevertheless, the right of derogation is not absolute. Article 4 permits States to take measures derogating from their obligations under the Covenant only 'to the extent strictly required by the exigencies of the situation' and 'provided that such measures are not inconsistent with their other obligations under international law and do not involve discrimination . . .' Consequently, there are many circumstances in which the prohibition of forced or compulsory labour will still apply, so that it may be claimed that one more humanitarian right is, as a general rule, protected by Article 8, paragraph 3.

Four other rights protected by the Covenant are 'sacrosanct' and not subject to derogation. As indicated in the list given above, these are: freedom from imprisonment for debt, prohibition of the retroactivity of the criminal law, the right to recognition as a person before the law, and freedom of thought, conscience and religion. But these are perhaps less relevant to our present enquiry about the relationship between humanitarian law and the law of human rights.

The affirmation that a number of important humanitarian rights are protected by the U.N. Covenant – and *a fortiori* by the European Convention on Human Rights – is not meant in any way to disparage, or diminish the value of, the humanitarian Conventions. Our only object at the present stage is to show that there are a number of areas of common concern to the two disciplines and that, if humanitarian law was developed earlier in time, human rights law is coming to cover some of the same ground and is likely to continue the process. This has consequences to which we shall return shortly.

The fact that there is a growing measure of convergence between the two subjects has been amply illustrated at international meetings during recent years. The Tehran conference in 1968 was an 'International Conference on Human Rights' and one of the major events of International Human Rights Year. It is generally agreed that one of the more important texts adopted by the conference was its Resolution XXIII, to which it gave the title 'Human rights in armed conflicts'; this was based on the fundamental precept that 'peace is the underlying condition for the full observance of human rights and war is their negation'. Resolution 2444 (XXIII) of the General Assembly, adopted later in the same year, is a resolution 'on respect for human rights in armed conflicts', and the same title was given to the report prepared by the Secretary-General as a result of the adoption of this resolution. We thus see that humanitarian law is coming to be recognised as the particular branch of human rights law which relates to human rights in times of armed conflict.

This convergence – one may even say interpenetration – of the two disciplines was underlined by the 'Istanbul Declaration' of the twenty-first International Conference of the Red Cross in 1969, which read, in part, as follows:

The twenty-first International Conference of the Red Cross,
  Aware of the unity and indivisibility of the human family,

Declares:
    That man has the right to enjoy lasting peace,
    That it is essential for him to be able to live a full and satisfactory life
    founded on respect of his rights and of his fundamental liberty,
    That this aim can be achieved only if human rights as set forth and
    defined in the Universal Declaration of Human Rights and the
    Humanitarian Conventions are respected and observed.
    That it is a human right to be free from all fears, acts of violence and
    brutality, threats and anxieties likely to injure man in his person, his
    honour and his dignity,
    . . .
    That the universally recognised general principles of law demand that
    the rule of law be effectively guaranteed everywhere . . .

The Red Cross, therefore, is concerned with human rights,
fundamental freedoms, non-discrimination and the rule of law, just
as the United Nations is concerned with humanitarian law and
respect for human rights in times of armed conflict.

What practical consequences can we draw from this convergence
and interpenetration of the two disciplines? The U.N. Covenant on
Civil and Political Rights, as we have seen, affords a new legal basis
for the protection of several humanitarian rights. Moreover, it will
have two, and possibly three, further consequences. The entry into
force of the Covenant means that the contracting parties are under
the obligation to report to the United Nations on the measures they
have adopted to give effect to the rights in question. Under the
provisions of Article 40 the procedure involves examination by the
Human Rights Committee of the reports of governments, possible
consideration of them by the Economic and Social Council and by
competent Specialised Agencies and, under Article 45, an annual
report by the Human Rights Committee to the General Assembly,
via ECOSOC, on the work it has accomplished. This therefore
constitutes the basis of a modest system of international supervision
as regards certain humanitarian rights.

Another possible consequence is that if the States concerned have
accepted the optional procedure for inter-State complaints under
Article 41 of the Covenant, this also will enter into play, and other
States may bring a violation before the U.N. Committee; if they are
parties to the Optional Protocol to the Covenant, then they accept
that the U.N. Human Rights Committee can 'receive and consider
communications from individuals subject to its jurisdiction who
claim to be victims of a violation . . . of any of the rights set forth in
the Covenant'. This would constitute a further step in the direction

of international supervision.

The third consequence is that acceptance of the Covenant – with or without the optional provisions – necessarily implies that respect for its provisions is a matter of concern to international law – and therefore of concern to the international community – so that a State party to the Covenant cannot properly object that the question of respect for the rights protected is a matter 'essentially within the domestic jurisdiction of the State' within the meaning of Article 2 (7) of the Charter. To sum up, therefore, it may be said that the inclusion of a certain number of humanitarian rights in the U.N. Covenant will have the result of subjecting them to a greater measure of international control than is the case under the existing humanitarian Conventions.

NOTES

1   This chapter is based in part on a report presented by the author to a conference organised by the International Institute of Humanitarian Law held in San Remo in September 1970 and published under the title *Human Rights as the basis of International Humanitarian Law*, Lugano, 1971. A great deal has, of course, been written about humanitarian law and the Red Cross. I may mention particularly the following works: H. Coursier, 'L'évolution du droit international humanitaire', A.D.I. *Recueil des Cours*, I, 1960, p. 357; *idem*, *The International Red Cross*, Geneva, 1961; G. I. A. D. Draper, 'The Genva Conventions of 1949', A.D.I. *Recueil des Cours* I, 1965, p. 63; J. S. Pictet, *The Principles of International Humanitarian Law*, Geneva, 1967; *idem*, *Le Droit Humanitaire et la Protection des Victimes de la Guerre*, Leyden, 1973; Stephen P. Marks, 'Emergency situations arising from the existence of internal disturbances and armed conflicts', in *UNESCO Manual*, Part I, chapter 8, section 3; Christian Dominicé, 'The implementation of humanitarian law', in *UNESCO Manual*, Part II, chapter 14. An extensive bibliography is *International Humanitarian Law: Basic Bibliography*, compiled by Jiri Toman and Huynh Thi Huong, Henry Dunant Institute, Geneva, 1979.

2   Draper, *op. cit.* n. 1, p. 66.

3   Figures quoted by Pictet, 'Armed conflicts – laws and customs', *I.C.J. Review*, 1969, p. 30.

4   Figure furnished by the I.C.R.C.

5   For such an analysis see the lectures at the Hague Academy of International Law by H. Coursier and G. I. A. D. Draper referred to in n. 1.

6   See particularly G. I. A. D. Draper, *op. cit.* n. 1, pp. 82–100.

7   J. S. Pictet, 'The twentieth International Conference of the Red Cross', *I.C.J. Journal*, VII, No. 1, 1966, p. 15.

8   See particularly Resolution 2444 (XXIII) of 1968 reaffirming that it is prohibited to launch attacks against the civilian population as such; the Secretary-General's report on *Respect for Human Rights in Armed Conflict* (U.N. doc. A/7720, 1969); Resolution 2597 (XXIV) of 1969 requesting the Secretary-General to consult the International Committee of the Red Cross about further action; Resolution 2603 (XXIV) of 1969 declaring the use of chemical and bacteriological weapons contrary to international law; and the discussions in the Commission on Human Rights in 1970, doc. E/CN.4/1039, pp. 24–6.

9   The text of the two Protocols may be found in various collections and are published as a separate booklet *Protocols additional to the Geneva Conventions of 1949* by the International Committee of the Red Cross, Geneva, 1977. See also Stephen P. Marks, *op. cit.* n. 1; and Yves Sandoz, 'La place des Protocoles additionnels aux Conventions de Genève de 1949 dans le droit humanitaire', *Human Rights Journal*, 1979, pp. 135–161.

10 The General Assembly was far from unanimous on the subject. The Resolution was adopted by eighty-three votes in favour, thirteen against and nineteen abstentions.

11 Two of the problems which arise are the following. In any international conflict there are two (or more) governments which are parties to the conflict and can assume the obligations resulting from the Geneva Conventions. In struggles against colonial domination, etc., there is a government, on the one side, and the insurgents, on the other. Are the insurgents legally capable of assuming international obligations and materially capable of enforcing respect for them? Article 96 (3) of Protocol I attempts to deal with this problem by stating that 'the authority representing a people' engaged in such a conflict may make a declaration undertaking to apply the Conventions. But will this work in practice? Who decides whether the 'authority' is capable of assuming international obligations and whether the government represents 'colonial domination, alien occupation or a racist régime'? Secondly, what happens when there are several different liberation movements (as in Angola before independence) which do not constitute or recognise any single 'authority'?

12 When signing the Protocols the United Kingdom and the U.S.A. declared that they interpreted the First Protocol as not relating to the prohibition or use of nuclear weapons. They considered that such questions should be settled at other meetings and not in the framework of humanitarian law.

13 110 governments were represented at the Diplomatic Conference, 1974–77.

14 By 31 December 1980 the Protocols of 1977 had been ratified by seventeen states: Ghana, Libya, El Salvador, Ecuador, Jordan, Botswana, Cyprus, Niger, Yugoslavia, Tunisia, Sweden, Mauritania,

Gabon, Bahamas, Finland, Bangladesh, Laos.

15 On the operation of the system of the protecting power and of the International Red Cross see Christian Dominicé, 'The implementation of humanitarian law', *UNESCO Manual*, Part IV, chapter 14. See also U.N. doc. A/7720, paras. 202–27. This document is a report by the Secretary-General to the General Assembly in 1969 which examines many of the problems discussed in this chapter.

16 *Ibid.*, para. 212.

17 *Ibid.*, para. 215.

18 *Ibid.*, paras. 221–7.

19 For further suggestions aimed at strengthening the 'measures of implementation' of humanitarian law see the first edition of this book at pp. 181–4.

20 On this subject see Sean MacBride, 'The interrelationship between humanitarian laws and the law of human rights', *Revue de Droit Pénal Militaire et de Droit de la Guerre*, summer 1970; *Human Rights as the basis of International Humanitarian Law*, Proceedings of a conference on the subject organised by the International Institute of Humanitarian Law, San Remo, Lugano, 1971; Stephen P. Marks, *op. cit.* n. 1; Yves Sandoz, *op. cit.* n. 9 at pp. 149–59; T. S. G. Bissell, 'The I.C.R.C. and the protection of human rights', *Human Rights Journal*, 1968, p. 273. A distinct but interesting subject is the relationship between human rights law and military law. The International Society for Military Law and the Law of War organised a conference on this subject at San Remo in 1976. The proceedings are published by the Society under the title *Les Droits de l'Homme dans les Forces Armées*, Brussels, 1978.

21 J. S. Pictet, *op. cit.* n. 7, p. 22.

22 Article 27 (2) of the American Convention, in which there are eleven 'sacrosanct' rights.

POSTSCRIPT

As we said at the beginning of this book, our aim has been, while recognising the lamentable state of human rights in many parts of the world, to show that more and more people in the modern age are aware of this situation and are endeavouring – whether as individuals or in voluntary associations or in international organisations – to do something about it. During the period when this new edition was in preparation we have seen ample confirmation of both assertions. Reports presented to the Commission on Human Rights and the General Assembly of the United Nations, the investigations of the Inter-American Commission on Human Rights into the situation in certain countries of Latin America, evidence produced to the C.S.C.E. conference in Madrid about the treatment accorded to human rights activists in Eastern Europe, the report of Amnesty International published in December 1980, that of the U.S. State Department to the Congress in February 1981, all confirm the picture of systematic and repeated violations in many countries. On the other hand, the fact that these reports are made and widely publicised – and some of them show improvements in certain countries – the debates and discussions which follow their publication, and the number of people concerned with these problems in the international organisations, national and international parliamentary bodies and non-governmental organisations – Amnesty International has a quarter of a million members in 134 countries – afford the proof that people do care about human rights. The mounting pressure of public opinion in the years to come is likely to have a cumulative effect in persuading – or shaming – the governments which systematically violate human rights to mend their ways. In this struggle international organisations and international lawyers have a particularly important role to play, one might say a special responsibility. The Universal Declaration called on every individual and every organ of society to 'strive by teaching and education to promote respect for these rights and freedoms and . . . to secure their universal and effective recognition and observance'. If this book can make a modest contribution in helping them to do so, by explaining the international procedures which exist and, in some cases, the deficiencies which should be remedied, then it will have achieved its object.

INDEX